M000289583

SHIP
OF
BLOOD

By Charles Oldham

SHIP OF BLOOD
Mutiny and Slaughter Aboard the Harry A. Berwind,
and the Quest for Justice

THE SENATOR'S SON
The Shocking Disappearance, The Celebrated Trial,
and The Mystery That Remains A Century Later

SHIP
OF
BLOOD

MUTINY AND SLAUGHTER
ABOARD THE *HARRY A. BERWIND*,
AND THE QUEST FOR JUSTICE

CHARLES OLDHAM

Published by Beach Glass Books, 2022
Printed and manufactured in the United States of America
First Printing January 2022
Also available in eBook and audiobook editions

1   3   5   7   9   10   8   6   4   2

Front cover illustration, Los Angeles Herald, Nov. 4, 1906
Back cover photograph, Daily Arkansas Gazette, March 10, 1912
Author photograph supplied by the author
Book and jacket design by Ray McAllister

Charles Oldham, 1974-
Ship of Blood: Mutiny and Slaughter Aboard the Harry A. Berwind, and the Quest for Justice / by Charles Oldham
Library of Congress Cataloging-in-Publication Data applied for
ISBN 978-1-7361321-4-2

To the memory of my grandparents,

Charles M. Oldham Sr. and Madge Hardy Oldham
&
P. Eric Cotter and Lutie Tyler Moore Cotter

They loved the North Carolina coast, and especially
the Brunswick Beaches. Many thanks for all the stories.

CONTENTS

CONTENTS

PUBLISHER'S NOTE

In the early 2020s, following the police killing of George Floyd and the emergence of the Black Lives Matter movement, the publishing industry both sought and was beset by warehouse-loads of books on social and racial justice. That may have spoken to opportunism—2021 sales of such books, after all, were nearly three-fold those of the previous year. But many works emerged that needed to emerge. Their stories needed to be told.

Ship of Blood, though already in the works, is such a book—and then some. At heart, it is a true crime mystery from early in the twentieth century, as was Charles Oldham's previous acclaimed volume, *The Senator's Son*. This one is a page-turner, too, a deconstruction of a monstrous and seemingly unresolvable crime. Many of a state's elite make appearances, as do two United States presidents. The story rests in part on issues of social and racial justice. No tale such as this, at this place and time, could be otherwise (though, as you'll see, some attempted to present it as otherwise).

Ultimately, however, it is a story simply of justice.

All true. All meticulously researched. All compellingly told.

In theory, this important book could have been written at any time during the past hundred years. All it would have taken was a dedication to rigorous research, a keenly analytical legal mind, an unerring sense of justice, an innate sense of decency, and a consummate storytelling prowess. Unsurprisingly, that combination did not emerge. Until now.

Trust me. It was worth the wait.

Ray McAllister
for Beach Glass Books

SHIP
OF
BLOOD

INTRODUCTION
CAPE FEAR

For someone who doesn't hail from North Carolina, it may come as a surprise to learn that Cape Fear is more than a title for a fictional adventure film. The movie made in 1962, about a vengeful rapist stalking the attorney who sent him to prison, starred Robert Mitchum and Gregory Peck; the 1991 remake featured Robert DeNiro and Nick Nolte. Cape Fear is a real place, a conspicuous spot of land on the coast where the state's largest river—of the same name—empties into the Atlantic about twenty-five miles south of Wilmington.

Native Americans lived in the area for centuries. The first European to see the river was Giovanni da Verrazzano, who sailed by on an exploratory voyage for the King of France in 1524. Like Columbus just a few decades before, Verrazzano was searching for the fabled water route to Asia, and, failing to find it in the Carolina Coastal Plain, he did not stay long.

Not until June 1585 did the area appear by name on a map. Sir Richard Grenville, while scouting the river as part of the Sir Walter Raleigh and John White expedition that led to the famous Lost Colony of Roanoke, recalled that his ship was in "great danger of a wreck on a breach called the Cape of Feare." He was describing the inlet where the river finally meets the ocean, and the treacherous shoals lying all about. Later explorers, like James Hilton, who ventured up the river in 1663, wanted to encourage further settlement by making the area seem more hospitable; instead of playing on trepidation, they labelled it "Cape Fair."[1]

Verrazzano "discovered" it, Grenville named it, and Hilton glossed over it. But James Sprunt was, for many years, the man most influential in defining the history of the Cape Fear. Wilmington's wealthiest merchant at the turn of the twentieth century, Sprunt was also a diplomat and a comprehensive author. Shortly before World War I, he published his nearly six-hundred-page *Chronicles of the Cape Fear River*, a collection of essays and anecdotes dating back to the early explorers. Throughout his work, one can see how James Sprunt liked to give his stories an adventuresome flair, befitting the Rebel blockade runner he had been in his youth.

He wrote,

> Looking then to the Cape and the reason for its name.
> . . . It is the playground of billows and tempests, the
> kingdom of silence and awe, disturbed by no sound save
> the seagull's shriek and the breaker's roar. Its whole aspect
> is suggestive, not of repose and beauty, but of desolation
> and terror. Imagination cannot adorn it. Romance cannot
> hallow it. Local pride cannot soften it. There it stands
> today, bleak, and threatening, and pitiless, as it stood three
> hundred years ago, when Grenville and White came nigh
> unto death upon its sands. And there it will stand bleak,
> and threatening, and pitiless, until the earth and the sea
> shall give up their dead. And, as its nature, so its name
> is now, always has been, and always will be, the Cape of
> Fear.[2]

By the time James Sprunt wrote his magnum opus in 1914, the communities alongside the river had grown fast and settled down. Plantations, growing rice and other crops, had sprouted along its banks. They had grown wealthy through slave labor, and then adapted painfully to its abolition after the Civil War. Wilmington had grown to be the largest town in North Carolina, an international seaport where commercial vessels docked and embarked with regularity.

Local folks retained their penchant for adventure, centered along the river and its treacherous allure. They regaled their children with tales of Stede Bonnet, the pirate from Barbados who fought a battle in 1718 with the Royal Navy near the mouth of the river at present-day Southport, and of Confederate heroes like Sprunt and Rose O'Neal Greenhow, the glamorous female spy who drowned off Fort Fisher while trying to escape the Yankee blockaders in 1864.

Most of them, or at least most who were white, held on to nostalgia for the Rebel ideology as well. The Reconstruction years were tense, so much so that in 1898 Wilmington saw one of the nation's bloodiest race riots, which left dozens dead and ushered in the long, dark night of Jim Crow. One former Confederate leader vowed, "We will never surrender to a ragged raffle of negroes, even if we have to choke the current of the Cape Fear with carcasses."[3]

Imagine then, the scene of a shipboard killing spree off the coast of Cape Fear in 1905, just a few years after the violence that occurred on land: four officers shot dead, the decks stained red, and only three sailors left to account for it, telling contradictory tales and blaming one another.

The Cape lived up to its name. It's the kind of human maelstrom that Shakespeare could have imagined, a shocking tale that Coleridge's Ancient Mariner might have shared with the awestruck Wedding Guest.

Imagine further that those three sailors were put on trial in Wilmington for mutiny and murder. Imagine that all four murdered officers were white, and all three accused sailors were Black. Naturally, it would have been the easiest thing in the world to execute all three of them.

The story does *not* end with a triple hanging, but along the way there are plenty of billows and tempests, desolation, and terror.

New-York Tribune.

NEW-YORK, THURSDAY, OCTOBER 12, 1905.—SIXTEEN PAGES.

PRICE THREE CENTS.

UNITARIANS SHUT OUT.   KILLED BY "BLACK HAND"

CHURCH AMITY SPLIT.   MONEY DEMAND SCORNED

FRANK A. VANDERLIP

FIVE KILLED IN MUTINY.

CREW NEARLY WIPED OUT

Three Negroes, Found on Schooner,
Held for Wholesale Murders.

ITALY'S CUBAN TREATY.

MOST FAVORED NATION.

She Has Secured All the Rights Objected to for Great Britain.

THE MORNING S

WILMINGTON, N. C., THURSDAY, OCTOBER 12, 1905.

LOCAL DOTS.

ABRUPT END OF SUIT

Much Suit Involving The City
Rock Quarry Will Now
Begin Anew

HORNE VS. CONSOLIDATED CO

Interesting Damage Case Begun in
Superior Court Yesterday After-
noon, Will Last Probably
Balance of Week.

VETERAN PILOT IS GONE

Crossed the Bar left Scull Beyond
Yesterday—The Funeral.

MUTINY AND MURDER

Wholesale Slaughter of White
Members of Schooner Crew
By Negro Seamen

HORRIBLE TALE UNFOLDED

Negroes, Their Hands Red With Blood
Brought Into Southport To Chains
Yesterday—Killed Companion
Who Dared Expose Them.

PERSONAL.

VETERAN ARTILLERYMEN
HOLD THEIR REUNION

Hartford Courant

HARTFORD, CONN., THURSDAY MORNING, OCTOBER 12, 1905.—18 PAGES.

PRICE 3 CENTS.

Rain and colder today; fair
tomorrow.

THIS MORNING'S NEWS.

KEPT A QUORUM
BY AID OF POLICE

Drastic Measures by Omaha
Mayor to Pass Gas Or-
dinance.

DOORS BARRED TO PREVENT
ESCAPE OF COUNCILMEN

Strong Epithets Passed Between Mayor and Minor-
ity Members

LET PRETTY
GIRLS BITE YOU.

More Deadly than Ser-
pents'—Fright for Wes-
leyan Students.

MUTINOUS CREW
MURDERS FIVE.

Captain and Men Killed and
Bodies Thrown Over-
board.

THREE NEGROES SEIZE
SCHOONER H. A. BERWIND.

Captured Off Cape Fear and
Brought to Port in
Irons.

CLINGS TO CRIPPLE
WHO DESERTED HER.

BRISTOL P.O. WILL BE MOVED.

YALE FRESHMEN WILL
FRAME AN APOLOGY.

BAR UNITARIANS
FROM FEDERATION

Officials Planning Church
Union Draw the
Line.

ONLY TRINITARIANS
TO BE ADMITTED.

Dr. Hale, Dr. Eliot and Ex-
Secretary Long Among
Those Excluded.

EXPRESS ROBBER
ELUDES DETECTIVES

Man Resembling Cunliffe Seen
By Fisherman Clipping
His Hair.

The Washington Post.

WASHINGTON: THURSDAY, OCTOBER 12, 1905.—FOURTEEN PAGES.

THREE

AT THE FIRST SESSION OF THE BANKERS.

Weather—Fair and cooler
to-day and to-morrow; light to fresh
northwesterly winds.

TO ANNUL

Family of Co
Order S

MARRIED

Warrant w

MURDER ON THE SEA

Mutinous Negro Crew Butcher Officers of Schooner.

THROW BODIES OVERBOARD

Ghastly Scene on Deck Tells Story
of Desperate Fight.

Mutineers Captured by Another Schoon-
er and Brought to Southport, N. C., in
Irons—One of the Negroes Killed by
His Companions for Signaling for Aid
from the Ill-Stated Berwind—Trouble
Started in Squabble about Coffee.

Special to The Washington Post.

Wilmington, N. C., Oct. 11.—The
mutiny of four Negro members of the
crew of the schooner Harry A Berwind,
bound from Mobile to Philadelphia,
Rumil, her mate, cook, and three seamen were
killed and their bodies thrown overboard
somewhere off the Negroes who committed the
deed.

According to the stories told by the mutineers, the mutiny arose as the result of
a quarrel aboard the Berwind early Tues-
day morning about some coffee. They
had brewed for breakfast. The schooner
Blanche H King, Capt. J. W. Taylor, bound from Brunswick,
Ga., to Philadelphia, ran in Southport
this afternoon, bringing in irons the three
negroes.

Signaled for Aid.

The Harry A. Berwind left Mobile September thirty with a cargo of yellow pine,
bound for Philadelphia, when attention was
attracted to the vessel in a...

The North Ca

Volume XIII. Number 30.

RALEIGH, NORTH CAROLINA, THURSDAY

R ILROADS RAISE ONE MIGHTY HOWL

Gagging at the Esch-Townsend Bill.

'TIS UNFAIR, THEY SAY

It is Equivalent to Providing by Statute for the Enforcement of Commercial Lynch Law. President Spencer Addresses the Newark
Board of Trade.

(By the Associated Press.)

FLAT DENIAL

Relations with
law Neve

STORIES TOL

Lumber Men Call on President and
Commend Railroad Rate
Legislation.

(By the Associated Press.)

Washington, Oct. 11.—President
Roosevelt today received further assurances of the attitude toward the
enactment of railroad rate legislation
from the big lumber interests of the
country. Lewis Dill, president and
Robert W. Higbee, a member of the
National Wholesale Lumber Dealers'
Association and George P. Gardiner
and Alba Gardiner representing the
Central Yellow Pine Association of
Mississippi, said the President that
their association approved heartily of
his course in the rate legislation question, and urged that upon the Inter-
state Commerce Commission might
be conferred more power to deal
with discriminatory railroad rates.
The President told the railers he
hoped that the legislation they advocated might be enacted at the approaching session of Congress.

MUTINY DYED THE DECK WITH BLOOD

Three Negroes in Irons at Southport.

FIVE MEN ARE DEAD

These Three Negroes Are All That Re-
main of the Crew of the Berwind
Found Thirty Miles Off
the Cape Fear
Bar.

(By the Associated Press.)

Wilmington, N. C., Oct. 11.—A special to the Star from Southport to-
night says the schooner Blanche H.
King, Captain J. W. Taylor, Brunswick, Ga., September 23rd, to Philadelphia, put in there this afternoon,
bringing in irons three negroes, all
that remain of the crew of the four-
masted schooner Harry A. Berwind.
Captain Rumill, from Mobile, September 23rd, to Philadelphia, the captain, mate, cook, and all engineer having been murdered in a mutiny
at sea and their bodies thrown
overboard. The body of a fourth
negro of the crew was found lying on
deck where he, too, had evidently
been murdered.

Captain Taylor, of the schooner
King, sighted the Berwind early this
morning about thirty miles off the
Cape Fear bar, and was attracted to
her by the manner in which she was
being steered, having several times
come very near running down the
King. A nearer approach to the Berwind showed that she had been prac-
tically abandoned. Captain Taylor
and crew boarded the vessel and placed the three negroes in irons, bringing the two vessels off the bar,
whence one of them was towed in by
Wilmington tug, which chare now
gone for the other schooner, a prevailing on the outside.

The Berwind being from a territory against which this city is quar-
antined for yellow fever, the three
negroes in irons are held in quarantine until arrangements can be made
for their detentions by the Federal
authorities.

Story of the Mutiny.

It develops from the stories of the
negroes brought in irons by the King
that the mutiny arose as the result
of a quarrel aboard ship early Tues-
day morning about some coffee they
was being brewed for breakfast. The
King was signaled by the Berwind
50 miles east of Frying Pan light-
ship, and in response to a signal Captain Taylor sent his mate, engineer
and others to board the Berwind, the
decks of the schooner were crimson
with blood, giving evidence of a fierce
encounter. The berth of the mate, it
is reputed with blood indicating that he
was murdered in bed. One of the
prisoners says the mate begged pit-
eously for his life, but the savage
lchres for blood would not spare
their pardon.

A FOULED ERMINE

Judge Baker Solicited Campaign Funds.

A Violator of the Civil Service Rules,
This Federal Judge's Case Re-
ferred to the Department of
Justice.

(By the Associated Press.)

Washington, Oct. 11.—The charge
of soliciting and accepting campaign
contributions in the campaign of 189
made against United States Circuit
Court Judge Baker, of Indiana, by the
Civil Service Commission, has been

CONCORDIA DAILY KANSAN.

VOLUME I

CONCORDIA, CLOUD COUNTY, KANSAS, OCTOBER 12, 1905.

THURSDAY

NUMBER 185

THURSDAY

BR SUGGESTS REMEDY

HEAVY TAX
NATIONAL BANK NOTES

FLEXIBLE CURRENCY SYSTEM

Pretty Belleville Girl to Become Bride
of Former Concordia Boy.

BETRAYED BY JEALOUS WIFE

THEY HAD A BIG TIME.

THE PRIZE CREW.

Seamen Light and Open Modern
the Winner.

UNFAIR TO RAILROADS

SPENCER'S VIEWS OF PROPOSED
RATE REGULATION.

PREDICT INDUSTRIAL PARALYSIS

American Order of Protection Fails to
Organize New Members.

CREW MURDERS OFFICERS

Mutiny on Schooner Harry A. Berwind Results in Death of Five Men

Wilmington, N. C.—

The Bangor Daily News

— ESTABLISHED JUNE 18, 1889.

BANGOR, MAINE, THURSDAY, OCTOBER 12, 1905.

PRICE

ANGOR
AILWAY & ELECTRIC CO.
rty Year 5% Bonds
00 and $1000

**BIGGEST CROWD
EVER AT TOPSHAM**

**BATES SCORED
ON HARVARD**

DECKS OF SCHOONER
CRIMSON WITH BLOOD

BRITISH FLEET
AT YOKOHAMA

as Officially Welcomed Wednesday Amid Scenes of
General Enthusiasm.

DOUGLAS MAKES
FULL CONFESSION

Shot Kimball to Lay Him Up
so He Could Get Job On
the Farm.

Mutiny Aboard the
Four Masted Harry
A. Berwind.

CAPT. AND FOUR
MEN MURDERED

Was Result of Quarrel About Coffee
at Breakfast.

WILMINGTON, N. C. Oct. 11—The
murder of Captain Rumill and four of
his crew of the four masted schooner
Harry A. Berwind in a mutiny while
he vessel was bound from Mobile to
Philadelphia, in the story told in a
special to the Star from Southport to-
night. The schooner Blanche H. Kar,
Captain J. W. Taylor, bound from
Charleston, Ga., to Philadelphia, put
into Southport this afternoon bringing
nind of the crew of the Harry A. Berwind. The captain, mate, and an
engineer, who did have that ...

---

arolinian

Y, OCTOBER 12, 1905.   Price ...

BANKERS APPLAUD
SHAW TO THE ECHO

Need of Financial Legis-
lation Emphasized.

A FLEXIBLE CURRENCY

Shaw Suggests a Remedy for Present

THE MORNING NEWS.

LANCASTER, PA., THURSDAY, OCTOBER 12, 1905.   TEN CENTS A WEEK

NO. 4918.

MUTINY AT SEA
ON BOARD SCHOONER

The Captain and Four of His
Crew Murdered.

BODIES THROWN OVERBOARD.

Three Negroes Who Were Bringing the Boat
Up the North Carolina Coast Now
Imploring Captured and Taken

POSITION OF ROADS
ON RATE LEGISLATION

ARE OPPOSED TO DEBATES

D. A. R. CONFERENCE

DR. ABRAM S. MILLER
EXPIRES SUDDENLY

Died in a Chair While Convers-
ing With Friends.

HEART TROUBLE THE CAUSE.

York Daily.

Established 1870

YORK, PA., THURSDAY MORNING, OCTOBER 12, 1905   4 PAGES.

Today's Weather Fair colder

EXPRESS CLERK
STILL AT LIBERTY

$100,000 IS PAID OVER

RAMSEY FAILS UTTERLY
IN FIGHT WITH GOULD

MONETARY SYSTEM
NEEDS REVISING

SHAW POINTS A REMEDY

NEGRO SAILORS MUTINY
MURDER A SHIP'S CREW

Captain and Four Men Slain, Bodies
Overboard—Three Negroes
in town at Wilmington, N. C.

CANAL COMMISSION
ANNULS A CONTRACT

MARKEL CONTRACT
HAS BEEN REVOKED

INVOLVES HALF MILLION

THREE COLLEGES
TO ABATE FEVER

The *Harry A. Berwind*,
after being pulled into port.

CHAPTER ONE

DISCOVERY BY MOONLIGHT

When it comes to adventure stories, Jack London wrote some of the most enduring classics in any language. For *The Call of the Wild* and *White Fang*, probably his two best known titles today, he famously drew from his experience as a greenhorn miner in the Klondike Gold Rush of the late 1890s. Yet, before London ever ventured into the Great White North, he was a sailor. And whenever he wrote about sailing, he wrote about the dangers it posed, to both human and non.

London was born in San Francisco in 1876. Through much of his youth, when he was not filling his head with books, he explored the waterfronts of northern California, seeking work or adventure. As a boy, he bought a small boat and worked as an "oyster pirate" (or poacher) in San Francisco Bay, until the game wardens caught him, putting an end to his short-lived enterprise. Soon after, at seventeen, London joined the crew of his first oceangoing sailing vessel, the *Sophia Sutherland*, a three-masted wooden sailing schooner, for a seven-month seal-hunting trip toward Japan. It was a turbulent voyage on a rickety vessel, and the young sailor no doubt encountered many trials along the way, from aggressive fellow sailors to violent storms in the cold North Pacific waters. Later, he depicted the experience in his 1901 short story, *Chris Farrington: Able Seaman*:

> So small and insignificant the schooner seemed on the long Pacific roll! Rushing up a maddening mountain, she would poise like a cockle-shell on the giddy summit, breathless and rolling, leap outward and down into the yawning chasm beneath, and bury herself in the smother of foam at the bottom. Then the recovery, another mountain, another sickening upward rush, another poise, and the downward crash.[1]

Not long after, Jack London set his best-known sailing novel, *The Sea-Wolf* (1904), on another seal-hunting schooner. Both the characters and the plot are, in a word, brutal, with the title character especially so. Captain Wolf Larsen comes across like a figure from mythology, a man with superhuman strength and a complete lack of sympathy for other people's suffering. Throughout the story, he is willing to terrorize, torture, or humiliate any person he encounters, so much so that some literary scholars view him as London's symbolic incarnation of the ocean itself: ferocious, capricious, and indifferent to human struggle.[2]

Jack London did his writing at a time when the sailor's life was on the cusp of change. In the very late nineteenth and very early twentieth centuries, the wooden sailing vessels that he knew best were already on their way out, being replaced with sleeker steel models powered by steam or, increasingly, gasoline. But for a taut, psychological adventure tale, it was hard to create a finer locale than a creaky wooden ship that sways in the breeze and groans with every wave. It's not surprising that London set his stories on the type of ship he knew best, the sailing schooner. And while his youthful voyages took place on the Pacific, ships very much like his could be found on the Atlantic Ocean as well.

Some of the sturdiest schooners, and certainly some of the

best known on the East Coast, were built in shipyards along the coast of Maine. That far northeastern region was a mecca for shipbuilding, dating back to colonial days. Geography had much to do with it, as well as the abundant timber that grew there: mostly white pine, but also ash, locust, and many types of oak. The Maine shore was pocked with countless coves and bays, which made for safe harbors. Towns like Bath, Camden, and Belfast grew up along the coast, and especially along rivers that could be used for floating cut logs. By the mid-1800s, Bangor was known as the Lumber Capital of the World, processing more than two-hundred million board feet of wood per year. Between 1800 and 1920, more than three thousand sailing ships were built along Penobscot Bay alone.[3]

Schooners came in various sizes, ranging between two and five masts; the largest ever constructed, the five-mast *George W. Wells*, was built in Camden, Maine in 1900. It broke the record at 342 feet in length, forty-five feet beam (width). Most schooners were far smaller, though all were built with two primary factors in mind: durability and flexibility. Unlike the huge clipper ships, designed for the most difficult shipping lanes across oceans or around Cape Horn, for example, Atlantic schooners were intended for shorter voyages along the coasts or across smaller seas like the Caribbean. Unlike the clippers, schooners were built with a shallow draft, often with a retractable centerboard that could be raised or lowered instead of a fixed keel. The schooner was intended to access any harbor, even the most shallow; or even, if necessary, to be grounded on a beach in an emergency.[4]

For sailors who manned the schooners, the work was arduous under the best of conditions, even those that did not compare with a Jack London story. Maintaining a ship was a constant battle against equipment wear and tear, for seawater could cause just about anything to rust or rot. The crew constantly had to scrub the decks, keep all exposed wood sanded and painted, patch the sails when they ripped, waterproof ropes with tar, and work the bilge pumps necessary for even the soundest wooden ships. And that was to say nothing of the minute-to-minute operation of the ship: steering it, maintaining watch, hoisting and furling the sails, climbing the rigging when necessary, all while keeping one's footing on the deck, which was pitching to and fro with the waves.

Not surprisingly, captains often had a tough time keeping their ships' crews intact. The pay for schooner crewmen was low, even while much safer and less demanding work could be found in factories onshore. On a voyage that might include stops in four or five harbors, it was not unusual for a crewman to request his pay and quit midway. In such cases, the captain would have to scramble to replace him, with predictable results. Sailing-ship crews were not drawn from the highest social ranks.

In fact, crewmen on board more glamorous, ocean-crossing clipper ships had a pejorative for those who served on their slower, shore-hugging counterparts: "schooner trash."[5] An unfortunate stereotype, perhaps, but as with many stereotypes, one could find cases to validate it.

One such was the evening of October 10, 1905, when the four-masted schooner *Blanche H. King* was working its way north off the coast of North Carolina. It was headed for Philadelphia, carrying a load of wooden railway ties it had picked up in Brunswick, Georgia, a moderately sized port about halfway between Savannah and Jacksonville. It was standard cargo for such a ship to be carrying in that area. The lumber industry was booming in many parts of the South, including the Carolinas and Georgia, as the white pines of the Northeast had largely been depleted by the early 1900s. Logging companies then turned their eyes to the longleaf pine forests of the South, decimating them in short order to build the houses, factories, and railroads that served America's burgeoning economy in the Industrial Age.

The master of the *Blanche H. King* was Captain John W. Taylor, a native of Providence, Rhode Island, with more than thirty years of seafaring experience. He led a complement of eight officers and crew, some white and some of African descent, which was fairly typical of the time. It was sometime between 9:00 and 10:00 p.m. that evening when, at a spot roughly thirty-two miles south and one-half mile west of the tip of Cape Fear, Taylor caught sight of another vessel just ahead of him, also moving north in the same general shipping lane. In the darkness, he noticed the other ship only when he saw a red lantern hanging from its rigging, which struck him as odd. That kind of signal was not permitted at nighttime, and it led Taylor to suspect the vessel was in distress. His suspicions were aroused further after he watched the other ship's movements for a while; it was taking "very peculiar actions, running off and running to" in a zigzag pattern.[6]

Had it been daylight, Taylor might have been able to read the other ship's nameplate, and noticed that it was a similar vessel to his own. The *Harry A. Berwind*, like the *King*, was a four-masted wooden sailing schooner built in Maine. It originated in the Sawyer Brothers Shipyard in Milbridge, a fairly small village on the Narraguagus River, about midway between Penobscot Bay and the Canadian line. The Sawyer Brothers operated from 1858 until 1920, producing an average of two or three ships per year. Thus, the launching of a new vessel was an event for the local papers. When the *Berwind* rolled down the planks in October 1895, they reported a christening ceremony accompanied with a broken bottle of seawater instead of French wine. The owners thought it only proper, since the ship was destined to "sail through floods of saltwater," not wine.[7]

Naturally, the *Berwind* had been built with "all the latest improvements." It had a steam engine, often called a "donkey" engine, which interestingly was used not to propel the ship, but only to power the windlass (winch) that was used to hoist heavy loads, including the sails. All propulsion came from the sails, which hung from the four pine masts. The outer structure was built of white oak, and the deck cabins finished with ash, cherry, and "whitewood" (likely white pine). With a length of 175 feet in the keel, 204 feet on the top deck, 38 feet of beam, and six feet of space between the decks, the *Berwind* was a moderately sized ship, although hardly a spacious one.[8] Of course, one would be hard-pressed to find any sailor of that time period who would call any ship spacious.

Nor would anyone ever call this particular ship a lucky one. A superstitious man, as many sailors were, might have thought the owners would have been wiser to christen it with something other than plain water.

Feeling the need to investigate, Taylor and his crew maneuvered the *King* close to the *Berwind*. In the darkness, they could see little activity on board the ship's deck. But once they came within hailing distance, Taylor shouted over to the other vessel, asking its

A newspaper depiction of the struggle onboard the *Berwind*.

crew to identify themselves.

Over the dark waves, barely illuminated by the moonlight, someone shouted back a chilling revelation: "One man aboard here has killed the captain, mate, engineer, steward, and one colored seaman, and we want to abandon ship." That carefully phrased sentence might not have been the actual words, but it is what the captain later testified. The same voice also pleaded with the newly arrived vessel to send a boat over to the *Berwind*, so that he could be evacuated from it.[9]

Dispatching a boat would be a risky maneuver in the dark, to say nothing of what the *King*'s crew might encounter upon boarding this stricken vessel. But Taylor knew he could not leave the situation unaddressed. He gathered his first mate, Theodore Simmons, and four other crewmen, and sent them over to the *Berwind* on one of the *King*'s lifeboats (often called a "yawl"). One can visualize them approaching the mysterious vessel, and then climbing up the side ladders in the dark with no more than lanterns in hand, bracing themselves for possible ambush once they set foot on deck.

The men met with no ambush, but they did find a shocking sight.

Only three of the *Berwind*'s original complement of eight officers and men remained alive on board. Two of them were fully mobile, but seemingly distraught. The third man was sitting on top of the ship's cabin roof, bound hand and foot with a rope and chain.

And another man, obviously dead, lay just a few feet away from the captive, sprawled on the roof with a trail of blood oozing down onto the deck.[10]

CAPT. EDWIN B. RUMILL,
Murdered During Mutiny on Board His
Schooner, the Harry A. Berwind.

18

CHAPTER TWO

SHIP OF BLOOD

I n the days long before detective shows or true-crime podcasts, there was no sense of gathering evidence or "securing" a crime scene, as law enforcement officers are trained to do today. And the men of the *Blanche H. King* were not cops but sailors who had happened upon the killing of at least one man. But a crime scene it was, and since it was aboard ship, the first order of business was to secure the vessel.

First Mate Simmons watched over the three crew of the *Harry A. Berwind* while his own men carefully fanned out over the ship, to see if anyone else was aboard or alive. Gingerly, in the dark, they made their way across the deck, which was stacked quite high with boards; like the *King*, the *Berwind* was transporting a cargo of lumber. They also ventured belowdecks, not searching in detail, but just to see who was there. After just a few minutes, they reported back, finding no one.

It was not yet clear which of the *Berwind* sailors had done what, but Simmons knew all three of those sailors needed to be taken securely into custody on his own ship. Apparently two of them had overpowered the third and tied him up, and so it would be wise to keep the third man restrained. After loosening the chain and rope that secured the captive sailor, later identified as seaman Henry Scott, they retied his hands before escorting him and his two cohorts, Arthur Adams and Robert Sawyer, back to the yawl boat. As they did so, Adams willingly turned over to Simmons a small, white-handled revolver. Then they all rowed back over to the *King*.[1]

For the time being, they would have to leave the dead body on the cabin roof where it lay. Not until later would they ascertain the name of the deceased: sailor John Coakley.

When Simmons brought all three of the apprehended sailors before Captain Taylor, the first thing he asked them was the whereabouts of the *Berwind's* captain; legally, he could not take control of another vessel unless he knew its commander was indisposed. Whereupon the bound Henry Scott spoke up and said, "He is killed and overboard." Neither Adams nor Sawyer said anything to refute Scott's statement, which gave Taylor all the jurisdiction he needed. The captain of the *Berwind* was dead, nor was it looking good for the ship's other officers who were yet to be found or accounted for. If the captain had been murdered and his body cast into the ocean, then they likely had been as well. Taylor ordered all three sailors handcuffed and locked away in the *King's* lazarette, while sending Simmons and three of his men back in the yawl boat to take full charge of the *Berwind*.[2]

For the *King*, their cargo voyage to Philadelphia would be interrupted. Taylor ordered Simmons to follow him in the *Berwind* to the nearest point on the Carolina coast, where both the prisoners and ship could be turned in to the authorities. That point was Cape Fear. The first place to embark would be the small town of Southport, situated at the mouth of the river on its west bank.

It was not until morning light that Simmons and the other men had a chance to inspect the *Berwind* in further detail. The ship had been through something rough, and it was more than just a fight between sailors, a mutiny, or a shoot-out. Obviously, the ship had been through stormy weather at sea. One of its sails, the foremost topsail, was missing. Worse, the ship's rudder was disabled, with water leaking in around it. That likely accounted for its erratic movements that had drawn the *King*'s attention and would now make it a tricky task to steer the vessel into port.[3]

Simmons and company took a brief look through the ship's living quarters, although they would need to dock the ship before they could do a detailed search for weapons or other clues of the crime (or crimes). Since the belowdecks portion of the ship consisted almost entirely of the cargo hold, the men lived, ate, and slept in structures built upon the main deck.

The cabin, occupied by the captain and mate, stood very near the stern (rear) of the ship, just in front of the steering wheel. Walking forward toward the bow, one would pass by the main hatches leading into the hold, and then come to the galley. That was where the meals were prepared and eaten, and where the cook slept. Be-

The *C.A. Thayer*, restored lumber schooner owned by the National Park Service and docked in San Francisco as a tourist attraction. Built about the same time as the *Berwind*, it has a very similar size and design. Clockwise from upper left: ship at harbor, captain's cabin, forecastle, galley.

yond that came the engine room, which likely was also where the "donkeyman"—an unflattering nickname for a ship's engineer—had his quarters. Finally came the forecastle, a small space that served as bunkhouse for the four lower-ranking sailors, all of African descent. Just outside the forecastle, on the very bow of the ship, was the ship's bell, which was rung regularly to mark the time. When the bell sounded, the crew were signaled to begin and end their regular watches, which were scheduled throughout every day and night.

No doubt the most relevant find, at least at first, was the ship's logbook. It was found in the captain's cabin, which both Taylor and Simmons would later describe as "very much disordered," with papers, books, and bedding strewn about. Yet if someone deliberately tried to trash the cabin, they surprisingly had left the logbook sitting there in plain sight, revealing a rough outline of the *Berwind*'s fatal voyage.[4]

The vessel began the trip with four crewmen (Scott, Sawyer, Adams, and Coakley), led by four officers: specifically, Captain Edwin B. Rumill, a first mate, cook, and engineer. They departed Philadelphia on July 6, 1905, carrying 975 tons of Pennsylvania coal. It was bound for Cardenas, a town on the north shore of Cuba, roughly a hundred miles east of Havana, where the much-remembered U.S.S. *Maine* had famously met destruction in 1898. Cuba had won its nominal "independence" from Spain in the resulting war and was now in a confused transitional period of American occupation. Each year, it was exporting larger and larger crops of sugar, and Cardenas was one of the major ports of exit.

But before reaching Cuba, indeed almost as soon as the voyage began, there were some ominous signs. Apparently, tempers were flaring under the hot summer sun on board that vessel, as duly noted in the log in the handwriting of both the captain and first mate:

- July 9, 6 p.m.: Henry Scot very insolent, inciting insubordination, saying he would kill the captain before voyage ended if he didn't look out and several other threats

- July 19, 7:30 a.m.: Hen. Scot came to galley at breakfast and began abusing the cook about the food…. Hen. Scot took up the beans and threw them down into the galley, making mess, wasting food, cursing, and swearing at cook

• July 30, abt. 7 p.m.: Robert Sawyer came aft for some water, steward told him not to use so much of the drinking water since they had gone through 4 bucketfuls that day. . . . Sawyer became very abusive, called steward a goddamn white son of a bitch, attempted to strike, threatened to beat steward, captain stopped the row, sent the sailor off forward where he continued using abusive language, trying to incite the other sailors to insubordination

•July 31, 4:30 a.m.: Hen. Scott came aft into galley and commanded the cook to cook the allowance of provisions given to him, then catching the steward by the collar, shook him,

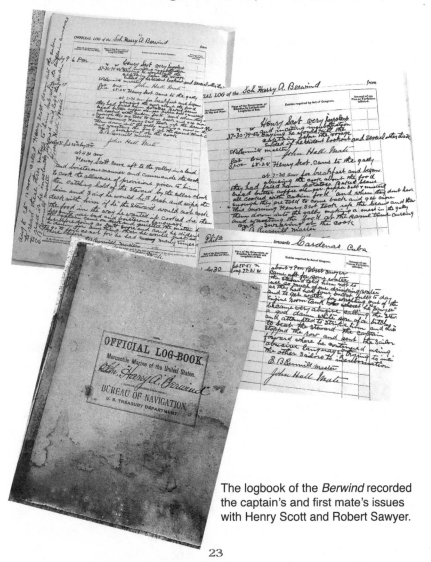

The logbook of the *Berwind* recorded the captain's and first mate's issues with Henry Scott and Robert Sawyer.

said he would wipe the deck with him if he (the steward) would not cook the food in the way he wanted; used bad and boisterous language; captain came on deck and quieted the matter, but before he did so Scott swore and said he didn't care a damn for anything, would "just as leave and go to jail" as he had done many times before

• August 5, 12 noon: Captain called Scott down into cabin to read these 3 [?] entries to him, but when captain did so, Scott insolently turned and left the cabin[5]

Eventually the ship reached Cardenas, and as all three surviving sailors would later attest, they spent ten days laboriously offloading the coal, the tropical heat no doubt continuing to wear upon them. There are no further written records of disciplinary action in the log, although all three men agreed that "grumbling" continued among the officers and crew. There was, however, vehement disagreement about who was doing the grumbling.

After leaving Cardenas, the *Berwind* travelled to Mobile, Alabama, another Southern port known for its sawmills. There, they picked up their cargo of lumber intended for Philadelphia, which took several days to stack on deck. They did not depart Mobile until September 23, heading across the Gulf of Mexico, around the Dry Tortugas, through the Straits of Florida and up the Atlantic Coast.

Again, by the account of all three men, it was on October 6 that the ship encountered a fierce storm off Cape Romain, South Carolina, which lasted for two days. The wind tore away one of the topsails and sprung the "rudder head," the top portion of the rudder that connected to the steering cables. Consequently, the crew had to jury-rig to replace the lost sail, as well as contend with the damaged rudder, all in addition to the personal tensions previously noted in the log.

Between that time and the night of October 10, when the *King* encountered the *Berwind* off of Cape Fear, the sailors' accounts diverged profoundly. However, this would not become definite until the three prisoners were brought ashore at Southport, where they could be questioned in detail by federal port authorities who had jurisdiction to interrogate the living and identify the dead.

A s for the deceased officers, the sad fact is that history has preserved very few details about them, except for the captain. Chances are that they had served on any number of previous voyages, possibly with Captain Rumill, and very likely on the *Berwind* or other vessels owned by the same company. John T. Hall, the mate, had been the overall second-in-command. The cook, alternatively called the "steward," was John Falbe. And C.L. Smith was in charge of manning the engine, plus the cables, bilge pumps, and other equipment associated with it. His formal title was engineer, although donkeyman was used just as often.

Aside from their names, and the fact that they were white— about which the press never tired of making mention and contrasting with the four African-descended sailors—barely anything is to be found about those three men.

But the personal background of Captain Edwin B. Rumill is well documented. Not only because he was the commander, but because he had a wife and two young children identified by the press at the time as "prostrated with grief" and descendants as having maintained a faithful legacy since.[6]

Rumill, like many of the ships on which he served, came from Maine. He was raised in the small waterfront village of Pretty Marsh on Mount Desert Island. In the early 1900s, it was a hardworking community located on the edge of seaside estates owned by mega-wealthy families like the Rockefellers. Fishing was the primary trade, but there also were several lumber mills and granite quarries in the area, and in winter there was a lively business in cutting massive blocks of ice from local ponds, so they could be shipped to New York and Boston for use as refrigeration.[7] Pretty Marsh still has its picturesque houses and storefronts, and tourism, not industry, is the name of the game today. It lies next to Acadia National Park, created out of the Rockefeller land in 1916 and phenomenally popular with summer hordes of lobster-feasting day-trippers and cottage renters.

Forty-five years old when he was murdered, Captain Rumill had been at sea since age fourteen, when he signed on as a cabin boy for his father, who was also a seafarer. His many voyages took him away from home for months at a time, to destinations as varied as South America, the Ivory Coast, and China. Departures were always sad and filled with some trepidation for Rumill's family. But his homecomings were joyful occasions, often accompanied by exotic gifts for the children.

In 1905, he was living in a fine mansard-roofed house in Pretty Marsh with his wife, Lettie, twelve-year-old son George, and eight-year-old daughter Edna. That house remained the home of Edna Rumill Hysom, where she lived surrounded by a beloved assortment of family memorabilia, until well into her nineties. In a retrospective story for the local paper in 1989, she thought back to her last memory of her father. Just before he departed for his final trip on the *Berwind*, Rumill presented young Edna with a chain necklace, adorned by a carved ivory elephant that he brought back from India.[8]

In addition to the jewelry, Ms. Hysom carefully guarded a photograph of her father. It suggests that Captain Rumill was every inch the classic New England ship's officer. He stands tall in his blue uniform coat with two vertical rows of buttons, wearing his braided officer's cap and a handlebar mustache. In every way, the image bespeaks a personality to be reckoned with.

As for the four Black lowerdecks sailors who were suspected of killing Rumill, they also had histories to be reckoned with, some better documented than others.

John Coakley, the only one of them not to survive the voyage, is unsurprisingly the least known. One of his cohorts, Sawyer, would later testify that he had known Coakley since 1904, and had served on several other ships with him. Aside from that, he apparently was from somewhere in the English-speaking "West Indies," a large region that included the Bahamas, Jamaica, and any number of Caribbean islands.[9] If so, then Coakley shared at least some kinship with two of the accused.

Robert Sawyer himself was about thirty years old, and by all accounts was born in Nassau, on New Providence Island of the Bahamas. His later correspondence with his mother, recorded by his jailers, suggests that his family still resided there on Shirley Street.[10] If so, they lived one block back from Bay Street, the main route circling Nassau harbor that today greets dozens of cruise ships every year and faces the Atlantis mega-resort on Paradise Island.

Yet, the present-day atmosphere of the Bahamas reveals vir-

tually nothing of what the islands were like at the turn of the twentieth century. There were no resorts. The Bahamas were a little-known
corner of the British Empire that thrived only occasionally when
conditions in the United States sent illicit commerce their way. Confederate blockade runners found a profitable safe harbor there during
the Civil War, and, much later when Prohibition was in full force, the
isolated islands and cays were a paradise for liquor smuggling boats.
Most of the other times, the "Over-the-Hill" neighborhood of Nassau where the Sawyer family lived was a poverty-stricken quarter inhabited by the descendants of slaves who either escaped from the
Southern states or were deposited there by the British Navy after
being "liberated" from slave ships.

Nassau would have presented little opportunity for young
Sawyer to better himself. By his own account, he attended school
long enough to read and write, apprenticed as a ship's carpenter, and
then took to sea.[11] He first came to the United States in October
1895, on board the *James A. Garfield*, a three-masted lumber-car-
rying barque named after the assassinated president. According to
what he later told the U.S. Naturalization Service, Sawyer's first entry
point was Union Island, Georgia, near the town of Darien, where
there were at least two major sawmills owned by the Lachlison family, later bought out by the Hilton Timber and Lumber Company.[12]
Over the next ten years, Sawyer served on many other American
ships and voyages. But at the time of his arrest on board the *Berwind*,
he was still legally a British subject.

The same was true for Sawyer's cohort, Arthur Adams.
Somewhat younger at twenty-three, he had first gone to sea two and
a half years before.[13] Adams identified as a native of Saint Vincent,
another British territory far down the Windward Island chain, much
closer to Venezuela than to the Bahamas. As with Sawyer, Adams's
prison mail records provide some hint as to where he was raised.
Both his parents still resided on Bequia,[14] one of the Grenadine islets just south of the main island of Saint Vincent, and just north
of Mustique, which is well known today as an ultra-exclusive private
resort island favored by Princess Margaret, Prince William, Princess
Kate, Mick Jagger, Johnny Depp, and other celebrities when they
desire a Caribbean getaway.

Much like the Bahamas, those islands a century ago bore

no hint of the rampant tourist development to come. If anything, they were even more of a backwater. Through the seventeenth and eighteenth centuries, the volcanic hills of Saint Vincent were home to sugar plantations, where multitudes of slaves toiled under the tropical sun, chopping cane, worked to death in a ruthless industrial meatgrinder that can only be described as mass murder. Slavery was abolished in 1834, but freedom brought little prosperity since the cane fields became less profitable for owners or workers. Cuba had picked up much of the sugar market, and by 1886, two-thirds of all the former plantation lands on Saint Vincent were no longer being farmed at all. In 1902, about the same time that Arthur Adams first enlisted as a sailor, La Soufriere volcano erupted, killing more than 1,500 people and devastating the main island.[15] He would have needed no other excuse to flee the islands and seek his fortune elsewhere.

And that left Henry Scott, the sailor who had been tackled, tied up, and chained by his fellows, and the only one who was an American citizen. By his own telling, he was thirty-one years old, born in Baltimore but raised in Philadelphia, and had worked as a sailor off and on for about fourteen years. He also claimed to be married, and that his wife was then living in Philadelphia with his daughter and son, aged three and two years, respectively.[16] That is what he claimed, although no verification is to be found, and no woman ever came forward to acknowledge she was married to Scott.

Not surprising, in light of everything eventually to be revealed about him. As the inquiry began, it seemed clear that the other men's fingers were going to be pointing at Henry Scott, and that he would be the pivotal figure in this affair.

CHAPTER THREE

ONCE BROUGHT ASHORE

The first order of business was to bring the *Harry A. Berwind* into a port where the damage to its masts and rudder could be repaired and, more urgently, the three implicated sailors could be handed over to the authorities.

Southport, North Carolina, some thirty miles away, was the first point of land that a ship would see after passing through the mouth of the Cape Fear. It has always been a tricky bit of navigation, requiring a captain to negotiate the shallow water and constantly shifting sandbars surrounding the inlet, with Fort Caswell to the west and Bald Head Island to the east. Fortunately, Southport was well staffed with river pilots, local sailors who would venture out in their own boats to meet incoming vessels and guide them in with their unique expertise.

At the time, Southport—known as Smithville until just a few years earlier—was the quintessential seafaring town. It was home to just fewer than a thousand people, virtually all of whom relied on the water in one way or another.[1] If they were not fishermen or sailors themselves, their jobs were based on oceangoing commerce. The riverfront was lined with weather-beaten piers, wharves, and warehouses. Moving back from the water, there were several blocks of sandy lanes paved with oyster shells, shaded with live oak trees, and lined with wood frame houses. The larger ones either were boardinghouses frequented by sailors or were owned by the more prosperous ship captains. Even the smaller houses gave the town the genteel look of an orderly southern county seat.

Life in Southport tended to revolve around the seasons and tides, as well as the shipping schedules. There usually was a vessel of some sort coming or going, and so there were few times when the waterfront was not bustling. Consequently, that was where most of Southport's able-bodied men could be found, either bringing in fish or processing them, or shipping out cargoes of products like lumber or turpentine.

Today, the wharves and warehouses are gone, and the piers now are used to dock pleasure boats, not commercial ones. The harbor is known as the Yacht Basin, and the old frame houses are now meticulously restored, painted white, and have historic markers on the porches to describe who built them and when. The older houses are accompanied by ever-growing numbers of massive new homes, which, although they are built to look like something as historic as a Tara or Twelve Oaks, clearly are not old. For Southport is now a town for tourists and affluent retirees, rather than salty fishermen. On a summer weekend, traffic jams plague Howe Street, the main

Whittler's Bench in
Southport today.

thoroughfare leading down to the river through the sandwich shops and antique stores.

Yet one charming feature of Southport's riverfront has remained authentic for more than a century. Right at the foot of Howe Street one will find Whittler's Bench, a set of simple wooden rails arranged in a circle. In years past the benches were arranged around a windblown cedar tree that provided shade on hot days. It has been there since 1898, a place where the elder men of the town would sit and carve on sticks with their pocketknives, and talk about the latest gossip, especially politics.[2] The cedar tree is long gone, but Whittler's Bench is a reminder that a sense of community still can be found in this formerly small town.

People certainly were gossiping in October 1905, when Captain Taylor and the crew of the *Blanche H. King* brought the three *Berwind* prisoners and one of their deceased shipmates ashore.

Once the sheriff was notified, a call went out for one of the local physicians to come along and perform an autopsy. It was a brief affair, conducted right on the deck of the *Berwind*, where the body of John Coakley had remained undisturbed since the ship was intercepted. The cause of death was quite evident, and so the finding was uncontroversial. All the doctor had to do was note where the bullet had lodged in the body and then remove it, as medical protocol would require.

What to do with the corpse posed more of a question. Coakley had no relations anywhere nearby; they were miles away in the West Indies, and even the ship's owners likely had no means of contacting them. There was nothing to do but give the man space in the local potter's field. No written record exists of Coakley's burial, but chances are that the town fathers would not have buried him in the stately, oak- and Spanish-moss-shaded Old Smithville Burying Ground, which was used by Southport's white families.

More likely, Coakley's unmarked grave is in the John N. Smith Cemetery, the primary resting place for Southport's Black community at that time. One can find quite a range of grave markers there, most of them unassuming pieces of stone or brick, some of them bordered with rows of seashells. The cemetery fell into a sad state of neglect for a number of years, although recently the locals have made a point to restore its landscaping and update its burial records. A recent survey uncovered at least 758 unmarked graves there.[3]

In the early 1900s, Blacks and whites in Southport lived in separate neighborhoods and divided social spheres. Whites owned most of the property and virtually all the businesses, yet there also was a cohesive Black community in town. By necessity, all had to work together. Even today, memories remain of some of the African-American watermen who worked the fishing boats side by side with whites. They included George Wortham, who served as a fishing guide for more than fifty years and was an oarsman on one of the pilot boats. There was also Captain Eugene Gore, who worked his way up from a kitchen boy in the early 1900s to serve as one of the first Black captains in Southport's menhaden fishing fleet.[4]

Regrettably, the background of the John N. Smith Cemetery reveals the travails that Southport's African-American community has endured over the years. Just as the twentieth century began, racial tensions in Brunswick County were at their height, as they were throughout North Carolina. Starting then, and throughout the rest of the segregation era, Black people in Southport would find themselves increasingly marginalized, to the point that many saw that their best option was to move away.

The Smith Cemetery lies on Leonard Street, just around the corner and a few blocks from the building known today as the Old Brunswick County Jail at the corner of Rhett and Nash Streets. Nowadays it is a local history museum, but in 1905, when Henry Scott, Arthur Adams, and Robert Sawyer were brought ashore and incarcerated there, it was a state-of-the-art building constructed only one year earlier. From the outside, today it looks just as it did then: the jail is a squat, rectangular, two-story building with thick brick walls, and iron bars across all the windows. The second floor was divided into several casemated cells, so the three sailors could be kept separated from each other with no opportunity to talk or collaborate. For a sleepy small town, it seemed a secure enough place to house a few prisoners, whatever they were charged with.

But even so, one of the local court commissioners wrote to Harry Skinner—the federal district attorney who would eventually prosecute the case—that the Brunswick jail was a security concern.

Brunswick County Jail and railroad station in Southport, early 1900s.

He described it as a "new brick building, and in every way apparently safe as a place of confinement," and yet it was "rather remote from the business section of town, and without police protection." The commissioner suggested moving the *Berwind* prisoners to the New Hanover County Jail in downtown Wilmington, which might be more secure.[5]

The Brunswick County jail in reality was not remote at all; it was no more than two short blocks from the business section of Southport, such as it was at the time. And it was protected by the Sheriff's Department, located on the ground floor of the building. The problem was that Brunswick County, like much of eastern North Carolina at that time, was not unfamiliar with vigilante justice.

The Brunswick County Jail today is a history museum. The jail was one year old in 1905, when Henry Scott, Arthur Adams, and Robert Sawyer were incarcerated.

33

Once the sensational story of the shipboard murders got around, a lynch mob might very well gather to raid the jail and administer capital punishment to the three accused Black men, dispensing with the time and expense of a trial.

Not many years earlier, in November 1897, several North Carolina newspapers carried a horrific tale of a local 23-year-old Black man named Nathan Willis who was apprehended for having robbed and killed a white man named Stephens. As Stephens was travelling through Brunswick on his way to Windy Hill Beach, just across the South Carolina state line, he apparently was shot in the back of his head, with his body left in the adjacent woods. Suspicion fell on Willis when he was seen wearing clothes that were stolen off the murdered corpse.

A sheriff's posse was formed to escort the prisoner to the jail in Conway, the seat of neighboring Horry County, South Carolina. But right at the state line, the story went, the posse was intercepted by a mob of local farmers who seized Willis and "carried [him] off into the woods and chained between two pine trees. Lightwood was then piled around him, and he was burned to death, thus suffering an awful fate to pay the penalty for his terrible crime."[6]

It was a very unsettled time throughout eastern North Carolina. Race was the greatest source of friction in Brunswick County, and had been since the Civil War. But by the 1890s, there was economic upheaval added to the mix. As hard times usually do, they made the racial tensions all the more volatile.

Until then, Brunswick County had long been a land of plantations dating back to the early colonial days. In the east, along the marshy Cape Fear riverbank running north from Southport towards Wilmington, it was all about rice cultivation. Very wealthy men such as "King" Roger Moore, a descendant of some of Charleston's original founders, and Eleazar Allen, an immigrant from Massachusetts, turned major profits with huge acreages along the river. Moore's opulent Orton Plantation—after going through a series of owners—remains today as the area's most notable manor house. Allen's nearby plantation, which he named Liliput in obvious tribute to Jonathan Swift, had a home that was nearly as impressive, but is less known today because it, like the industry that supported it, is long gone.[7]

That industry, of course, was slave labor. Rice planting and harvesting was brutal work, and the plantations required dozens, if not hundreds of slaves to make it economical. Once the "peculiar institution" of slavery was gone, so were the rice canals dug into the riverbank.

Inland and to the west, the hot, humid coastal plain was home to another type of large plantation. Like the ones along the river, many dated back to ancient land grants from eighteenth-century kings. But they focused less on rice than on a naturally growing crop, one of the few things that grew well in the sand. It was the longleaf pine tree, whose sticky resin could be tapped and boiled down into "naval stores," products such as rosin, tar, and pitch that were needed to waterproof wooden ships in the days of sail. While slaves were available to do the sweltering grunt work, there was much profit to be made. The William Gause family built themselves a fine estate on their land near present-day Ocean Isle Beach, where George Washington once spent a night on his tour of the South in 1791. Also, the French-descended Bellamy family, originally from South Carolina, had a huge turpentine plantation that they called the "Grist," probably the most lucrative of all the properties they owned in southeast North Carolina.[8]

Slave emancipation was not the only factor in the demise of the pine plantations. The constant pattern of slashing the trees, draining their sap, and burning the undergrowth around them was not ecologically sustainable. It was this confluence of events that brought about the end of the agricultural planter economy.

At any rate, the post-Civil War decades are remembered in Brunswick County as the "Tough Years," when everyone of all colors had to adjust to a new social and economic reality. With the plantations gone, and newly freed slaves jostling to make their way, many people had to find new ways to survive. For those in Southport, the only town of any size in the county, that typically meant working on the water. In the interior, most were very small farmers relying on subsistence agriculture.[9]

Then in 1893, a national economic slump seemed to bring everyone's fortunes even lower. Farmers were especially hard-hit, as the value of their products tumbled. Cotton prices, in particular, had fallen by more than half between 1868 to 1893. At the same time, railroads charged farmers their usual fees to ship their products to market, and banks refused to grant any relief on their interest rates. For many farmers in eastern North Carolina, it was a ruinous time.[10]

It was enough even to shake the foundation of North Carolina's partisan political loyalties, which had stood since the end of the war. The Republican Party, long seen as the tool of Yankee Reconstruction, consisted almost entirely of Blacks by the 1890s, while the predominant Democrats were the white man's party, the upholder of the Confederate tradition. Yet the Democrats were conservative, financially as well as socially. The party apparatus was heavily influenced by railroad and industrial interests, who saw no need to extend any help to the agricultural sector. Many farmers, in sheer desperation, began looking for a political new deal.

They found it in the lead-up to the 1894 midterm elections, when many white farmers broke with the Democrats and joined the Populist Party, which remarkably enough decided to merge with the largely Black Republicans. Known as the Fusion campaign, they set forth a sweeping platform calling for controls on railroad fees and interest rates, lighter working hours, and more education funding. This biracial coalition, as improbable as it seemed, met with great success. In 1894 and 1896, they won control of the General Assembly, the governorship, and both of North Carolina's U.S. Senate seats.[11]

The Fusion campaign was an awkward coalition of disparate groups, born only out of exceptional economic hardship. Many of the white Populist farmers were as virulently racist as anyone, and insecure about governing in partnership with Blacks. But now eleven Blacks had been elected to the General Assembly, in addition to hundreds more as county commissioners, magistrates, policemen, and other officials. For the Fusionist experiment to work, those whites would have to accept Black people in positions of everyday legal authority. From the outset, it was a challenge for the Fusionists to remain fused.

One man who embodied those conflicts was the leader at the top: Daniel L. Russell, whom the Fusionists elected as governor in 1896. Russell was a Brunswick County man, a Confederate veteran, and scion of an affluent plantation family. Quite surprisingly, given that background, he was a white Republican who supported public schools and vocally opposed the influence of "railroad kings, bank barons, and money princes." But although Russell had appealed to Black voters to help him win in 1896, he had never been friendly toward them personally. When he served earlier as a county judge, Russell sometimes remarked on the pervasive criminality of Blacks, calling them "largely savages," as unqualified to govern white men as "their brethren in African swamps."[12]

Democrats were infuriated at having been thrown out of their accustomed seat of power, and they could easily see the best way to regain it. They would disrupt the tenuous Republican and Populist coalition by appealing to white voters solely on the grounds of race. Thus was born the White Supremacy Campaign in the midterm year of 1898.

The leading light of the campaign was Josephus Daniels, editor of the Raleigh *News and Observer*, the most widely read paper in eastern North Carolina. He had grown up in Wilson, a farm town in the Coastal Plain where Confederate nostalgia ran high. The Daniels family lived with rumors of a past disgrace: Josephus's father (also Josephus, though sometimes called Jody) had supposedly been anti-secession, and he had been killed by gunfire from Confederate troops while sailing on a trading boat on the Pamlico River. For years afterward, rumors circulated that the elder Daniels was engaged in treasonable commerce with the Union army.[13]

From that, editor Josephus Daniels may have felt a certain compulsion to prove his Rebel *bona fides*, and so he did in 1898. In his newspaper, he urged white voters to flock to the polls and vote Democratic, claiming the Fusionist government was riddled with corruption, incompetence, and most of all, with Black people. North Carolina's government had been sullied by Black hands and needed to be "redeemed." Virtually every front page carried a sensationalist story about Blacks abusing whites. Some alleged violent crime, especially the tired trope of the Black rapist preying on white women. (One of many such reports, from Greene County near Wilson, told of "burglary and attempted rape by a negro.") Perhaps even more troubling were stories of Black government officials lording their authority over whites. In Vanceboro, white ladies were supposedly required to visit a Black clerk in order to list their taxes, while "young white women in Wilmington [were] pushed off the sidewalks by Negro policemen on their beats."[14] Such everyday occurrences took on hostile meaning for white southerners long used to being in power.

Just as provocative as the stories were cartoons carried by the *News and Observer*. Many white North Carolinians were illiterate, and so Daniels sought to reach them with images they could easily grasp. The drawings were crude, but the message was clear. One showed a heavy black boot, labeled simply "The Negro," crushing a white man underfoot, with the caption, "A Serious Question—How Long Will this Last?" Perhaps the worst of them all showed a menacing Black demon with wings marked "Negro Rule," and outstretched claws clutching helpless white ladies above the title, "The Vampire That Hovers Over North Carolina."[15]

Along with the media blitz, the Democrats had a lineup of speakers who canvassed the state, giving rousing speeches at every rail depot and crossroads where they could draw a crowd. The constant themes were whiteness, womanhood, and redemption. The organizer was Furnifold Simmons, an attorney who came from an affluent plantation family near New Bern, and the unquestioned star was Charles B. Aycock, a boyhood friend of Daniels who loved to regale crowds with Lost Cause memories of his older brothers who served in Rebel gray. The success of the 1898 campaign would be revealed in the future destinies of both men.[16] In 1900, Aycock was elected governor, and Simmons won a United States Senate seat.

The campaign's success was due partly to the fact that it had an armed partisan militia supporting it. Known as the Red Shirt brigade, this Democratic paramilitary unit was composed of white troopers on horseback, toting Winchester rifles, and bringing the threat of gunfire to Democratic campaign rallies. Even Daniels, writing in his memoirs years later, admitted how the Red Shirts "could carry terror to the Negroes in their quarters . . . their appearance was the signal for the Negroes to get out of the way, so that when the Red Shirt brigade passed through the Negro end of town, it was as uninhabited as if it had been a graveyard."[17]

The Red Shirts were so brazen, and tensions so high by the end of 1898, that Governor Russell came within a hairsbreadth of being lynched himself. As the governor was travelling by train through the small towns of Hamlet and Maxton, on his way home to Wilmington to cast his vote, the train was rushed by a contingent of mounted troopers, shouting for the governor and threatening to swing him from the nearest utility pole. Russell escaped death only by hiding in the train's baggage compartment.[18]

As shocking as that was, it was a pale harbinger of violence to come after the votes were counted.

In those closing months of the campaign, the White Supremacists received an unwitting gift from an unlikely source. Alexander "Alex" Manly was the editor of the only Black-owned newspaper in eastern North Carolina, the *Wilmington Daily Record.* The light-skinned editor was, in all likelihood, the mixed-race grandson of Charles Manly, a Wake County plantation owner who served a term as governor of North Carolina in the pre-Civil War years, and who fathered children with several of his enslaved women. Being personally familiar with the subject of miscegenation, Alex Manly stepped up to answer the accusations about Black men preying on white women.

In an editorial responding to a speech given by Rebecca L. Fulton of Georgia, in which she advocated the lynching of Black rapists, the *Daily Record* shockingly asserted that not every Black man who slept with a white woman was a rapist, that many Black men were "sufficiently attractive for white girls of culture to fall in love with them." And even among poor whites, the editorial claimed that "the women of that race are not any more particular in the matter of clandestine meetings with colored men than the white men with colored women." And to add menace to the insult, Manly warned whites, "Don't think ever that your women will remain pure while you are debauching ours. You sow the seed—the harvest will come in due time."[19]

North Carolina's white press immediately seized upon Manly's purported words, republishing them at every opportunity. They pretended to be shocked and offended, but in fact they loved it. Nothing could better motivate white Democratic voters to vote "white" than to show that Blacks were openly advocating not just equality, but interracial sex. Poor white men, who earlier had voted Fusion, did not appreciate the hint that they were attracted to Black women. Thus, the fate of the Fusion experiment was sealed. On Election Day 1898, the Democrats swept both houses of the state legislature and North Carolina's congressional delegation, setting the stage for the decades of white segregationist rule that followed. It would last well into the 1960s.

In fact, the *Daily Record* editorial was so inflammatory that some have questioned who actually wrote it. Some remember Alex Manly as an assertive firebrand who frequently challenged Wilmington's white economic establishment, although at least one historian, Philip Gerard, believes the infamous editorial is not characteristic of Manly. It does not fit his writing style: many of his editorials dealt with bread-and-butter mundane issues like building city bicycle paths, and conditions in black hospitals.[20] Some believe that William L. Jeffries, Manly's assistant editor, wrote the offending article. A few even claim that Josephus Daniels bribed Manly to print it, knowing the white backlash that would ensue; that, however, is likely getting a bit too conspiratorial.

The mystery still remains as to who exactly wrote the *Daily Record* editorial, which just goes to show how the events of those tumultuous days can be obscured by confusion, bias, and outright falsification.

Consider also the statistics on lynching that occurred in that period. It is difficult for historians, even with the best of intentions, to take an accurate count of how many people were terrorized or murdered by extrajudicial mobs. Those who committed the violent acts did not keep legal records, and victims usually were too terrified to seek redress. Estimates vary, but researchers from the Tuskegee Institute to the Equal Justice Initiative in Montgomery, Alabama, are certain that at least a hundred people were lynched in North Carolina between 1880 and 1950; in fact, there may have been dozens more.[21] No one doubts that hundreds more people were lynched in Georgia, Alabama, and Mississippi, where mob violence was more pervasive.

Newspaper coverage at the time, could be unreliable. The purported lynching of Nathan Willis, near Brunswick County as he was being escorted to Conway, South Carolina, in November 1897, is a case in point.

It turns out that Willis was indeed accused of murder, but he was not burned to death by a mob, as several papers reported at the time. That was a case of runaway gossip making its way into print. In fact, Willis was escorted to the jail in Conway, where he was duly put on trial, convicted, and executed in a legal hanging on April 1, 1898. It was not *technically* a lynching, although one can legitimately wonder how much due process the young Black man received. Willis was lucky to survive for even those few months between crime and execution. After he was hanged, the papers flat out admitted, "It is remarkable that there was not a lynching at the time. The men of Horry deserve credit for letting the law take its course in this instance."[22]

Taken with that example, few people in 1905 could have doubted what ultimately lay in store for the three men charged with five murders aboard the *Harry A. Berwind*. If they even lived to stand trial, their end would come with ropes around their necks.

Brunswick County Courthouse in Southport. Above: old postcard
photo of original 1844 courthouse. Below: courthouse today.

CHAPTER FOUR

THE
PRELIMINARY

The *Harry A. Berwind*, along with its now-infamous crew, had drawn the gawking attention of the locals as soon as it docked in Southport. As accustomed as they were to visitors passing through from distant locales, no one could remember an incident like this one. A shipboard mutiny, plus a quintuple murder, were enough to rivet the attention of everyone in the languid town.

Within hours of the ship's arrival in port, many onlookers were taking it upon themselves to board the ship and rummage through its quarters. Newspapers would write later of the "public taking a keen interest in all developments of the case," and the "morbid curiosity of at least some of the visitors was interesting if not despicable. . . . Hundreds of souvenirs were being carried away from the ship."[1] Obviously a matter of great concern, if the authorities had been seriously interested in securing the crime scene.

As the Brunswick County seat, Southport was no stranger to the sort of small-town legal spectacles that one might find anywhere in the South. Usually, they did not amount to much. In 1905, still very much the horse-and-buggy era, there was not much traffic to be found in the "business district." On days when court was in session, the courthouse was the social center of town. Like Whittler's Bench, it was a good place just to sit around and shoot the breeze, and, depending on what cases were on the calendar, one might also find interesting free entertainment. Moonshining, deer poaching, and the random drunken brawl: those were some of the local judicial matters that might be heard in a North Carolina county courtroom. Most such cases were informal affairs, dispensed within a few minutes with a plea, a fine, and often some colorful words of wisdom from the presiding judge.

A murder trial, however, was exceptional. And this particular crime promised to be a complex one to deal with, not least because of jurisdiction. It turned out that the ultimate judicial proceedings in the *Berwind* case would not be held in the state court at Southport, even though it was the point of land nearest to the alleged crime, because it was not a state court case.

Then as now, when a homicide takes place aboard a vessel on the "high seas," rather than on the soil of a particular state, it becomes a matter for the federal courts. The situation was not common, but when it did arise, courts followed the general rule that state jurisdiction did not extend more than three miles offshore from its low-tide mark. The *Berwind* had been roughly thirty-two miles from land when it was intercepted. That, combined with the fact that the ship flew the American flag, was enough to bring these five alleged killings under the definition of "murder on the high seas," as defined in Section 5339 of the United States Code.

Aside from the killings of four officers and one sailor, there was another federal legal issue that could be raised. Mutiny and piracy were rarely encountered in North Carolina waters, at least in the two centuries since Blackbeard and Stede Bonnet had their heyday. But when they did occur, courts recognized that they were federal crimes. The takeover of a ship by its crew was a mutiny, and if the act also resulted in theft of a vessel, it constituted piracy.[2] Either such crime was to be governed by the law of the nation under whose flag the ship sailed, and the *Berwind* was undoubtedly an American vessel (although some of her crew were not).

Mutiny or piracy, though, would require the element of conspiracy. For the government to prove either, they would have to show that at least two of the charged sailors had plotted together to seize the ship. Before long, it was clear that there was serious dispute on that score.

At any rate, the trial could not be held in the Brunswick County Courthouse. If it came to that, the *Berwind* sailors would be tried before a jury in the Circuit Court for the Eastern District of North Carolina, as it was called then. The federal court sat upriver in Wilmington. And yet, there was a preliminary legal matter that could be handled in Southport, and would provide the first detailed account of what had occurred on board the ill-fated ship.

When a federal crime was alleged, it was standard for an evidentiary hearing to be held before a commissioner, a court appointee very much like a federal magistrate today. The commissioner would hear testimony from the witnesses, or at least the most important ones. Like a grand jury, the commissioner would determine whether there was sufficient evidence of a crime for a case to be bound over for trial. As it turned out, there were two local men who had previously been appointed to the part-time job of federal commissioner: William T. Pinner of Southport, and S.P. Collier of Wilmington. It was not often that they were called upon to fulfill this duty; apart from smuggling, there just were not that many federal crimes that occurred in the area. But this hearing promised to be a spectacle.

The commissioners, with William Pinner taking the lead as presiding officer, called their hearing to order on the morning of October 12, 1905, only two days after the *Berwind* was intercepted offshore. Here again, time was of the essence, as was security. They assembled the hearing in the Brunswick Courthouse at the corner of Moore and Davis streets, only a few hundred yards away from the jail where the prisoners had been placed as securely as possible, and just blocks from the cemetery where John Coakley lay in his one-day-old grave.

The building was a nondescript, utilitarian structure, built out of brick in 1854.[3] Surprisingly it still stands, even though Southport is no longer the county seat. That would change in 1978, when the county government offices were moved—amid considerable controversy—to the more centrally located town of Bolivia. The old courthouse then served for a while as the Town Hall, although it now sits mostly vacant. Unlike most historic buildings in a town where appearances are so important for attracting visitors, it sits in a sad state of disrepair. But the spacious old courtroom on the second floor still has the basic appearance it did a century ago. The old wooden pews still face toward the council table at the front where the judge's bench used to be. Yet it also has a "pebble-board" ceiling, a much more recent addition, which now sags with water damage and disrepair.

As the hearing began, it was clear that the public's morbid curiosity had travelled from the dockyard into the courthouse. The courtroom was packed to capacity, so much so that it was "almost impossible for His Honor to quell the crowd." The spectators tried to muscle their way to the front of the courtroom so they could hear the witnesses' testimony clearly, despite Commissioner Pinner's threats to hold them in contempt.[4]

The proceeding was brisk, despite the excitement. It was finished within one day, consisting basically of the commissioners questioning the various witnesses: the captain, mate, and sailors on board the *Blanche H. King*, followed by the survivors from the *Berwind*. Sadly, there is no stenographic transcript; the newspaper accounts are the best ones to be found. Yet the hearing revealed "one of the most bloodcurdling and awful stories of butchery known since the days when piracy reigned supreme on our coast."[5] Granted, newspaper writers of the day were given to exaggeration and purple prose. But the description fit.

The officers from the *King* testified first. Captain Taylor and First Mate Simmons both described how their vessel had come alongside the *Berwind* after noticing its curious movements, as well as the red lantern. And after they boarded and saw Coakley's bloody corpse, they took what seemed to be the only responsible course of action, to apprehend all three men aboard. For the *King*'s crew, it was more than a matter of civic duty. They also wanted to stake a salvage claim: a financial share of the value of the *Berwind* and its cargo, which they had retrieved for the *Berwind*'s owners by seizing it back from the mutineers who had apparently tried to steal it.[6]

Yet, if the newspaper accounts of the hearing are accurate—and they might not be entirely so—Captain Taylor also made a curious statement. He said that once his men boarded the *Berwind* and saw that Robert Sawyer and Arthur Adams had subdued Henry Scott and chained him, they proceeded on the assumption that Scott had committed the murders on his own.[7] If it were true that one of the sailors was more guilty of the crime than the others, then that would have legal ramifications for the *King*'s salvage claim. Later, Captain Taylor would give other testimony on that point, which would not be entirely consistent.

Arthur Adams then took the stand and presented the first direct account of the events on board the ship. The youngest of the *Berwind*'s surviving sailors, he also gave the most favorable impression by his physical appearance. Reporters, who never tired of focusing on the racial elements involved, and who were conditioned to equate intelligence with good looks and light skin, described Adams as a "bright mulatto."[8] Although many folks by the end of the day would think Adams's story questionable, they did not doubt that he looked relatively sympathetic. His caramel-colored skin and straight hair contrasted noticeably with the other two, much darker accused.

As Adams related the tale, the crime on board the ship was no mutiny. There was no conspiracy involved. One man alone had conceived the plan to murder all the ship's officers, and that man alone had carried it out. That man was Henry Scott.

The trouble began in the dark, early morning hours of October 10, nearly a full day before the *King* met up with the *Berwind*. From 12 midnight until 4:00 a.m., Adams stated that he and Sawyer had served watch on deck, one of them at the wheel and the other stationed near the bell at the ship's bow. At 4:00, he and Sawyer were relieved by Scott and Coakley, who were assigned to the next watch, which would last until 8:00 a.m. Going off duty, Adams and Sawyer headed to the forecastle, where they ordinarily would climb into their bunks for sleep. On the way, Adams said he passed by the engine room, where he saw Captain Rumill laboriously working the bilge pumps. It was necessary, because the some of the ship's seams were leaking after having passed through heavy weather days earlier.[9] This was the last time Adams would see the captain alive.

Around 5:00 a.m., Adams said that Coakley came rushing up

to the forecastle door, and said to him and Sawyer, "Come out here, they are shooting!"

But before they could do so, Scott appeared at the door with a pistol in his hand, and ordered all three of them, "Not a damn one of you come out of the forecastle; if you do I will kill you." Scott left and headed toward the stern of the ship, leaving the other three—who had no firearms, and were shocked to see Scott carrying one—standing in the forecastle.

Moments later, they heard more shots, and Sawyer ventured out onto the deck to see what was happening. Then Adams heard Sawyer exclaim, "My God, don't shoot!" as he rushed back to the forecastle, followed by Scott, who then announced that he was the "master of this damn ship," and the others must do as he ordered. Immediately, Scott began issuing commands for Adams, Sawyer, and Coakley to come on deck and tend to the ship's wheel and rigging.[10]

None of the other three sailors saw at whom or what Scott was shooting, but in light of what happened next, it became all too clear. Scott had killed Captain Rumill and tossed his body overboard.

If Adams was being truthful, Scott apparently walked the deck for some time, brandishing his pistol, ordering Adams, Sawyer, and Coakley here and there. It is not clear how long that went on, perhaps as much as an hour. As it was still dark in the early morning hours, the men were limited in what they could see. But there were three other officers onboard the ship, and at some point, Scott must have gone looking for them.

The next officer to appear was the engineer, C.F. Smith. Apparently, he came staggering up the deck in some distress, because Adams called out to Sawyer, "Oh God, look at the engineer coming up washed in blood!"

Smith was crying out with indistinct words, but it sounded like he was pleading for mercy while Scott pumped him with bullets. The next sound Adams heard was Smith's voice, "crying in the sea astern" after Scott cast him over the side.

"After a little while," Adams continued, "I saw the mate and Scott come up." Scott and John T. Hall were grappling with each other, with Scott attempting to throw him overboard, but Hall managed to slide under some of the board lumber stacked on the deck as he cried out, "Scott, have mercy on me!" Again, it is tantalizingly unclear how long the struggle continued, but according to Adams, he and Sawyer gestured to each other, trying to find a way to distract Scott.

Sawyer called out for Scott to desist, but Scott shouted out to them, "Damn you, if you come up here, I will shoot you!"

To underline the threat, Scott raised his pistol, and took a shot at Sawyer, but missed. The mate called out, "For God sake, help me, Sawyer!" Scott replied by firing two more shots at Hall, even though the mate had his hands upraised, pleading. The mate fell dead, and Scott tossed him over the ship's rail, into the lolling waves.

After that, Scott headed off to the galley, apparently in search of his final victim. Adams claimed that he and Sawyer heard two shots in quick succession, and then four more. Scott then emerged from the galley, carrying the body of cook John Falbe—"a very small white man," according to Adams—in his arms, and then threw the corpse overboard like the others.

All this time, Coakley had been at the ship's wheel, steering. Someone had to do so, for otherwise the vessel would veer off course. At some point later in the day, when Scott was not looking, Adams and Sawyer approached Coakley and said that somehow, they must overpower Scott. They would have to await just the right moment, as Scott was armed and they were not; moreover, it was not clear how much ammunition Scott had for his gun. But if they did not do it, Scott was certain to kill them all. Again, if Adams is to be believed, Coakley agreed.

It was not until "late in the evening" of October 10 that someone made a move against Scott. Adams claimed he heard someone call out to him for assistance, and then when Adams ran toward the stern, he saw that Sawyer had tackled Scott. The two of them subdued Scott, grabbed his pistol from him, tied his hands, wrapped a chain around his ankles, and tied him down to the roof of the captain's cabin. Coakley was at the wheel, located just above the cabin, where he had been most of the day.

Around this same time, in the gathering darkness, Adams and Coakley thought they saw the lights of another vessel approaching. Adams then went into the rigging to hang the red signal lantern, wanting to draw the other ship near. But as he did so, he was shocked to hear a new gunshot, and Coakley's anguished cry of, "My God, he's shot me!"

Scrambling down the ropes, Adams saw Coakley's limp body lying across Scott, who somehow had managed to free his hands and draw another pistol from within his clothes. Although Adams and Sawyer both claimed to have searched Scott for additional weapons after they tackled and tied him, they apparently failed to do so completely.

Either Sawyer or Adams then picked up a belaying pin and smacked Scott with it, immobilizing him before he had a chance to fire again. They tied him down to the cabin roof for a second time and laid the dead body of Coakley beside him. Before long, the *King* arrived alongside, and Sawyer and Adams both shouted to its crew that they wanted to be evacuated from the *Berwind*.

Thus completed the narrative of Arthur Adams, followed immediately by that of Robert Sawyer, who took the stand and gave an account that was "exactly same" as that of Adams. Both men were adamant that they were compelled to cooperate with Scott until they had their opportunity to subdue him physically, because he had two pistols and they had none. But they were adamant they themselves had never killed anyone, nor did they conspire with anyone to do so.

When Henry Scott took the stand, the press was not quite sure what to make of him. Reporters' descriptions of him were ambivalent, to say the least. Some white folks thought that Scott, with his piercing eyes, pointed eyebrows, and whiskers, looked like the stereotypical devious Black man that haunted their imaginations. They characterized him as a "powerful negro," "indifferent and insolent in his manner." Yet when he testified, Scott revealed enough charisma that some thought him almost charming. One reporter was impressed enough to praise him as "rather above the intelligence of his race, of powerful physique and a smooth talker."

Scott would have to be a smooth talker to combat everything that had been said against him. And so, he confronted Adams's and Sawyer's accounts head on, essentially flipping the script on them. While they had placed blame for all the killings on him, Scott would claim that Adams, Sawyer, and Coakley had colluded together in the murders. Yes, Scott admitted to shooting Coakley, but claimed to have done so only in self-defense.

By Scott's telling, the other three sailors—being all West Indians, unlike him—had sailed together on other ships prior to the *Berwind* and were "pals." The entire voyage had been long, hot, and filled with backbreaking labor, and by the time the ship reached Mobile, all the sailors were in a foul mood. They had been complaining about the quality of food and water on board ship—and the ship's log did, in fact, seem to support that, although the captain's notes suggested Scott was the primary instigator of the trouble. Yet, according to Scott, the other three were the men who had finally had enough. When they went ashore on liberty in Mobile, Adams, Sawyer, and Coakley all went to a store and purchased pistols, saying they intended to kill the officers if they inflicted any further abuse on them. They also asked Scott to take part, but he refused, and declined to purchase a gun.

Once they were back at sea, the grumbling continued among the men, up to the fatal day of October 10. Scott said it was true that in the early morning hours, he and Coakley took over the deck watch at 4:00 a.m.: Coakley at the wheel, and Scott on lookout on the bow. Then, at 5:00, Scott briefly took the wheel so that Coakley could go to the galley, where the mate and cook could usually be found, to get some coffee.

A few minutes later, Scott said he heard shouting from the direction of the galley: it sounded like someone was complaining the coffee was too cold. Scott left the wheel and ran forward. On the way, he encountered Sawyer, who was brandishing a pistol, and said to Scott, "Let's start this business now." Reaching the galley, Scott said he witnessed Coakley shoot the mate, and Sawyer shoot the cook. From the direction of the engine room, they first could hear Adams wrestling with the engineer, then a shot. Scott ran back toward the wheel in fear. When he got there, he found a pistol, loaded, lying on the cabin roof. He did not know where it came from, but he shoved it in his pocket, and took the wheel.

As Scott claimed, all the officers were shot dead, and their bodies were thrown overboard within ten or twelve minutes. It was not long enough to leave many traces of a struggle—including bloodstains—on the ship.

After the shooting stopped, Scott said, all four sailors went about in a sort of a daze, manning the ship for most of the day, wondering what they would do. It was not until late afternoon, supposedly, that Sawyer and Adams revealed a plan: they would set the *Berwind*'s yawl boat adrift, waterlog the ship by opening its scuttles, and then beach it somewhere along the Carolina shore. When asked, they would claim that during a storm, all eight men had attempted to abandon ship in the yawl boat but all four white officers drowned and only the four Black sailors managed to get back to the ship. In their imagination, Scott claimed, they thought the recent storm damage to the ship's rudder and masts would corroborate the story. The four of them would be awarded the prize money for the ship.

Scott claimed that he dismissed the idea, thinking the white authorities would never believe such a story—whereupon Sawyer supposedly struck Scott and knocked him down. The other three men proceeded to tie Scott hand and foot, and chain him to the cabin roof. After a while, when Scott managed to get his hands free, Coakley noticed this and ran to subdue him, brandishing a club as well as a gun. Coakley got off a shot at Scott, which missed, and Scott had just enough time to draw the pistol that he had kept concealed in his pocket and shoot Coakley, who fell dead. Sawyer and Adams seized their own clubs, beat Scott into submission, and tied him up again. When they saw the *King* approach, they resolved to hoist the signal lantern and invent a story, laying all the blame for the murders on Scott.

Scott did not mention what had happened to Captain Rumill, leaving the impression that one of the other three must have killed him earlier, before Scott went on duty.[11]

What to make of it all?

There were two basic accounts of the massacre, one from Adams and Sawyer, and one from Scott. At first blush, one might think Adams and Sawyer's story a bit more credible, if not overwhelmingly so. Scott's account of finding a loaded pistol, discarded so perfectly on the cabin roof when it had not been there minutes before, was not plausible.

Yet if Scott had killed all four white officers plus Coakley, would he have done so entirely by himself? Would one Black sailor have undertaken a mass murder without any of his other three fellow Black sailors having *any* foreknowledge? That, too, seemed implausible, if only due to the close quarters and the shared experience of working together on a small vessel for three months, and particularly implausible given the prejudiced views held by most white Southerners, who tended to view Blacks as naturally violent and conspiratorial.

Plus, how much blood was found on the ship? The press stated the *Berwind* had been searched thoroughly and, aside from the cabin roof where Coakley's body lay, not a "drop of blood or sign of struggle" had been found.[12] Later, that "fact" would come into serious question, as others would describe blood spatters in several other places. But as reported at the time, the lack of disorder on the ship suggested that the shootings were finished in a matter of minutes, as Scott claimed, rather than over a full day, as Adams and Sawyer said.

One reporter, who managed to get a direct quote from Scott after the hearing concluded, thought that he had put forth a "rather straightforward tale," and that "public opinion throughout the state implicates the whole three negroes" in the murders.[13] The smooth-talking Scott himself posed a rhetorical question:

"Now if you will look at this matter from a reasonable standpoint there were four White men and three Negroes besides myself aboard, does it look reasonable, if the three Negroes, Coakley, Adams, and Sawyer, had been in sympathy with the White sailors, do you think that I could have overcome them all? And even after the captain was killed, does it look reasonable that I could have overcome the six remaining men, if they had resisted?"[14]

To the surprise of no one, the commissioners ruled that there were sufficient grounds to indict all three sailors—Scott, Sawyer, and Adams—with murder on the high seas. Juries would have to sort it all out. The charge was the same, but since the defendants were telling such widely varying stories, they would not be tried together in federal court. Adams and Sawyer would be tried in one joint proceeding, and Scott in a separate one.

Wilmington, North Carolina, was about to witness one of the most spellbinding courtroom dramas in its history. In fact, it would be the biggest spectacle of any kind that town had seen since 1898.

A white mob gathers outside the charred remains of
The Daily Record after the 1898 massacre.

CHAPTER FIVE

A City
Undone

When Scott, Adams, and Sawyer were taken to Wilmington, they were immediately locked away in the New Hanover County Jail. Built in 1850, on the corner of Princess and Third streets downtown, it was just next door to the county courthouse and police department.[1] As federal officials intended, this jail would be at least as secure as the one in Southport. Whatever danger there may have been from mob violence on the outside, there was slim chance of anyone making a break from the inside.

The old jail no longer stands, but news accounts from the time paint a stark picture of the setting within. The hulking stone structure was divided into cell blocks, with Scott occupying one, and Adams and Sawyer in another. Since the men were clearly at odds with each other, the jailers thought it best to separate them, lest one might try to attack another. At night, when the iron cellblock doors were locked and bolted, the clang of shifting metal could be heard throughout the jail. Each cell door was covered with iron bars, with barely enough space for one to slip through his hands or a dinner plate. The windowless space was pitch black, except occasionally, when a jailer would make his rounds carrying a lantern.[2] For the three unfortunate sailors, it must have seemed like they had been cast into the Black Hole of Calcutta. Or they might have likened it to a slave ship, not the kind of vessel to which they were accustomed.

Beyond the jail walls, Wilmington was perhaps the most inhospitable town where they could fear to be put on trial. The White Supremacy Campaign was over and done by 1905, and whites now reigned indisputably supreme. The judges, sheriff, prosecutors, police, and virtually all the attorneys—whatever their specialty—were white.

What a difference seven years had made—seven years of living in the aftermath of a deadly armed insurrection that was, in the view of many historians today, the only successful governmental *coup d'état* that ever occurred in the United States, an insurrection that would remake not only the politics, but the very population of a city.

In 1898, Wilmington had been a moderately sized city of just more than twenty thousand people, which made it the largest town— and commercial center—of a stubbornly rural state. Throughout North Carolina, most still lived either on small subsistence farms or, increasingly, in cotton mill villages that were found mostly in the central Piedmont rather than on the coast.[3] Even in places where manufacturing was growing, the mill towns were self-contained communities where nearly everyone worked at the mill, and all commercial activity revolved around it. No one would have likened them to cities.

North Carolina had started to industrialize long before it ever made much progress with urbanizing, which is what made Wilmington an anomaly in the state, a fully developed city with all the modern conveniences of the day. The marvel of electricity was well established by 1898. Telephone service began in 1879, streetlights in 1886, and electric streetcars began running in 1892.[4] In a port town, most of the business naturally was centered along the riverfront. Wilmington was the world's largest cotton exporting center, much of it around the Cotton Compress owned by James Sprunt, the local business baron and historian. His company alone employed more than eight hundred men, almost all African American, working long hours to load huge bales of cotton onto ships headed to European ports.[5]

Just more than three decades past Emancipation, the color line was very much evident in Wilmington. Two years earlier, in 1896, the Supreme Court had issued its infamous decision in *Plessy v. Ferguson*, which placed a legal imprimatur upon the social order that most people already recognized. Segregation was law, as well as a fact of life. Whites and Blacks lived in neighborhoods that were closely adjacent, but mostly separate. Schools and churches were strictly segregated. That reality had never changed, despite the political breakthrough of the Fusionist years.

Yet even though African Americans in Wilmington were second-class citizens, they had economic clout. They were a majority of the city's population, at roughly fifty-six percent. And not all were unskilled laborers or domestic servants. Wilmington's Black middle class was relatively small but growing, and it included college-educated professionals like teachers, ministers, and funeral directors.

One could even find African Americans among Wilmington's legal and business elite, and not all were as politically provocative as Alex Manly, the newspaper editor. Thomas C. Miller, for example, was a pawnbroker, real estate investor, and moneylender who extended loans to whites as well as Blacks. At his death, his estate was valued at approximately $280,000.00 in today's dollars, making him one of the wealthiest men in town. Attorney William E. Henderson, who represented himself as a Black man although he was actually a half-blood Cherokee, was known as the best lawyer for whites to retain when they needed to do business with the Black community.

Overshadowing them all was John C. Dancy, a Howard University graduate who in 1897 had been appointed by President William McKinley as the federal customs inspector for Wilmington. The prestigious job netted him a salary of four thousand dollars per year, while the governor of the state earned only three thousand. Having grown up the son of a free Black man in Eastern North Carolina, Dancy was always cautious not to put on airs or provoke the suspicions of whites. He was a friend and follower of Booker T. Washington. Whenever he was asked by whites, Dancy would promote education and entrepreneurship, not political activism, as the keys to Black social advancement.[6]

Although not all of their leaders were equally enthusiastic, Blacks in Wilmington were able to flex their political muscles, especially in the mid-1890s as the Fusionist experiment swept the state. Blacks could vote, and many did in 1894 and 1896. The Populist/Republican coalition in the state legislature granted new home rule to the city government, which enabled Fusionists to elect a new mayor and six of the ten city aldermen, including two Blacks. The coroner, superintendent of streets, deputy clerk of court, as well as a justice of the peace, were also Black. The police force and fire departments also had African Americans serving openly.[7]

If the three Black sailors from the *Harry A. Berwind* had been booked into the New Hanover County Jail in early 1898 rather than late 1905, they would have found the political environment far less intimidating, if not actually favorable. At that time, even the jailer was Black.[8]

But that period of African-American political influence could never last. By the end of 1898, all of it would be swept away with barely a trace.

It has taken far too long for the history of the Wilmington Insurrection—there really is no other name for it, unless one goes further and calls it a massacre—to become known. For North Carolinians who love their state and cherish its reputation for fine schools and sound government, it is hard to swallow the idea that a violent coup occurred there. The story was shamefully suppressed for decades, and when finally mentioned, it was with mythmaking and rationalization. For years afterward, the textbook account was that Blacks provoked the violence by firing the first shots at whites, who reacted only to restore order.[9]

Not until the 1990s, as the centennial of the insurrection approached, did many historians give serious attention to the events of 1898. What they learned was that there was nothing extemporaneous about those events. The white Democratic leadership of Wilmington—aided and abetted by the business establishment, which was much the same thing—plotted for many months to suppress Black voting as part of the statewide White Supremacy Campaign, and then to trigger an armed riot to overthrow the city's elected Fusionist government.

The strategy could not have been more calculated. Throughout the summer, as Furnifold Simmons and his campaign team, including Charles B. Aycock and others, crisscrossed the state on the Red Shirt barnstorming tour, they also relied on local clubs to promote the White Supremacist cause. Often known as White Government Unions, these groups were intended to spread propaganda as well as gather intelligence on the activities of Blacks. There were as many as eight hundred such clubs across the state, with some of the most vociferous of them in Wilmington. Among locals, there was much social pressure to join up. One white Wilmingtonian, Benjamin F. Keith, recalled people being marched out of their homes and told to sign onto the Democratic Handbook. "Those that did not were notified that they must leave the city…. As there was plenty of rope in the city."[10]

One of the Union's leaders was George Rountree, the chair of the county Democratic Party, and a prominent attorney with a Harvard degree. Although not originally from Wilmington, Rountree had married as highly as possible into the city's legal and political elite. His wife was the daughter of George Davis, who had served briefly as attorney general of the Confederacy during the Civil War. As a lawyer, Rountree was most comfortable with business cases, and he was much more familiar with conference rooms than with the rough-and-tumble of local elections. But in 1898, he sensed the political winds, and could see how anti-Black sentiment had been whipped up by coverage of Alex Manly's writing. Rountree made no effort to discourage it. He wrote later that in meetings of the White Government Union, "I started to endeavor to inflame the white men's sentiment and discovered that they were already willing to kill all of the officeholders and all of the negroes."[11]

Even though Rountree and other white leaders were growing more brazen about their intentions, they could not just announce plans to overthrow a city government without providing some excuse for it. Not surprisingly, they would blame their victims for precipitating the assault that awaited them. The press was setting the narrative for them.

The *News and Observer*, which could always be relied upon

to fan the flames of white apprehension, spread the idea that Blacks were arming themselves for battle. On October 18, it ran the headline, "The Wilmington Negroes Are Trying to Buy Guns," and the subhead, "But the Dark Scheme Has Been Detected." The paper claimed it had cleverly intercepted a copy of a written order for pistols and rifles, filled with misspelled words, proving that it had come from uneducated Blacks. Shortly after, the *Wilmington Messenger* claimed, "Sambo is seeking to furnish an armory here." John D. Bellamy, a descendant of the family that owned the Brunswick County turpentine plantation—and also the Democratic candidate for Wilmington's congressional seat in 1898—spoke of the tendency of Blacks toward stealthy violence. "They constantly carry concealed weapons—the razor, the pistol, the slingshot, and the brass knuckle seem to be their inseparable accompaniments as a class."z[12]

In truth, Wilmington and other towns in Eastern North Carolina *were* being flooded with weapons. But it was the whites, not Blacks, who were doing the stockpiling. In cities like Baltimore and Richmond, gun manufacturers were shipping so many weapons to North Carolina that they were facing shortages. From Richmond alone, more than a thousand shotguns, Winchester repeating rifles, and .32 and .38 caliber revolvers were sent to Wilmington and the surrounding area. The *Richmond Times*, sensing a story, sent a reporter to Wilmington, who wrote that whites were primed for action as Election Day neared. On one city block, he counted thirty-two white men armed with twenty pistols, eighteen rifles, and ten shotguns, while Blacks possessed only a few "old army muskets, shotguns, or pistols."[13]

If handheld firearms were not enough, they brought in artillery. One group of white merchants, calling themselves the Secret Nine and led by Hugh MacRae, president of the Wilmington Cotton Mills Company, procured a Colt rapid-fire Gatling gun. It was an early form of multibarreled machine gun, capable of firing more than two hundred rounds per minute. It was the sort of weapon used on the battlefield to mow down waves of charging infantry, such as at San Juan Hill in Cuba months before. The gun was mounted on a wagon that could be towed through the streets, to intimidate anyone in its path. The wagon would be manned by a team of gunners led by Captain William Rand Kenan Sr., a Confederate veteran who previously served as Wilmington's customs inspector, until he had been replaced, unforgivably, with the Black John C. Dancy.[14]

Blacks and Republicans in Wilmington could easily see that the white Democrats intended to hijack the election by force. They appealed to Governor Russell to act, but he could see few options. White voters throughout the state were coalescing around the Democrats, and Russell knew that if violence did erupt, the federal administration in Washington—even though it was Republican—had no appetite to intervene.

George Rountree saw an opportunity to flex his political and paramilitary strength. He sent James Sprunt to Raleigh with a message for the governor. They demanded that the Republicans remove from the ballot all of their candidates seeking local office in New Hanover County. Everyone knew the demand was backed up with threat of violence, but even so, Rountree added an inducement to make the deal seem a little more reasonable. If Russell would withdraw the Republican slate of candidates, then the Democrats would remove from the ballot two of their candidates for the state legislature, George L. Peschau and J.T. Kerr, known to be especially opposed to Russell and who were calling for his impeachment.[15]

Russell, angry and humiliated, agreed to the deal, seeing it as the only way to avoid bloodshed. Democrats followed through and did remove Peschau and Kerr as promised. Yet, their places on the ballot were taken by two Democrats no less vociferous about white supremacy: one was Rountree himself.

In those last weeks before the election on November 8, Wilmington and the entire state teetered on the brink of conflagration. Furnifold Simmons, accompanied by Red Shirt cavalry and a retinue of other speakers including U.S. Senator "Pitchfork" Ben Tillman of South Carolina, travelled through the state, rousing rabble in every town and hamlet they visited. Simmons had usually been the organizer behind the scenes, and more often let his surrogates do the speechmaking. But in those final days of the campaign, he gave a speech that focused on Alex Manly's editorial with almost Freudian imagery. Simmons assailed Manly for daring to sully "the virtue of our pure white womanhood," reminding white men that "the issues involved are pregnant with momentous consequences . . . there was thrust to the front the all-absorbing and paramount question of

White Supremacy."[16]

Tillman was even more blunt. He chastised North Carolinians for being needlessly timid in dealing with Manly, "who ought now to be food for catfish in the bottom of the Cape Fear River."[17] Surely, Tillman said, if a Black man had written any such heresy in South Carolina, he would be dead already.

And yet the most incendiary—and persuasive—speech of all, the one that threatened to "choke" the river with Black "carcasses," came from one who was viewed by many as a political has-been. "Colonel" Alfred Moore Waddell came from plantation gentry, the great-grandson of one of the very first justices of the U.S. Supreme Court. He served as a proud Confederate cavalry officer and later went to Congress, but in 1878 he was defeated for re-election by Daniel Russell, now the scalawag governor. By 1898, Waddell was long out of office and treated skeptically by Rountree and other leaders of the white cabal. But he was eager to redeem himself and, for good measure, his entire race.

On the evening of October 24, Waddell strode to the stage of Thalian Hall, Wilmington's ornate opera house, which in earlier years had hosted speakers as disparate as Buffalo Bill Cody, Frederick Douglass, and Oscar Wilde. Before a crowd of cheering white militants, he urged them to break the political influence of "savage" Blacks, and to prove themselves worthy of the respect of civilized mankind. "We are going to protect our firesides and our loved ones, or die in the attempt. . . . We will have no more of the intolerable conditions under which we live," and, if bloodshed were to be required, Waddell said, "I trust that it will be rigidly and fearlessly performed."[18]

One out-of-town reporter, Henry L. West of *The Washington Post*, minced no words when describing the speechmaking, the hoarding of weapons, and how the Red Shirt militias were dividing Wilmington, block by block, into military districts commanded by "captains" and "lieutenants." The city was preparing for armed battle, not an election. The whites intended that "(1) The Negro must either be frightened away from the polls or else (2) he must be forcibly resisted when he undertook to deposit his ballot."[19]

Over the next few days, Red Shirts and other white horsemen rode unrestrained through the streets, brandishing their weapons and firing them into the air, drunk on adrenaline as well as cheap whiskey. The day before the election, Waddell gave another impassioned speech before another armed throng at Thalian Hall:

> "Men, the crisis is upon us. You must do your duty. This city, county, and state shall be rid of negro domination, once and forever. . . . Go to the polls tomorrow and if you find the negro out voting, tell him to leave the polls. And if he refuses, kill him! Shoot him down in his tracks!"[20]

When November 8, 1898, finally dawned, there was surprisingly little overt violence. The word had been passed effectively from the leadership through the rank and file. Their plan was to maintain the façade of order through election day, win the vote, and save the bullets for the coup afterward.

White gunmen, from the Red Shirt militia as well as the White Government Unions, rounded up white men on every city block and escorted them to the polls to secure their ballots. At the same time, they pulled their guns on any Black whom they saw on the street walking anywhere near a polling place. "Pistols were held in the faces of Negro poll holders who had to leave to save their lives . . . and they knew not what moment they would be killed," recalled Reverend J. Allen Kirk, a Black minister. *The Washington Evening Star* reported, "There is no doubt that the negroes have been thoroughly overawed by the preparations which have been made by the whites to carry the election."[21]

Those preparations included voter fraud as well as intimidation. Late in the evening, after the polls closed, the white armed troopers surrounded several polling places and held the registrars at gunpoint while they stuffed the ballot boxes. They remained standing guard outside, guns at the ready, while the counting continued. In one precinct with a total of 343 registered voters, the Democratic ticket impossibly received 456 votes.[22]

The final result need come as no surprise. In New Hanover County, much as throughout the state, the Democratic White Supremacy campaign was triumphant. It won 134 of the 170 seats in the North Carolina General Assembly, which the Fusionists had dominated for the past four years. Democrats also picked up five congressional seats. In Wilmington itself, where the Fusionist ticket had won by five thousand votes in 1896, the Democrats now won by six thousand votes, an eleven thousand vote swing.[23] It was too incredible, of course, to be credible. Yet it was official.

That took care of the state government, but Wilmington's inter-racial city government was still technically in office, as municipal elections were not scheduled until 1899. But not for long. The second phase of the insurrectionist plot began November 9, the day after the 1898 election.

By prearrangement, and with notices published in all of Wilmington's white papers—"ATTENTION WHITE MEN"—the militants gathered in front of the county courthouse uptown. Colonel Waddell stepped up to the rostrum—on the spur of the moment, he would later claim. He began reading out a lengthy document, which had been drafted in advance, to the cheering crowd. Entitled the "Wilmington Declaration of Independence," it announced a new political order for the city, a corollary to the United States Constitution which had been drafted generations ago by men who "did not contemplate for their descendants a subjection to an inferior race."

Henceforth, said the Declaration, Black people were no longer to participate in any way in the governmental affairs of the city. "Unscrupulous white men" who allied themselves with Negroes were to be banished. Since Black employment had restrained the economic growth of the city, most jobs held by Blacks were now to be handed over to whites. Blacks now would be treated "with justice and consideration," provided that they remained servile to "the intelligent and progressive portion of the community."

Then came the bloodiest scrap of red meat, which the crowd was longing to hear: *The Daily Record* was to end publication immediately, its printing press to be seized and shipped far away from town. Alex Manly, as punishment for "publishing an article so vile and slanderous that it would in most communities have resulted in the lynching of the editor," was ordered to leave Wilmington within twenty-four hours lest he "be expelled by force."[24]

The crowd was behind the curve. Alex Manly had fled town the night before the election, apparently alerted by someone that

Alexander Manly

Left to right: Albert Moore Waddell, James Sprunt, George Rountree.

the lynch mob was headed his way. The identity of the tipster is uncertain, although from the recollections of Manly descendants, it may have been the Reverend Robert Strange, rector of St. James, Wilmington's most upscale white Episcopal church. Strange was well respected by Blacks and whites alike for his moderation and sense of justice. He also was chaplain to the Wilmington Light Infantry, an organized state militia whose legal mission was to enforce state law, but now was firmly in control of the white militants. As such, Strange would have known the password that would allow someone to travel through the roadblocks that the militants had set up around town in anticipation of the coming battle.

Manly packed up his horse and buggy and headed out of town, going north, destination uncertain. Though everyone knew his name, few whites in Wilmington knew what he looked like, and his skin was light enough that he could "pass" when necessary. When he met the armed sentinels along the road, Manly gave them the password, and they waved him along, saying they were planning a "necktie party" in town for that black editor.

Noticing Manly was unarmed, one of the sentinels gave him a rifle and said, "If you see that nigger Manly up there, shoot him." He nodded, no doubt mumbling a brief word of thanks, and prodded his horse onward.[25]

In addition to their new Declaration of Independence, the militants passed a drumhead resolution demanding that the Fusionist mayor and police chief, Silas Wright and Joseph Melton, respectively, resign from office. Then they summoned a group of the city's leading Black residents to meet with them. Now designated the "Committee of Colored Citizens," they included the prosperous attorney William Henderson, as well as Frederick Sadgwar, a successful homebuilder whose daughter was married to Alex Manly.

This Black Committee—"cowed and terror-stricken," by at least one news account—met with Waddell and his junta at the Seaboard railroad office uptown that afternoon. Waddell presented them with his full set of demands, including the Declaration and the call for Fusionist resignations, and sternly demanded a written reply from the committee no later than 8:00 the following morning, November 10, 1898. Whatever their response, Waddell told them, the white coup would proceed as planned.

The committee, no doubt with trembling hands, composed a pitiful handwritten note, in which they pleaded lack of authority to comply with Waddell's demands. But they made it a point thoroughly to disavow Manly, denying responsibility for his "obnoxious article," and "very respectfully" promising to use their influence to see the white men's wishes carried out.[26] It mattered not one whit.

The next morning at the appointed hour, a throng of nearly a thousand whites gathered at the city's Armory on Market Street. Virtually all carried a rifle, many, pistols as well. Waddell then organized about five hundred men, and lined them up with military precision, four abreast, to march the seven blocks to the *Daily Record* office at the corner of South Seventh and Church streets. As they did, other whites stood cheering by or joined the procession, while Black children and adults fled behind closed doors. They knew what was coming; it was what the junta had been planning for months.

Once they reached the newspaper office, Waddell called out "Halt!" to the paramilitary column he led. As if it made a difference, he knocked twice on the door; hearing no reply, the column battered it down and streamed inside. They looted or smashed everything in sight, most importantly Alex Manly's printing press. Finding a jug of kerosene in a corner, they splashed it all around and finished the work with a lit match.

As the flames shot through the roof, sparks spread to several nearby houses and buildings, including the St. Luke's AME Church. Not all the mob intended that, and one of them sounded the alarm at a nearby firebox. But the first firefighters to respond were from the Cape Fear Steam Fire Engine Company, an all-Black outfit formed in 1871. The mob prevented the Black firemen from approaching the scene until the *Daily Record* was burned beyond salvage. Afterward, whites posed for photos in front of the gutted shell of the building, grinning and brandishing their guns.[27]

Waddell later claimed that, once the offending newspaper office was destroyed, he ordered his military column to march back to the Armory, and thence to their homes. Some went home, but most did not. From there, premeditation merged together with panic, confusion, and a little ineptitude to create a massacre.

At James Sprunt's Cotton Compress building, Black workers could hear the fire alarm and gunshots, as well as see the smoke from the fire. They thought a white mob was torching Black homes, killing their wives and children. Fear arose within the building, and many workers filtered outside, wondering what to do.

About the same time, George Rountree was headed toward the Sprunt building, and when he saw the crowd of Blacks gathered outside, he feared they would disperse, head home and grab guns of their own. Rountree located a phone and called the leaders of the Light Infantry to bring the Gatling gun to the Cotton Compress, and "to have it convenient for use if necessary." They brought the gun, and a white mob with it. Later, Rountree admitted he acted in haste, calling it "a fool thing to do."[28]

Sprunt, fearing loss of a day's productivity at his factory, climbed up on a stack of cotton bales and urged his employees to stay on the job. He promised to protect them from vigilantes and to ensure they could travel freely back home to their families. Some claimed later that Sprunt challenged the machine-gun vigilantes himself, shouting out, "Shoot if you will, but make me the victim!"[29] That likely was an exaggeration, but Sprunt did in fact give his workers signed passes allowing them to walk the streets past vigilante checkpoints. That allowed the Cotton Compress to keep operating, and fed into Sprunt's reputation as a genial, relatively moderate white plutocrat.

The white mob withdrew from the scene, headed to other hot spots. Near the corner of Fourth and Harnett streets, some in the mob encountered a nervous group of Black men, some of whom were armed. It is not clear who fired first, nor does it matter. It is perfectly clear who instigated the struggle and had been planning it. At least one white man and six Blacks were shot, two fatally, which set off a running battle through the adjacent streets.

With that, the alarm went out far and wide by phone, telegraph, and word of mouth for the ethnic cleansing to commence.

Mounted companies of Red Shirts and Light Infantry were already massed on the outskirts of the Brooklyn neighborhood north of downtown, where many Blacks resided. The goal was to kill as many Blacks as they must in order to neutralize them as a community. They charged in with guns and sabers, with standing orders "to kill every damn nigger in sight." Much of the killing was indiscriminate: one refugee later described how one white marksman

68

single-handedly killed nine Blacks after setting their home on fire, and picking them off one by one as they tried to flee.[30]

Some of the victims, though, were specifically targeted. Daniel Wright was known to the militants as a Black troublemaker and was suspected of taking part in the shoot-out at Fourth and Harnett. When the white troopers approached his house, they immediately opened rifle fire into the attic and walls. Wright ran out of his house and was immediately cut down by another shot. As he begged for mercy, one of the vigilantes proposed hanging him, but they could not find a rope. Instead, they turned him loose, only for him to stumble down the street as they called out, "Run, nigger, run!" Finally he fell with thirteen bullet wounds, five of them in his back.[31]

As night fell on November 10, skies clouded over and a cold rain, buffeted with gusty winds, blew into town. For many terrorized Black men, women, and children who were trying to sneak out of town, the nasty weather added to their misery. The refugees huddled together under crude blankets in the dense woods and pocosin swamps on the outskirts of town. Another hiding place was Pine Forest Cemetery, known as Wilmington's colored potter's field, where they imagined white men would not seek them out.[32]

The final butcher's bill was never conclusively determined, and never will be. The *New York Times* reported nine Black men killed, while some witnesses estimated one hundred dead in the street fighting. Reverend J. Allen Kirk, a Black Baptist minister, claimed hundreds of Black bodies were tossed into the Cape Fear, likely an exaggerated claim inspired by Waddell's rhetoric about choking the river. When the victims of the crime were so thoroughly deprived of their political power—and their voice—in the aftermath, it made a full accounting virtually impossible. The true number of dead likely lies somewhere in between.[33]

After the shooting subsided, Alfred Waddell and the rest of the junta located Mayor Silas Wright and the rest of the Fusionist city officeholders and informed them they must leave town in addition to resigning. Wright knew his life was in danger, and by some accounts he appealed to James Sprunt for protection. The Scottish-born Sprunt was not only Wilmington's cotton exporting

Historic marker near the Alex Manly Historic Market in Wilmington today.

king, but the local vice-consul representing the British government. Wright thought that by claiming British citizenship—it was not true, he was from Massachusetts—he might get some legal immunity. Ultimately, Wright and many other troublesome Blacks and scalawag whites were herded onto trains and banished from Wilmington permanently. Waddell was sworn in as mayor, in a ceremony that lacked any legal basis whatsoever, but no one was in a position to question.[34]

Many other people, virtually all Black, followed Wright and company into exile. They can hardly be blamed for not wishing to stick around. Blacks could see which way the winds were blowing, and they voted in the only way they now could: by fleeing. The town that was fifty-six percent Black in 1898 was only forty-nine percent so in the 1900 census, and forty-seven percent black by 1910.[35] Within a few days, Wilmington had been transformed from a political and economic center of African-American life into a bastion of segregation, thoroughly dominated by whites.

So it would be, in November 1905, when three Black men from out of town—two of them from out of the country, no less— would face a trial for their lives.

CHAPTER SIX

THE COUNSELS
LINE UP

The trials of the three *Berwind* sailors began on November 1, 1905, only three weeks after the ship was intercepted off Southport and the crime discovered. Today, of course, it is inconceivable that a murder case in federal court could be conducted with such haste. Defendants must have ample opportunity to meet with attorneys, plan strategy, receive discovery from the prosecution, and file motions accordingly. All of that takes months at the very least, and usually longer in a case like this one, which involved multiple codefendants and conflicting defenses.

But federal officials in Wilmington wanted to get the business over and done. For one reason, the defendants seemed easily convictable, even if the details of the mutiny and killings were ambiguous. There was no doubt that four white men had been brutally killed by at least one Black man, and even if not all were equally complicit, surely they must all have been in on it somehow. That, at least, appeared a safe assumption.

The Black community in Wilmington had no reason to think otherwise, and at the outset, little inclination to try and advocate for the three Black sailors. The defendants were not Wilmington natives, and did not have families in the area who might support or comfort them as they awaited trial—not that their families could have helped very much, even if they had been local.

Black influence in the political and legal affairs of Wilmington, as throughout North Carolina, had shrunk to virtually nothing by 1905. Many hundreds of Blacks who fled to the swamps and surrounding forests during the insurrection never returned, a path followed by many more in the intervening years.

Of those who remained, few dared to challenge the new political order. Safety and security were of paramount concern, and Blacks continued to find it in their churches and schools. Although they were segregated, many thrived, often with financial support from whites in Wilmington and elsewhere. For example, Professor Hugh M. Browne, a Black academic who was a follower of Booker T. Washington's accommodationist Tuskeegee Institute, visited Wilmington shortly after the insurrection. He noted how some of the "best white men" had contributed to Black schools by purchasing land in their vicinity and selling it to Blacks on good terms, and urged Blacks to reciprocate by working hard, obeying the law, and not making waves. Browne was not alone. Other Black leaders in North Carolina, including James B. Dudley, a Wilmington native and president of the Black Agricultural and Mechanical College—the present-day North Carolina A&T State University)—urged Blacks to abandon political involvement in favor of promoting education in the Tuskeegee mold.[1]

John C. Dancy, who held the lucrative position of Customs Collector prior to the insurrection, wanted to be sure he kept it. He gave an interview to the *New York Times*, in which he placed full blame for the bloodshed on Alex Manly and his incendiary writing. He said that the "intelligent colored people of the state," among whom Dancy desperately wanted to be included, were greatly offended by Manly's comments on race and sex. If Manly had retracted his editorial, as Dancy claimed he had urged, "there would have been no race war in Wilmington."[2]

When reading the obsequious pandering of men like Dudley and Dancy, one must remember that they lived in North Carolina. Unlike Black activists who lived up north and were actively calling for redress of the Wilmington atrocities, such as the writer W.E.B. DuBois and poet Paul Lawrence Dunbar, these local men were having to eke out their existence in a South where they now feared for their lives on a daily basis.

Moreover, they had to stand by and watch as the right to vote was systematically eliminated for most of their fellow Blacks. As white Democrats seized control of the North Carolina General Assembly, one of their first acts was to redesign the state's voting qualifications. In February 1899, they wrote an amendment to the state constitution, commonly called the Disenfranchisement Amendment, which required all voters in the state to be newly registered, pass a literacy test, and pay poll taxes. Those requirements were sufficient to restrict poor and uneducated men from voting, whether Black or white. But the real intent was to let white men vote, whether rich, poor, literate or not. For that purpose, the amendment included a grandfather clause allowing any man whose father or grandfather had voted prior to 1867—before Reconstruction—to avoid the literacy test and poll tax.

The amendment was drafted by New Hanover County's new state representative, George Rountree, the attorney who was so instrumental in planning the insurrection. Once passed by the legislature, it was submitted for a public referendum in August 1900, which the White Supremacists were now confident they could win.

Thus followed another statewide campaign blitz, as Furnifold Simmons, Charles Aycock, and company crisscrossed North Carolina to drum up support for the amendment, much as they had in 1898. Simmons, who also would be elected to the U.S. Senate in 1900, told a crowd in Burlington, "There is no use mincing matters. This amendment discriminates against the Negro in favor of the white man . . . and I am here today to defend that discrimination. This is a white man's state. We have raised the white flag here. Who will haul it down? The Negro can't do it, and the white man that does, spot him. Write on his brow, traitor—Let him be an outcast upon the face of the earth."[3]

The amendment carried statewide, by a vote of fifty-nine to forty-one percent. Oddly enough, it prevailed by wide margins in some parts of Eastern North Carolina where Black populations were highest. In Wilmington itself, it supposedly carried by 2,967 votes to two: A result impossible to take seriously and only a sign of massive fraud accompanied by coercion.[4]

The new voting rules worked precisely as intended. In 1896, there had been 126,000 Black registered voters in North Carolina; by 1902, there were only 6,100.[5] The most obvious results were in the passage of new segregation laws, governing everything from schools to cemeteries. But they also had a major impact on who was eligible to serve on juries—only males, of course—and those who were eligible to vote and own property, now almost exclusively white.

So it was in the trials of Scott, Sawyer, and Adams when the first case was called in early November 1905. The jury pool consisted of white males drawn from the federal judicial district in Southeastern North Carolina, counties such as Brunswick, Bladen, Robeson, Richmond, and Duplin, as well as New Hanover.[6] This was the heart of Red Shirt country, where the White Supremacist campaign had been at its most brutal. With men like that serving on the juries, everyone expected that guilty verdicts would be delivered post haste.

As for the men who had the duty to conduct the trials—judge, prosecutor, and defense attorneys—time was also of the essence. Each for his own reasons, they wanted to get the case off their hands. It turns out that none of them was especially comfortable with the role he was called upon to play.

The presiding judge, Thomas R. Purnell, was a Wilmington blue blood through and through. His grandfather, Edward Dudley, had served as governor back in the 1830s, and was the primary investor in Wilmington's first railroad. The Dudley Mansion, built in 1825, was and still is one of the city's most beautiful pre-Civil War homes, situated on the riverbank near the wharf warehouses that today feature trendy stores and restaurants.[7] Purnell himself had served as a Confederate officer, practiced law, and held various state offices through the Reconstruction years. But somewhat surprisingly, and like Governor Russell, he allied himself with the Republicans.

In 1897, Purnell was appointed to the federal bench by President McKinley, largely on the recommendation of Jeter Pritchard, a Fusionist who served in the U.S. Senate for one brief term. Then came the upheaval of 1898, and although Judge Purnell still occupied the bench in 1905, his tenure had been marked by plenty of partisan controversy. In one case in 1900, Purnell found himself in a no-win situation when he had to preside over the trial of a Black postmaster in Rocky Mount who was accused of embezzling federal funds. Josephus Daniels, as one might guess, excoriated the defendant and other Republican federal appointees—including, by implication, the judge—in the *News and Observer* as "Jeter's Jailbirds" and "Pritchard's Pets."[8]

A bit later, in May 1904, Judge Purnell remarkably held Daniels himself in contempt of court, fining him $2,000, due to a particularly intemperate editorial. Daniels accused Purnell of corrupt dealings when he ordered the assets of the Atlantic & North Carolina Railroad, which was largely owned by the state, placed into a receivership. In the offending editorial, Daniels railed against "Federal court judges, appointed by hostile presidents upon alien recommendations."[9]

Judge Purnell's contempt order was later reversed on appeal, but the incident reveals just how precarious his position could be. He wanted to provide a fair hearing to the three *Berwind* sailors, and he had no personal interest in the cases one way or the other. But as an appointed representative of a despised federal government, Purnell knew he would have to be extremely careful with such a racially charged trial.

The same could be said for the prosecutor who would oversee the case. Harry Skinner, the United States attorney for the Eastern District of North Carolina, was another with the dubious distinction of being a federal appointee. McKinley gave Skinner the job in 1901 because he was a Republican, one of the few white men in Eastern North Carolina by that time who still identified as such.

For Skinner, the U.S. attorney post was the final government office that he would occupy in a tumultuous career. Although a Democrat in his youth, he joined the farmers' movement and later the Populist Party in the 1890s; in fact, he wrote several scholarly articles about how so many farmers had been ruined by the inflexible currency and banking rules of the time. He served in the state legislature and then Congress, but in May 1898 had a bitter falling out with Marion Butler, North Carolina's Populist U.S. senator. In a fratricidal state convention that foreshadowed the upcoming election disaster in November, Skinner was essentially drummed out of the party by Populists who thought him not progressive enough, too willing to cooperate with Republicans. After losing his Congressional seat that year, he joined the Republicans.[10]

Fifty years old in 1905, Skinner could not have relished the task of prosecuting Scott, Adams, and Sawyer for murder and mutiny. It was not that he was sympathetic toward Blacks. Skinner had been a supporter of white supremacy even during his Populist days, which helps illustrate just how impractical the Black-white Fusionist experiment had been all along. Rather, he just didn't want the drama. Skinner had never prosecuted anything like a capital murder case; he was accustomed to the mundane cases, like smuggling and ship salvage, which made up most of the federal court docket. Plus, he did not want to be seen as the white scalawag prosecutor in a bloody case that the white Democrats—whom he despised—might publicize to keep their voters stirred up at the polls.

Therefore, it may have been with a sense of *schadenfreude* that Skinner observed the dilemma faced by the young attorneys who were dragooned into representing the Black sailors. Their situation was even more uncomfortable than his own. It is not clear from the court records exactly how they were selected or appointed, or even how much they were paid. But both were prominent white Wilmington Democrats who were intimately connected with the insurrection and its plotters.

Henry Scott's attorney was William J. Bellamy, scion of the French-descended plantation family from South Carolina. His grandfather built the magnificent Grecian-pillared Bellamy Mansion at Market and Fifth streets. Finished in 1861, it remains today as Wilmington's most opulent example of antebellum

Prosecutor Harry Skinner.

Bellamy (left) and Dudley mansions today.

architecture, perhaps even more so than the Dudley Mansion. He also was the nephew of several attorneys, including John D. Bellamy, Jr., who was elected to Congress in 1898 and, by more than one account, assisted Alfred Waddell and George Rountree in coercing the resignations of the Fusionist City government.[11]

William Bellamy, age twenty-nine and coming from such a family of businessmen and lawyers, was obviously a man with a promising future in town. When called upon to defend the accused Black assassin, he may have put a positive spin on the task, thinking it would be a chance for valuable trial experience. But he would have wanted it over with as little fanfare as possible.

Likewise with George Ludwig Peschau, who would represent Arthur Adams and Robert Sawyer in their joint trial. Now thirty-two years old, he was the young man who, as a legislative candidate in 1898, had been so vocal in demanding the resignation of the scalawag Governor Russell. His father, Christian G.E. Peschau, had immigrated to America from Prussia before the Civil War and made his way to Wilmington, where he started a thriving dry goods business that evolved into a shipping partnership. Like James Sprunt, whose experience in international trade and Scottish roots led to his appointment as British consul in Wilmington, the elder Peschau served for many years as the Imperial German consul. When the father died in 1904, his son George took over that responsibility, in addition to his legal practice.[12]

In his law firm, known as Waddell and Peschau, George L. Peschau had an older partner and mentor. It was none other than Colonel Alfred Waddell, leader of the insurrection himself.[13] It is not clear whether Adams or Sawyer realized that their attorney was professionally affiliated with the man who had pledged to fill the Cape Fear River with Black bodies, but if they did, it must have been disconcerting.

T hus, the stage was set for the murder trials to begin less than a month after the alleged crime, and after minimal preliminary investigation. The accused also would have had little opportunity to confer with their attorneys, whose dedication to their clients would have seemed questionable at best.

And yet, even though the trials were a rush act, the legal procedures were followed to a surprising degree. The attorneys fulfilled their professional responsibilities. And there would be no lynching, as tempting as it might have been for some gathered in the streets outside.

The truth is that, even with all the horrific history in the seven years preceding the trials of Scott, Adams, and Sawyer, the rules were changing. The changes came slowly, almost imperceptibly at first, and it would be decades before African Americans could believe that serious progress was being made towards justice in the courtroom. But against all odds, those three friendless Black sailors from distant shores would find ways to avail themselves of legal options. And they would lead to surprising results.

CHAPTER SEVEN

GLIMMERS
OF HOPE

A t this time, new African-American voices in the media were beginning to advocate for a more active civil rights movement. Most of them could be found up North, in cities where segregation, while a reality, was not legally enforced as it was in Richmond or Memphis. In Boston or New York, for example, a Black journalist could ply his trade with a greater degree of safety than Alex Manly could have in Wilmington.

For years, Booker T. Washington had been the dominant—some would say the exclusive—public spokesman for the Black community. His best-known pronouncement, often called the Atlanta Compromise, came in 1895. As far as Washington was concerned, Blacks should focus on work and vocational school, not on political activism. Legal rights would come gradually, only after Blacks demonstrated their good character. Washington would have viewed the Wilmington massacre as a result of political overreach by Blacks.

But by the first decade of the twentieth century, several new Black writers had grown tired of Washington's brand of conciliation. It was in 1903 that W.E.B. DuBois published his landmark treatise,

The Souls of Black Folk. Part history, part fictional narrative, and part spiritual exploration, the book includes a chapter in which Du-Bois calls out Washington by name, urging Blacks not to follow his leadership unquestioningly. Although DuBois had been receptive to the Atlanta Compromise at first, the disenfranchisement campaigns of the late 1890s showed him how little trust could be placed in white good faith. The sheer oppressiveness of the new segregation laws was proof that whites had no intention of rewarding Blacks for good behavior.

In addition to the new laws, there was overt racial violence, of which the Wilmington coup was not even the most sadistic example. DuBois found inspiration in one especially horrific lynching. It was the 1899 case of Sam Hose, a young Black field hand in Coweta County, just outside Atlanta, where DuBois was teaching. Hose was accused of killing his employer with an ax, which he likely did, although it may have been self-defense after the employer threatened him with a pistol. He also was accused of gleefully raping the employer's wife and assaulting his child, which were surely false. Placed under arrest, Hose's death was planned in hideous detail; many folks from Atlanta boarded trains and travelled a short distance to watch it. A mob kidnapped Hose and marched him to a field outside town, where they chopped off his ears and genitals with knives before dousing him with kerosene, burning him at the stake, and dismembering his charred corpse.

As DuBois told it, he was walking down an Atlanta street when he saw Sam Hose's knuckles being sold as souvenirs in a grocery store. He knew at that point, if not before, that no meaningful "Compromise" could be expected to emanate from Atlanta.[1] If Booker T. Washington was not willing to lead the struggle for civil rights, then DuBois would do so in print and elsewhere.

One of DuBois's contemporaries—and sometimes rival—in the effort to oppose Washington was William Monroe Trotter, a son of a slave who grew up in Massachusetts. In 1901, Trotter created and began editing the *Boston Guardian.* The paper struggled financially but quickly gained attention as the city's Black newspaper due to its provocative stands. Trotter saw that even in Boston, as more and more Blacks moved to the city to escape segregation down South, white racial attitudes were hardening. Businesses were increasingly brazen about denying service to Blacks. Thus, Trotter became one of the first Black writers to point out that Washington's accommodationist approach to white racism was not improving the lot of Blacks.

Trotter and Washington got into a personal confrontation in July 1903, which grew into a longtime political rivalry. Washington came to Boston to give a speech, and the Black crowd turned out not to be as appreciative as expected. By the time Washington finished, the crowd was grumbling. When Trotter stood to ask Washington some pointed questions, a fistfight broke out on the floor. Although it was not clear who started the ruckus, Washington brought criminal charges against several men, including Trotter, who spent several weeks in jail.[2] It was not the first legal dispute between the two: Washington had sued the *Guardian* for libel, which hurt the paper financially but only enhanced its reputation as a voice for the dispossessed.

Trotter also used his newspaper's influence to assist Blacks facing legal trouble, as in one noted case that arose from North Carolina.

In April 1902, a young man from Durham named Monroe Rogers was charged with arson. The factual basis for the charge was murky. Some claimed Rogers had gotten into a pay dispute with his employer and tried to burn down his barn. Another account had it that the burned building was a house where Rogers's girlfriend worked as a maid, and Rogers had turned off a water valve. Rogers, not wanting to take his chances in state court, where arson was a capital offense, fled to Brockton, Massachusetts, where he had relatives.[3]

When North Carolina sought to have Rogers extradited back to Durham for trial, Trotter took up his cause in the *Guardian*. He solicited funds for Rogers's legal defense and urged readers to lobby Massachusetts Governor Winthrop Crane, asking him not to grant the extradition request. Trotter arranged for Clement G. Morgan and Butler R. Wilson, two local Black attorneys whom he knew well, to represent Rogers at a hearing. Aware of the proceeding, North Carolina Governor Charles B. Aycock issued a public statement guaranteeing safety to Rogers and a fair trial if he were handed over. Boston Black activists would have none of it.[4] At the habeas hearing, one of Rogers' attorneys pointed out that "The past history of North

Carolina along this line should not be forgotten," and said that no guarantee of safety could be trusted unless it was accompanied with armed troops. The Reverend W. H. Scott, a Black clergyman who grew up in Virginia but eventually escaped to the North, also spoke up for Rogers. He said there was simply no chance for any Black man in North Carolina, where "more than a hundred negroes were lynched" in Wilmington. Scott proclaimed, "I would rather be shot running away from an officer in Massachusetts than take the word of Governor Aycock."[5]

Eventually Massachusetts officials had to relent, with no statutory grounds to refuse the extradition. Rogers was returned to Durham for trial, which followed in late November 1902. Rogers was found guilty of attempted arson, not arson itself, and sentenced to ten years imprisonment. On passing sentence, the judge said expressly that Rogers could have been sentenced to death, "yet I will not give him the full limit of what I think is the law."[6] It was a surprising degree of forbearance on the part of the judge, as he was no doubt aware of the media attention that the Rogers case had drawn, North and South.

Governor Aycock recognized it as well. At the time, he was embarking on the political cause for which he was long known in North Carolina. He was committed to raising funds to revolutionize public education: he often claimed to have built nearly seven hundred new schoolhouses during his four-year term in office.[7] Much of the capital for that project came from Northern philanthropists such as the Rockefeller and Carnegie families, people who were sincerely interested in social progress for both Blacks and whites, and who might be dissuaded by too much press over racial injustice in the South.

In fact, if William Trotter's coverage of the Rogers case in the *Boston Guardian* can be believed, Aycock was worried enough about the media impact of the case that he corresponded by letter with Booker T. Washington, asking his input on how he should handle the extradition issue. Washington urged Aycock to persist with extraditing and trying Rogers, which again illustrates the rift between him and more assertive Black leaders like Trotter.[8]

The case of Monroe Rogers was a relatively small one, and extradition was a straightforward state court issue, not the type of case that federal courts would tend to weigh in upon. But at about the same time, some federal judges—even Southern ones—were beginning to voice concerns about the rights of defendants, even Black ones, in criminal trials. They did not amount to much at first, but a few court opinions in the 1900s started to lay the foundation for civil rights cases that would arise decades later in the Warren Court era.

Terms like the Bill of Rights, the Fourteenth Amendment, due process, and equal protection did not resonate in the early 1900s as they do today. The Supreme Court issued its infamous *Plessy* doctrine in 1896 that racial segregation in public facilities was perfectly constitutional; it did not violate the equal protection clause of the Fourteenth Amendment as long as one could pretend the facilities were "separate but equal." Moreover, the high court had maintained for some time that constitutional protections set forth in the Bill of Rights—such as the rights to counsel, against cruel and unusual punishment, or against unreasonable search and seizure—applied only to federal court proceedings. By the doctrine of *Hurtado v. California* in 1884, those protections had not been incorporated by the Fourteenth Amendment to apply in state court, where the vast majority criminal trials took place.[9]

Yet now there were a few cases in which Southern federal judges, mostly Republican holdovers from Reconstruction, were willing to take a chance on offering legal relief to Blacks.

In Macon, Georgia, for example, U.S. District Court Judge Emory Speer granted habeas relief to a Black man, Henry Jamison, sentenced to a chain gang in 1904 on a drunk and disorderly charge—without benefit of a jury trial. Such prosecutions were not unusual; many viewed it as a governmental policy to prolong slavery in the form of prison labor. But Judge Speer recognized the need for due process.[10]

Likewise in Huntsville, Alabama, Judge Thomas G. Jones—a former governor of the state, later appointed to the bench by Theodore Roosevelt on the recommendation of Booker T. Washington—empaneled a federal grand jury to investigate a particularly nasty lynching that occurred there in September 1904. The mob had set fire to the jail where the victim was housed, forcing him to jump out of a second-story window before they hanged him and riddled him with rifle shot. To the surprise of many, the grand jury brought back indictments. In his action, Judge Jones took his cue from a recent decision by Arkansas Judge Jacob Trieber, America's first ever Jewish federal judge, who had ruled that the 13th Amendment prohibition against slavery protected Black farm workers from harassment by the Klan.[11]

Blacks were not necessarily *receiving* justice in federal courts. In most instances they were not, and in fact all three decisions by Judges Speer, Jones, and Treiber were later overturned by the Supreme Court. But white supremacists could not assume their worst abuses would go unchallenged in court or in the press. There were cases in which Black defendants could find attorneys to raise valid constitutional arguments for them.

One such case, in which there were several surprising twists and turns, arose in Jones County. Jones was one of the most retrograde spots to be found in all of Eastern North Carolina. Just outside the old colonial capital of New Bern, by 1903 it was still basically plantation country, where the Klan had been active throughout Reconstruction and a white farming oligarchy held almost all the assets. As recently as 2000, African Americans were forty-three percent of the population of Jones County, but owned only three percent of the land.[12]

On a Saturday morning in September 1903, the owner of one of those plantations set out on foot into the thick woods that lay in the rear portion of his estate near Pollocksville. He carried his double-barreled shotgun because he had heard shots in the distance, and suspected someone was hunting without permission on his land. At seventy-seven, he was an elder gentleman but accustomed to being in authority; he was not only a wealthy planter, but a local political figure, having served in the General Assembly both before and after the Civil War.

By evening the old man had not returned to his house. He had planned to travel to town with some of his farm tenants to sell their cotton, and when he uncharacteristically failed to show, they searched the woods. They soon found his body lying dead on the muddy bank of the Trent River, a slow, meandering stream that formed his property line. Newspaper accounts reported he was shot several times in the stomach and chest with buckshot, and some claimed he was clubbed in the head as well. All concur that the decedent was a "quiet, peaceful, old gentleman."[13]

It was traditional in those days for papers to speak respectfully toward departed elders, especially if they were white, and especially if they had names like Furnifold Green Simmons. The dead man was the father of Furnifold McLendel Simmons, North Carolina's sitting U.S. senator who had spearheaded the White Supremacy Campaign five years earlier.

The locals jumped instantly to the foregone conclusion, summed up in the headline of one Wilmington paper: "Murdered: Senator Simmons' Father Shot To Death By Negro." Within two days, they had arrested Alfred Daniels, a "negro of desperate character" who supposedly had argued earlier with Simmons, saying that for some reason he was determined to hunt on the Simmons property even "if he had to kill the owner." As "mutters of lynching [were] often heard," Daniels was hustled off to the more secure Craven County Jail in New Bern, rather than the tiny one in Trenton, the Jones County seat with a population of fewer than five hundred people.[14]

It is difficult to imagine how a Black defendant could have found himself in a more hopeless legal situation. Daniels, in fact, did not deny killing the elder Simmons, although he pled self-defense. He claimed he had been paddling down the river in a boat when Simmons appeared on a fifteen-foot bluff overlooking the water, shouting and raising his shotgun to shoot Daniels, whereupon Daniels fired, fatally wounding the old man. Predictably, the white newspapers were filled with details now impossible to prove or disprove: that Daniels's footprints were found on the muddy riverbank, and that Simmons's wounds showed he had been shot by someone directly behind him, not shooting upward from a boat on the river as Daniels claimed.[15] Thus, the trial would hinge upon the credibility of the Black defendant, for what little that would be worth in that time and place.

Alfred Daniels lived to go to trial in Trenton in early November 1903, and he was represented by defense counsel of surprisingly high caliber. It was John E. O'Hara, born in 1844 in New York to an Irish father and an African-Caribbean mother, who moved to North Carolina after the Civil War as a missionary teacher. He later studied law at Howard University, served as a county commissioner in the 1870s, and was elected to Congress from the majority-Black Second District. He served there from 1882 to 1886, when he was defeated for reelection by the younger Furnifold Simmons. After his loss, O'Hara moved to New Bern and established his legal practice, keeping it going even through the worst days of the late 1890s.

O'Hara did not shrink from representing Daniels. He moved to quash the indictment, pointing out the mathematical fact that Blacks were underrepresented in the grand jury pool. The motions were taken seriously, at least for the record. O'Hara called the chairman of the county commission to the stand to testify about the property tax rolls from which the jurors were selected. In fact, the judge made it a point to examine the locked box from which the names were drawn. The trial had to be delayed for a day, since it took a while to determine who had the key, according to at least one news report. O'Hara also moved for the case to be removed to federal court, but in the end all his motions were to no avail.[16]

The state maintained that Daniels had ventured onto the Simmons property by boat, ambushed the old man with premeditation, then rowed to the other side of the river and fled through the woods. The defense called no witnesses and asked the jury to return a verdict of second-degree murder or manslaughter as an alternative to hanging. The jury thought about it for a half hour and returned with a verdict of first-degree murder.[17]

Placed under sentence of death, Daniels appealed with the aid of new counsels: Colonel John C.L. Harris and his son Charles Harris. The colonel was a longtime friend of Governor Daniel Russell and had been a primary architect of the Fusionist campaign. He also had experience in high-level litigation: in 1898, Harris represented Russell's state Board of Agriculture before the United States Supreme Court, arguing successfully that the state had the authority to tax goods produced out of state.[18] It was just the type of progressive reform that the Fusionists liked, and the corporatist Democrats hated.

Before the North Carolina Supreme Court, the Harrises raised several points. First was the fact that Blacks were completely excluded from judicial proceedings in Jones County. There also was some question about the truthfulness of Alfred Daniels's confession: he supposedly admitted the killing to the sheriff, while he was being transported by wagon from New Bern to Trenton. Daniels apparently thought there was a lynching party gathering near them, and he may have confessed falsely in the hope it would spare him.[19]

The state Supreme Court was unmoved, and Colonel Harris made a bold move for the era. He submitted an application for a Fourteenth Amendment writ of error to the United States Supreme Court, asking the highest court in the land to address the blatant racial issues implicated in the case. Strategically, Harris made the appeal to the justice whom he thought most likely to be receptive.[20]

Justice John Marshal Harlan was something of a maverick jurist. He had served on the Supreme Court since 1877, and, although he was the son of a Kentucky slaveholding family, he had shown himself to be concerned about the government racism spreading through his native South. He is best remembered today as the lone dissenter in both the *Plessy* and *Hurtado* decisions. Harlan's declaration in *Plessy*, that "our Constitution is color-blind, and neither knows nor tolerates classes among citizens," is legendary, and on balance he was more willing than his colleagues to accept the idea of incorporating the Bill of Rights into the Fourteenth Amendment, so that the states, as well as the federal government, must recognize equal protection and due process.

Even so, Justice Harlan could not save Alfred Daniels. In a brief letter to the attorneys Harris, he concluded simply "that the writ of error cannot properly be allowed." It would have been a bridge too far. It was not until the infamous Scottsboro cases from Alabama, in the 1930s, that the court seriously addressed the impact of race on jury selection and the appointment of defense counsels.[21]

The inevitable finally came about on May 19, 1904, when Alfred Daniels was hanged on the makeshift gallows outside the Jones County Jail. Shortly beforehand, he was baptized, and he made one final profession that he had shot the elder Simmons in self-defense. He had been in his boat on the river when the old man suddenly appeared on the shore, pointed his gun at him, and shouted, "God blast you, I am going to kill you!" Whereupon, Daniels said, he fired first.[22] No one will ever know.

Thus ended the saga of Alfred Daniels, who could have been lynched within hours of the crime, and yet lived long enough to be represented by some of North Carolina's most experienced litigators, and to have his case considered by the U.S. Supreme Court.

The precedent—and perhaps the memory of the Monroe Rogers case—would not have been lost on the judge and attorneys who handled the murder trials of Henry Scott, Arthur Adams, and Robert Sawyer just a year and a half later. Given the sensational nature of the quadruple murder, and especially since it was a federal case, they were going to have to follow the rules and provide some semblance of justice to those three men.

The press, and higher courts, were likely to be grading their papers.

CHAPTER EIGHT

THE
OPENING SALVO

When the trials of the three accused mutineers convened on Wednesday, November 1, 1905, all of Wilmington's attention was drawn downtown to one of its most handsome buildings, which stood at the corner of Front and Chestnut streets, just a block and a half back from the riverfront.

The United States Post Office and Courthouse, or just the Post Office as most folks knew it, actually looked a bit out of place. Built in 1891, it was a towering, Romanesque structure built of brownstone, unlike the New Hanover County Courthouse, which was built of native brick at around the same time, only three blocks away. With its dark profile, ornate clock tower, and gables, and a pitched slate roof, some might have thought it better adapted to a cold, northern industrial city like New York or Pittsburgh.

Its out-of-town appearance might be one reason why the building had a surprisingly short life. Unlike some of Wilmington's other architectural treasures such as Thalian Hall, and even the County Courthouse, which still stands today just across the street from it, the old Post Office stood for only forty-five years. It was demolished in 1936, having been supplanted during World War I by the massive new sandstone Federal Building that was constructed just behind it and still dominates the view of Wilmington from the riverfront today.[1] The newer building shares its Classical Revival style with Thalian Hall, and many would say it looks more authentically southern than the old one. The site of the old Post Office on Front Street is now populated by modern storefronts.

Yet the old Post Office was more than functional for its time. It had a spacious courtroom on the second floor that could accommodate a sizable crowd, which the trials of Henry Scott, Arthur Adams, and Robert Sawyer were sure to attract. From the first day, Wilmington papers were full of speculation about the "famous mutiny trial," which brought the "largest number of people ever in the federal courtroom in this city." Every seat in the courtroom was filled, they said.[2]

Spectators were packing the streets as well as the courtroom, which must have posed security concerns for the Wilmington police, and no doubt struck terror in the hearts of the three defendants. "Heavily ironed," the prisoners were transported in a horse-drawn wagon three blocks from the jail to the Post Office building. They travelled down Princess Street, through the same downtown that had teemed with rifle-toting vigilantes during the insurrection not long before. As the wagon pondered down the street, it was followed by a large throng of people, shouting out "There goes the mutineers!"— and likely other epithets that the papers were not comfortable in quoting.[3]

Once the prisoners were delivered to the courtroom, Judge Purnell got down to business. As had been determined, there would be two trials: Adams and Sawyer would be tried first, together, and then after their jury reached its verdict, Scott would be tried separately by a different jury. When U.S. Attorney Skinner read out the indictment to Adams and Sawyer, they seemed little affected by it, although Sawyer—likely in a journalistic understatement—"twitched with nervousness" a little.[4]

The trial could not start immediately; the court had to go through the process of summoning the pool of prospective jurors for both trials. It was a ponderous task, because the list included people who lived throughout the federal district, some of them a hundred miles or more away. Once their names were drawn by the clerk, they still had to be contacted—by "mail and telegraph," the only means available—and summoned to Wilmington by train or horse and buggy. Consequently, the opening statements and testimony could not begin until five days later.[5]

Yet even with technological limitations of the time, the judge made a point to ensure that the trial record would be carefully maintained. He arranged for G.C. Scherer, a court stenographer who worked for the U.S. Engineers office, to attend and take down the full trial proceedings in shorthand.[6] No doubt he wanted to ensure the integrity of the trials, in case any of the defendants later tried to appeal their almost certain convictions. Fortunately, this means that a verbatim transcript of the proceedings survives today, for historians to compare with the newspapers' coverage. Had the trials taken place in state court, that resource might not have been available.

Once jury selection was completed—and it did not take long, as neither the prosecution nor defense asked any especially probing questions of potential jurors—it was time for Adams and Sawyer to enter their pleas. When prosecutor Skinner asked them how they intended to plead to the charge of murder on the high seas, each responded with "not guilty."

And then, following a bit of archaic ceremony no longer practiced today but was well understood in courtrooms of that time, the prosecutor asked the defendants to answer another question for the record: "How will you be tried?"

To that, the two British West Indian defendants gave the routine response expected in all courts of the United States: "By God and my country." To which, the prosecutor said, "God bring you a true deliverance."[7]

The first prosecution witness was called to the stand, basically, to settle the court's jurisdiction. Captain Isaac F. Hewitt owned a one-eighth share in the shipping partnership that owned the *Harry A. Berwind*. He told the court that upon hearing of the mutiny and killings, he hurried down to Southport from his home in Vineland, New Jersey—near the partnership's headquarters in Philadelphia— to arrange repairs for the ship. He also described the ship's dimensions and gave an overview of its planned voyage on the Philadelphia-Cardenas-Mobile-Philadelphia route. After Hewitt noted that the ship was American-owned and American-flagged, it was clear that the murders were a federal case.

Hewitt also identified the four dead officers by name—Captain Rumill, as well as first mate Hall, engineer Smith, and cook Falbe—and confirmed they were employed by his company. When asked by Skinner whether the murder victims were white, he confirmed they were. As for the four Black seamen on board, Hewitt said he was not certain of their names.[8]

That was the extent of Hewitt's testimony in the trial of Sawyer and Adams, and later he did not testify at all when Henry Scott was placed on trial. But interestingly, he may have known something else, something that the prosecutor might not have wanted the jury to hear while they were weighing the guilt of Sawyer and Adams.

Just three weeks earlier, in the aftermath of the hearing in Southport—where Hewitt also did not testify—he had given a statement to at least one newspaper. The subject was Henry Scott. Hewitt recalled that about a year previously, he had been travelling on the *Berwind* as a passenger when it was under the command of another captain. He remembered a Black sailor on the ship at the time who was very "insolent," always wanting to stir up trouble. At one point, Hewitt claimed this sailor had told the captain, "Oh yes, d--- you, in less than two years I will make you take off your hat to me instead of having to take off mine to you."

Hewitt believed that rebellious sailor was the same man now known as Henry Scott, although he did not think the sailor went by that name at the time. That, as Hewitt supposedly told the press, would have been "nothing unusual, for negro sailors are always changing their names and especially if they happen to have a bad record."[9]

If Hewitt suspected Scott was more culpable in the murders than the other sailors, then why not say so during the trial of Adams and Sawyer, when the men's lives depended on it? Perhaps because Hewitt and the ship's other owners had a vested interest in seeing that all three defendants, and not just Scott, were found guilty. Although a small issue compared with the gravity of a capital murder trial, the ship's owners were liable for any back pay owed to their crews. If Adams or Sawyer were exonerated at trial, they would have to be paid for their service on the *Berwind*. Business was business, and the company had already lost enough through the deaths of their four officers.

Hewitt was followed on the stand by the captain of the *Blanche H. King*, John W. Taylor, and later by its first mate Theodore Simmons. Both led off with the now familiar story of how they and their crew spotted the *Berwind's* red signal lantern in the dark, and then boarded the ship after approaching it and hearing the shouts of distress about the ship's officers being murdered. Both mentioned their shock at seeing the bloody corpse of John Coakley lying on the cabin roof, as well as their surprise at how compliant Henry Scott seemed to be when he was handcuffed and removed from the ship.

Both Taylor and Simmons testified about their preliminary search of the *Berwind*, and it appears that Simmons played the larger role in it. He spoke about how, the night they first boarded, he found the disorder in the captain's cabin, with papers strewn all around, as well as the logbook in the captain's "secretary" desk. Taylor, who had served with first mate John Hall on another voyage from May to June 1905, testified that he recognized Hall's handwriting in the logbook, thus adding veracity to its contents.

Simmons testified he also went through the galley and found nothing unusual; specifically, he looked for any illicit liquor such as "bay rum," which might have been smuggled in from the Caribbean islands, but found none. The engine room, however, was in "bad shape." Simmons thought someone had deliberately poured salt water into the boilers, attempting to disable the engine. Additionally, Simmons identified two pistols recovered from the ship. One, fairly inexpensive, had a black handle. Another—which Arthur Adams had voluntarily handed over to Simmons when he came aboard—was ivory-handled.

In the forecastle—the crewmen's sleeping quarters—Simmons also found a blackjack in Scott's bunk. It was something that could only have been used as a weapon, a type of billy club made from wood and rubber, which an assailant might use to smack someone on the head at close range. Like the pistols, it would not have been standard issue for anyone on a commercial ship. Surely, whoever brought it aboard had some nefarious purpose in mind.

The blackjack was now sitting on the exhibit table, in full

view of the jury, along with the two pistols and all the other relevant objects taken from the ship. They also included the length of rope that Adams and Sawyer had used to tie Scott's hands after they tackled him.

And then there was the blood.

From the newspapers, it is not entirely clear what Simmons and Taylor had testified at the Southport hearing, although they may have left the impression that not much blood had been found throughout the ship aside from what was dripping from Coakley's corpse on the cabin roof. But now, Simmons was emphatic that he also found blood splotches in two places on deck: on a stack of lumber on the port side where Adams and Sawyer claimed Scott had shot first mate Hall, and also near the engine room where Scott claimed Adams had tussled with engineer Smith. That might be taken to support either of the conflicting accounts, but Simmons also said it looked like someone had taken the time to try and mop up the bloodstains. That, along with the damage Simmons and Taylor had witnessed in the captain's cabin and engine room, suggested a drawn-out affair consistent with Adams's and Sawyer's story, rather than the quick shoot-out that Scott claimed. Possibly, but far from certain.

Simmons concluded his testimony on that ambiguous note, and he had to acknowledge on cross-examination that he had no firm knowledge about which of the sailors carried out the murders. His commander, Captain Taylor, was a bit more emphatic in his view that all of them, not only Scott, had played a role.

Like the owners of the *Berwind*, Taylor probably had his eye on the financial side of the affair. His salvage claim, filed on behalf of himself and the entire crew of the *King*, was still pending in federal civil court. If they wanted to prevail, they needed to establish that the *Berwind* was legally an abandoned vessel with no crew. Essentially, they needed a verdict that all of the surviving crew were complicit in the killings.[10]

Toward that end, Taylor noted that on his inspection of the *Berwind*, it appeared that the mutinous sailors had tried unsuccessfully to launch one of the ship's yawl boats. That particular boat was intended as a lifeboat in case the crew ever had to abandon ship and was usually kept hoisted on davits alongside the vessel. According to Taylor, he found that the bow end of the yawl boat had been lowered about three or four feet toward the water, but the stern end had not been lowered. Someone may have been interrupted in the attempt to launch the boat, but at any rate, Taylor said that in his experience it was very difficult for a single crewman to operate the davits on either end of the boat. If any of the crew had tried to leave the *Berwind* behind, there must have been more than one man working in concert to do it.[11]

That was consistent with the testimony of Henry Scott, who testified next. Scott was, in effect, the star witness against Adams and Sawyer. If prosecutor Skinner was going to win a conviction against the two West Indian sailors, he had to rely on Scott's tale of how Adams, Sawyer, and Coakley had conspired without his cooperation to seize the ship. He simply had no other witnesses—from the *Berwind*'s owners to the crew of the *King*—who could say anything particularly incriminating against Adams or Sawyer.

For the moment, it mattered nothing to Skinner that, in only a few days, he expected to call Adams and Sawyer to testify as star witnesses against Scott. That would be another issue for a different jury.

Interestingly, before he began to question Scott, Skinner extended him a caution, which attorneys today might liken to a *Miranda*-style warning, more than sixty years before the Supreme Court enacted any such requirement. After reminding Scott that he was charged with "complicity for assisting in this murder and mutiny," he told him he therefore would "not be compelled to answer any questions incriminating to [him]." With that, Skinner asked Scott directly, "Are you willing to testify in this case?" He answered, "Yes, sir."

It might seem an unusual courtesy to offer to a Black murder defendant in that time and place, but it reflects the sense of decorum that prevailed in the courtroom throughout the trials. Although the case drew a crowd, neither the newspapers nor the trial transcript reveal any disturbances in the courtroom. There was no shouting and no slinging of racial epithets. Nor did the prosecutor or defense counsels seem to play to the gallery, cracking jokes for applause, as attorneys often did in that era. The attorneys, as much as they may have disliked the proceedings and wanted to get them over quickly, conducted themselves professionally. That may well have been due to Judge Purnell, who seemed determined to run his federal courtroom as a tight ship, unlike what one might find in any number of local county courthouses.

In fact, if the trial transcripts are credible, no one uttered the reprehensible n-word a single time. The judge and attorneys addressed the defendants by their surnames, Scott, Sawyer, and Adams, rather than by their first names as white professionals of that day were more wont to do when dealing with Black men.

Scott began, as he did in the Southport hearing, by describing how conditions on the *Berwind* had been lousy from the beginning. They had left Philadelphia on July 6, and within only a day or two, there were complaints that the food was "not suitable to us." The men's water supply was also at issue. Scott said that after they reached Cardenas, the cook stingily allowed the four sailors only four quarts of fresh water per day with which to drink and wash themselves as they laboriously offloaded the coal under the hot Cuban sun.

By Scott's telling, it was the other sailors who did the complaining, and Adams was the one who called the cook a "white son of a bitch." Scott also claimed that he personally had not been written up at all in the logbook, a claim that was easily refuted by the book itself, although that point was not raised until later in the trial.

Once in Mobile, Scott said, the other three men had the idea to go into a "Jew shop" located on a block of Government Street between Water and Commerce streets, and purchase firearms.[12] Sawyer and Coakley each bought a .38 Iver Johnson pistol, and Adams bought a Harrington and Richards model. Sawyer proclaimed, he recalled, "We have been treated very brutal," and "if the officers do any provocation to us we are going to shoot."

Which is just what happened, some three weeks later, on October 10. Scott maintained his story about how he and Coakley were on watch around 5:00 a.m., when Coakley, angry over the cold pot of coffee prepared by cook Falbe, rushed toward the galley, saying he intended to "give the cook hell." Supposedly that set off the ten-minute killing spree, in which Coakley shot the first mate three times, Adams shot the engineer once, and Sawyer shot the cook twice. The captain apparently had been killed earlier, his body already disposed overboard, although Scott was unsure who did it.

For the rest of the morning and afternoon, Scott swore, he

remained on the outside of the conspiracy among the three West Indians. "Sawyer and Coakley ran the ship all day," Scott said, as they tried to come with a plan for what to do with the ship. Scott claimed to have played along, afraid he would be killed if he tried to interfere, despite the fact that he was armed—by his own admission—with the pistol that he claimed to have found lying on the cabin roof.

Late that afternoon, it was Sawyer who first came up with the idea of setting the yawl boat adrift, as well as the story to accompany it. "This is what we will tell the white people," Scott claimed Sawyer said, as he, Adams, and Coakley began to work the davits to lower the boat. They would fabricate the story about the four officers drowning in the storm. The boat was only partially lowered when Scott claimed that he spoke up, saying the story "won't do," whereupon Scott claimed Sawyer knocked him down, and all three then chained him to the cabin roof.

Scott repeated his tale of how, several hours later, he managed to free his hands, and when Coakley saw he had done so, rushed forward to subdue him. Coakley was almost on top of Scott when Coakley drew his pistol and fired at Scott, almost at point-blank range. Yet, Coakley's shot somehow missed—the only shot fired by anyone who failed to hit its target—and instead put a hole in the soft pine cabin roof. Whereupon Scott drew his pistol, which he had kept concealed all that time, and shot Coakley dead in self-defense.

By the time he finished testifying, Scott may have been feeling satisfied with his performance. He probably believed he had successfully parried the defense's attempts to shake his story; and Peschau had made little attempt to do so, asking only a few questions on cross. But if Scott thought he had established any real credibility with the jury or spectators, he was wrong.

Among the questions Peschau did ask was about Scott's testimony in Southport, and how it may have differed in some details, such as whether Sawyer or Coakley had shot the first mate, or vice versa. Scott replied, with a grandiosity that suggested he was enjoying the attention fixed on him, that "the statement at Southport was only a small statement—this is a wide statement to the world!" Also, when Peschau suggested that Scott earlier had confessed the killings to Captain David Stetson, co-owner of the *Berwind*, stating that he did not believe in God or the hereafter, and was willing to go to the gallows for his crime, Scott replied with a bit of sarcasm. No, he had not confessed to anyone, and although he believed in God, "I don't believe as some people do, talk good, go off and take your money and your wife and so on."[13]

If the contemporaneous news accounts are any guide, Scott came across as he did after the Southport hearing. He was smooth and glib in his presentation, described as "very sharp" and a "negro with education." He was meticulous about detail, describing dimensions of the ship, and the heights and weights of the other sailors whom he had grappled with. Yet, that did not mean that he sounded believable. The same newspaper account described him as the likely "arch-conspirator."[14]

And therein lies the double-edged sword of white Southern racial prejudice of the day. When whites tended to view Blacks as naturally dull and slow-witted, it did not take much for one to exceed expectations. A Black witness, by taking the stand and answering questions in a calm, self-possessed manner, might come across as unusually "sharp." But at the same time, if he appeared too sharp, too confident in his bearing, he might be seen as lacking humility, or—to use the common pejorative—"uppity." And uppity Blacks were those likely to commit crimes.

Reporters noted that Scott talked "rather fast," and seemed in unusual control of his surroundings as he would swivel around in the revolving chair on the witness stand, frequently asking the stenographer, "Did you get that?" and "Am I too fast?" When he was asked to describe the height of those on board ship with him, Scott would direct white people in the courtroom, including the jurors and his attorney Bellamy, to stand up so he could use them as an example.

To modern ears, it would be no serious matter. But for a Black man accused of a quintuple murder in that time and place, it was presumptuous. Another reporter described Scott as testifying in "perfect self-possession and with the ultimate sangfroid," but his "attention to minute details and assignment of reasons for this or that statement did not create as favorable an impression as it otherwise would have."[15] His story sounded too precise, and likely rehearsed.

By the time Scott stepped down from the stand, the first day of the trial was over, and the government was ready to rest its case. The jury had not yet heard from the defendants, Adams and Sawyer, but already the papers were commenting that Scott's attempt to place the blame on them was falling flat. They predicted that although the jury was still likely to find Adams and Sawyer guilty, chances were that they would "recommend mercy and the result be that they will get life imprisonment." Yet as for the "arch-conspirator" who had just testified, "No one has the least doubt about Scott's being hanged."[16]

The press, as well as those in the courtroom, were coming to a surprising new realization. They likely had been too quick in assuming all three sailors were equally guilty due to skin color alone.

Mugshots of
Arthur Adams
(left) and Robert
Sawyer at the
federal penitentia-
ry in Atlanta.
Full booking re-
cords appear on
Page 156.

CHAPTER NINE

SWIMMING
AGAINST THE TIDE

The following morning, as George Peschau opened his case in defense of Adams and Sawyer, he likely harbored few illusions. Even if he had any sophisticated legal arguments that might favor his clients, which he did not, he knew they would carry little weight with the jury. His best option was to let his clients tell their own stories, in the hope that their earnestness—in contrast with the grandiosity that some had noted in Henry Scott—would move the jury to sentence them to prison rather than hanging.

Arthur Adams was the first to testify on his own behalf, after being advised—just as Scott was—that he had the right not to testify, and anything he did say would be counted against him by the jury. Adams did not appear to be fazed by the warning, nor did Robert Sawyer when he testified later in the day. Most in the gallery, in fact, were impressed by how both told their stories with composure, and consistently with what they previously testified in the Southport hearing.

According to Adams, Henry Scott had been the troublemaker from the beginning. Consistent with the notes in the logbook,

Scott started griping shortly after the *Berwind* left Philadelphia, mostly about the quality of the food. Another time, Scott had complained to the captain about why the sailors were being compelled to do so much grunt work, especially with raising and lowering the sails, when they had the "steam donkey" engine that could be used for the purpose.

After the ship deposited its load of coal in Cuba, picked up the cargo of lumber in Mobile, the ill will between Scott and the officers continued. According to Adams, the bad weather on the trip back toward Philadelphia added to the strain. The ship first encountered a storm near the Dry Tortugas keys, as they entered the Straits of Florida. It was not until they were off of South Carolina, however, that the real damage occurred. At that point, the topsail was torn away and the rudder was damaged, making it difficult to steer the ship at all.

As the jury and other spectators listened to Adams's testimony, they likely speculated that the storm damage was the spark that set off the killing. Whoever actually carried out the murders, the damaged sails and rudder might—in the killer's warped mind—have supported the false story about the officers drowning while trying to escape the ship.

Adams held fast to his—and Sawyer's—contention that Scott both committed the murders and concocted the story. Adams said he and Sawyer were alone in the forecastle at around 5:00 a.m. on October 10 when they first heard shots ring out, and then Scott appeared at the door with gun in hand, threatening to "shoot every man on board." After killing the captain, Scott pulled his pistol on engineer Smith while Scott was standing atop the cabin roof and Smith was standing below him on deck. In a most sadistic fashion, Scott held Smith under the gun, taunting and threatening to shoot him—for as much as a half hour—while Smith was begging for mercy, "praying to God," as Adams recalled it. Finally, Scott dispatched Smith with several gunshots, and then did the same to the first mate and cook. The first mate also grappled with Scott and begged for his life as Scott ordered him to jump overboard, and then shot him and tossed him over the rail anyway, when the mate refused.

All the while, Adams maintained that he, Sawyer, and Coakley were bystanders, trying to comprehend the horror while also tending to the ship's wheel and rigging, and imagining how they could over-power Scott while they had no firearms of their own.

Interestingly, Adams also recalled something on the stand that he apparently had not mentioned when he testified at Southport. He said that Scott, when he first encountered Adams and Sawyer with his pistol at the forecastle door (before he killed the engineer, first mate, and cook), told them, "I don't want you fellows to have nothing to do with this. When the white folks ask about it, I will tell them I did it." That would have been a helpful admission from Ad-ams's and Sawyer's standpoint, although it takes some imagination to guess how or why Scott would have said that to them in the heat of the moment.

Again, Adams claimed, it was not until the evening, after all the officers were dead and all four sailors had eaten a very tense dinner, that Scott announced his plan to launch the yawl boat and concoct the drowning story. "Boys," Scott said, "I want you to do as I tell you, or I will kill you all . . ." The others played along at first. But as they were lowering the boat, Sawyer seized the opportunity and jumped upon Scott when he had turned away from them briefly. The others joined in, overpowering Scott and taking his pistol. As they chained him in a seated position on the cabin roof, Scott said—although it is hard to credit—"Oh boys, don't do that. Just let me go and I will jump overboard."

The three sailors did not throw Scott overboard—or let him jump on his own—but not long afterward, Scott apparently com-plained of feeling cold while chained down. Scott cunningly asked Coakley to bring him his overcoat and spread it over him. Where-upon Scott, having secretly freed his hands and accessed the sec-ond pistol he had concealed in his clothing, shot Coakley dead as he stood over him. Coakley cried out, and Sawyer and Adams came running to subdue Scott again. And no, Coakley had not tried to shoot Scott, as Scott claimed.

When it came prosecutor Skinner's opportunity to cross-ex-amine Adams, the witness stood up to it remarkably well, repeating the sequence of events with striking consistency. The crux of the questioning was, why did Adams, Sawyer, and Coakley stand aside as Scott took his time in hunting down the officers one by one? And after the officers were dead, why did they wait as much as eight or nine hours before tackling Scott? Were there not plenty of belaying pins and other objects lying around, which they could have used as weapons?

Adams responded simply. A wooden stick is not an effective weapon to use against someone armed with a pistol, and Scott was the only man on board with a gun.

When Skinner asked him, "You seem to be mighty afraid of guns, had you never seen any guns before?" Adams replied, "I never saw any guns until I came to this country. . . . I only saw the big guns they use to kill whales." This might well have been true. When Adams first went to sea, at age twenty, his first voyage was a four-month tour on the *William A. Rosier*, a whaling vessel.

And in contrast with Scott, who had allegedly admitted that he had no fear of God because he did not believe in Him, Adams maintained that he had never been to sea without carrying his Bible with him.

All in all, it was a satisfactory performance by Arthur Adams, as the Wilmington press was surprisingly willing to acknowledge, with their usual tone of racial condescension, of course. Adams, the *Wilmington Morning Star* conceded, seemed like a "bright mulatto" who "does not impress one as a criminal."

As for Robert Sawyer, who immediately followed Adams on the stand, the same *Morning Star* account offered him similar backhanded praise. The darker-skinned Bahamian was "Black, thick-lipped, but reasonably intelligent. His nature and instincts from his appearance would seem rather to be more of a brute than his conversation would indicate."[1]

If the papers were willing to give Adams and Sawyer that degree of credit, it may have been partly for their humility and lack of presumption, to which white audiences might respond well. But most of all, perhaps, it would have been for their ability to keep their stories straight. Throughout that second day of the trial, as both men were examined and cross-examined thoroughly, their stories did not waver significantly from each other's, or from the testimony they had given in Southport. The reporters likely believed that a less "bright" Black man would have crumbled under the pressure if he were lying.

Sawyer concurred with Adams on the basic narrative of how Scott had carried out the quadruple murder of the officers, and then topped it off by killing Coakley as well. Sawyer also added some corroborating details. Like Adams, Sawyer remembered how Scott had wrestled with the first mate, rolling around on the deck for five or eight minutes. All the while, Scott was trying to force the mate through the rails into the sea, saying, "You won't go overboard, eh?" before finally overpowering and shooting him to death. Later, Scott resolved to head up the deck and hunt down the cook, saying, "That steward is in the galley yet. I want to get rid of him right quick—the bastard—shoot him."

Sawyer also agreed with Adams's surprising recollection that Scott—as the shooting began—had agreed to take the rap for it. Although Scott warned Sawyer not to interfere as he took out his wrath on the officers, Sawyer also recalled how Scott had promised, "When the white folks ask me, I can tell them I did it."

Later, when Scott revealed his plan for making up the story about the officers drowning, Sawyer maintained that Scott wanted to do more than just set the yawl boat adrift. He also intended to scuttle the ship halfway, opening up the hatches to allow the ship's hold to fill partially with water, to appear that it had been "waterlogged" by the storm. Sawyer and Adams both thought that was a reckless idea, as well as a story unlikely to be believed, and after that they were determined to take Scott down at the first opportunity. When they had their chance, and did manage to tackle and disarm Scott, he told them, "I did not think you fellows would do me like that. I ought to have shot all you negroes this morning."

But if Adams and Sawyer really were not culpable, could they not have overpowered Scott earlier? Skinner raised that same point with Sawyer on cross-examination, as he had with Adams. The prosecutor's theory was that after the storm damaged the ship, all four sailors together had come up with the plan to kill the officers, launch the boat, and blame everything on the storm; it was only when Scott proposed the scuttling that Adams and Sawyer had second thoughts about the plan and tackled Scott, resolving to pin the blame on him. Otherwise, why wait all through the morning and afternoon before making their move against him?

Moreover, why could Sawyer, Adams, and Coakley, plus the cook and the first mate, not have tackled Scott when they first realized he had a gun, when Scott pulled his weapon on the engineer and began threatening him? It would have been too late for the captain, whom Scott apparently killed and jettisoned earlier in the morning, before the others became aware of the danger. But surely the remaining five men could have armed themselves with belaying pins, or capstan bars, or any of the other tools lying around, and, as the prosecutor suggested, "demolished" Scott.

Sawyer responded much as Adams had to the insinuation. Scott was the only one armed with firepower, and apart from that, "we were not all together." There was no opportunity to coordinate a plan of action. Even though Scott held the engineer under the gun for a half-hour, taunting and firing at him, the first mate and cook were in other parts of the 204-foot-long ship, did not hear the shots, and so did not come running. When Scott then set out to kill the mate and cook one at a time, and even later, after all the officers were dead, the three remaining sailors could not gather together to take Scott down. The ship could not steer itself, and if it veered off track into the open ocean, the sailors— who, unlike the captain and first mate, had no navigational training—might be unable to regain course.

Sawyer, however, had a credibility issue. While he appeared to deny it when first questioned by Skinner, Sawyer acknowledged that he had a previous altercation with the cook about the drinking water supply on the ship. While the logbook showed there were at least four instances where Scott had been formally "logged" for insubordinate conduct, Sawyer also had been logged once, on July 30. That was the instance when Sawyer called the cook a "goddamn white son of a bitch." Sawyer admitted it was true on the stand, although he pointed out that the cook had first called him a Black SOB, "and I called him one in return."[2]

It was a relatively minor incident in the scheme of things, but it did establish some reason why Sawyer, like Scott, may have nursed a grievance against the officers. Toward the end of the second day of testimony, Skinner moved to admit the logbook entries as evidence. Defense attorney Peschau, doing what he could, objected to the written hearsay statements. He maintained the logbook was not admissible because it was not signed by all relevant parties, which would include Sawyer in this case. Also, Peschau argued that since the entry involving Sawyer referred only to a minor case of insolence, rather than a serious offense like desertion—which was mandatory for a captain to record in the log—it should not be admitted. Skinner countered that a captain was required to record any incident related to "mutinous conduct."

Judge Purnell recessed court for the day, instructing the attorneys to research the logbook issue and present any further arguments the following morning. When they returned, however, Skinner let the matter drop, electing not to pursue his motion to admit the log. It may be that since he already had read out the incriminating passage in the jury's presence, he believed he had gotten his point across.[3]

Thus, on the morning of the third day of the trial, the attorneys presented their closing arguments. All testimony and evidence related to the quintuple murder and mutiny had been finished up within two brief days of court.

George Peschau, for the defense, gave the first argument. The text of the arguments was not included in the formal trial transcript, and so the newspaper accounts must suffice. Peschau addressed the jury for about an hour, despite the "fearful odds" against an acquittal for Adams and Sawyer. He emphasized how plain and dull his clients appeared to be, compared with Scott, so "superior in intellect, audacious, and desperate." Clearly, Scott was the only villain, and when armed with pistols as well as a treacherous mind, he certainly could have held the other sailors captive for hours.

Skinner, of course, disagreed. In an address lasting one and a half hours, he maintained all four sailors, including Scott, took part in the killings. But then it was Adams and Sawyer who broke the bonds of conspiracy by tackling Scott and laying blame on him. In an odd twist, Skinner claimed that act was "almost as reprehensible as the mutiny and murder itself," as it violated the loyalty that sailors— serving together as they do on the treacherous sea—are supposed to feel toward each other. Although Scott had completely denied his own culpability, he had otherwise told the truth, and therefore he should be believed as to the guilt of Adams and Sawyer.[4]

As the trial concluded and the jury deliberated, there was a lingering sense of unease among the spectators, and even in the white-dominated North Carolina press. The *News and Observer*, of all sources, carried an account that it seemed "almost incredible" that Scott alone could murder five men without the assistance of his shipmates, and "yet the stories of Adams and Sawyer coincide so perfectly and are told in such a way as to inspire confidence."[5] The Wilmington *Messenger* said nearly everyone in the courtroom was impressed with Adams's and Sawyer's "ring of sincerity," as there was "nothing of the braggadocio" about them as there was when Scott testified. "There are extremely few who think Adams and Sawyer will be hanged for nearly every person who has heard the evidence has grave doubts about their guilt. As to Scott, no doubt is expressed."

If, the *Messenger* concluded, Scott had been armed with two pistols and Adams and Sawyer had none, then the only thing they could have done was seize the first opportunity to tackle Scott and then signal the other approaching ship for help. And Scott claimed Adams, Sawyer, and Coakley all had pistols of their own, and yet those guns had not been recovered from the vessel.

Where were they?[6]

Their objectivity towards Adams and Sawyer is surprising to note today. These same newspapers, seven years earlier, had been vocal cheerleaders for the White Supremacy Campaign and all the bloodshed that emanated from it. The *News and Observer* had led the way, but the Wilmington *Messenger* and *Star* enthusiastically followed along. It is no exaggeration to say that both Wilmington papers celebrated the killings perpetrated by the white insurrectionists in 1898. The *Messenger* had proclaimed, after the shooting ceased and the refugees fled, that "No more shall Sambo and Josh rule rough-shod over the white men who helped and befriend them." The *Star* said, "It was not a mob, it was simply a unanimous uprising of the white people against conditions that had become intolerable."[7]

For his own part, Judge Purnell was determined for the jurors to be as objective as possible. Before they began deliberation, he instructed them on the legal definition of murder, and explained that the death penalty was mandatory in such cases. However, he

SWIMMING AGAINST THE TIDE

also explained that the jury could qualify a guilty verdict by adding "without capital punishment," in which case the defendant would be sentenced to life in prison at hard labor. It was entirely up to the jurors whether the death penalty was "just or wise," and they could apply any considerations they wished, including, but not limited to "age, sex, ignorance, illness, or intoxication, of human passion or weakness." The judge also explained the presumption of innocence, the concepts of reasonable doubt, complicity, and conspiracy, and emphasized that Scott had been charged with the same murders as Sawyer and Adams, and the jurors could consider that when weighing his credibility as a witness.[8]

In substance, it was not much different from the instructions a judge might give to a jury in a murder trial today.

The jury retired at 1:40 p.m. and spent just more than two hours thinking it over. They came back at 4:00 with a verdict of guilty against Adams and Sawyer, and in a decision that caused "considerable surprise" among those gathered, the jury made no recommendation that the men be spared the death penalty.[9]

Therefore, Judge Purnell was left with no alternative. He sentenced both men to death by hanging, although before doing so, he asked each defendant whether they could give any reason why the sentence should not be imposed. Adams and Sawyer were each quoted as saying in reply, "Because I am not guilty."

The execution date was initially set for just two months away, on January 26, 1906. But it clearly would not take place at that time. There would be an appeal. George Peschau immediately asked leave of the court to file a writ of errors, asserting reasons why the verdict and sentence should be set aside. He also asked that Adams and Sawyer be allowed to proceed "in forma pauperis," without having to pay the costs of their own defense. To his credit, Peschau did not try to walk away from his clients, however little he was being paid, and however uncomfortable the case was for him politically.[10]

And thus, the jury box was cleared to make way for twelve new inhabitants. The trial of Henry Scott was to begin at 4:30 the same afternoon.

Henry Scott, likely photographed in the Wilmington jail

CHAPTER TEN

THE
SCOTT TRIAL

The Scott trial began with jury selection, and unlike that of the just-concluded trial of Adams and Sawyer, it turned out to be a rather haphazard process. The original pool of prospective jurors for both trials, who had travelled to Wilmington from all over the countryside, included only fifty men. Twelve had already served on the Adams and Sawyer jury, and, unfortunately, many of the others had been allowed to sit in the courtroom throughout the trial and already formed opinions about the case. Consequently, they could not attest that they could be impartial in deciding the case of Henry Scott.

Faced with a shortage of people, the federal marshal had to go out on the city sidewalks in the late afternoon and recruit "bystanders" to fill the jury box. The process took the rest of the afternoon and into the next morning.[1]

The prosecution opened by calling Captain David Stetson, who, like Captain Isaac Hewitt, was a part-owner of the *Berwind*. Just after the mutiny was reported, Stetson and Hewitt had travelled together from their Philadelphia-area homes down to Southport to take charge of the repairs to their ship. As Hewitt did in the trial of Adams and Sawyer, Stetson gave the jury a description of the ship, its legal registration, and its officers. But then Stetson related a new story, which Hewitt had not told when he testified.

Stetson said he had visited the three sailors in the cramped confines of the Brunswick County Jail on October 14, before they were brought upriver to Wilmington. He said Scott, who was kept in a separate cell from Adams and Sawyer, volunteered to speak with him. Scott, he claimed, told Stetson that Adams and Sawyer were not telling the truth in denying their involvement. Scott admitted killing the cook, Falbe, as well as Coakley, and also that "we were all in it with the other killings." He also said that all four Black sailors purchased guns in Mobile and brought them aboard, prepared to use them. The combination of the hot working conditions, bad food, and the racial arrogance of the white officers had finally pushed them too far.

In reply, Stetson claimed he said, "'Scott, you are a murderer and you will hang, and you deserve to hang,' and he agreed with me." It was also in this meeting that Scott made his infamous statement about not caring whether he was executed, as he did not believe in God or the Bible anyway.

When Stetson made his visit to the jail, he said, he was accompanied by several other men, although he did not name them. One might well have been his business partner, Hewitt, and yet Hewitt made no mention of Scott's supposed confession when he testified against Adams and Sawyer. With their company still on the line for the sailors' wages if any were to be acquitted, they may have decided not to mention Scott's confession until he was the one on trial.

Stetson also testified that when he inspected his ship, he succeeded in finding the logbook, although the captain's cabin was in much disarray. He had found blood stains in a couple of spots, on the ship's rail on the starboard side between the third and fourth masts, and on the port rail beside the fourth mast. There was also the large amount of blood near the cabin roof where Coakley's body lay, but none to be found in the cabin, galley, forecastle, or engine room. And for good measure, Stetson said he had examined the soft pine roof of the cabin and found no bullet hole there, although Scott claimed a bullet had struck the roof when Coakley supposedly fired at him and missed, before Scott shot back and killed him in self-defense.

After Stetson left the stand, he was followed by Captain Taylor and first mate Simmons of the *Blanche H. King*. Each gave a basic replay of their testimony in the first trial, describing how they boarded the *Berwind*, took charge, and brought the three surviving sailors into custody. Taylor also recalled how Adams had relinquished the ivory-handled pistol that he had from Scott, and how he had found the blackjack, plus the .38 cartridges wrapped in a sock, stowed within Scott's bunk in the forecastle. When asked how he knew it was Scott's bunk, Taylor said it was not only because Adams told him it was; Taylor also recognized the clothes that he found stored in the bunk as Scott's, because Scott was wearing them that very day in court.

Since Scott, unlike Adams and Sawyer, was charged with the murder of John Coakley as well as the four officers, the prosecution brought in some medical testimony about how Coakley died. It came from J. Arthur Dosher, a twenty-seven-year-old physician and Southport native who had recently returned to his hometown after finishing medical school. As a means of gaining experience, he took the position of Superintendent of Health for Brunswick County, whose job it was to perform autopsies in cases of homicide like this one.

It was the beginning of a distinguished career, in which Dr. Dosher would serve as a captain in the Army medical corps in France during World War I, be named supervising surgeon at the Quarantine Station, and be elected to the American College of Physicians and Surgeons. When he passed away in 1936, Dr. Dosher was the acknowledged dean of Southport's medical community. The town's hospital, Dosher Memorial, bears his name.

When Dr. Dosher went aboard the *Berwind*, after it was docked in Southport, he found Coakley's body still lying on the cabin roof where he had expired. He noted the gunshot wound in the chest, between the fourth and fifth rib, with the bullet lodged just under the shoulder blade. After extracting it, the doctor concluded it likely was a .32 or a .38 bullet, though he couldn't say definitively since he was "not acquainted to any great extent with firearms." He also noticed a bruise under Coakley's right eye, which was apparently inflicted prior to death.

(Also, though it was not pertinent to the legal question of homicide, Dr. Dosher mentioned that Coakley's teeth were irregular, suggesting he was "diseased by some venereal trouble." That, combined with a "shanker" sore somewhere on the body—Dosher did not elaborate—led him to suspect syphilis in the dead sailor.[2])

Adams and Sawyer then testified and gave critical testimony against Scott at the behest of prosecutor Skinner, who had won death sentences against them only the day before. Again, there were no significant variances in their testimony. Both described in detail how Scott had killed all five men, then held the two themselves under the gun until they could seize an opportunity to overpower him.

One Wilmington reporter noted how Adams' "words were broken and he spoke with difficulty," which was understandable due to the "strain of the past few days and the horrible realization of the fact that he had been found guilty of murder." Despite the strain, Adams remained firm in his story: "I said when I was first asked about it that I had killed no one, I said in my own trial I had killed no one, and I will say the same thing when I stand upon the scaffold."[3]

Both Adams and Sawyer were cross-examined by Scott's attorney, William Bellamy, who now strove to make the same point that Skinner had when cross-examining them in their own trial just forty-eight hours previously. How could they have just stood by while Scott went on his killing spree? Because they feared for their lives, they said.

"You are a timid kind of man, are you not?" Bellamy asked Sawyer.

"Not a bit so, sir."

"You are not afraid of anything?"

"I am afraid of some things."

"You are afraid of pistols?"

"Yes."

"You were so afraid that when you saw the mate in trouble, and you saw Scott standing up there talking to the engineer for a half hour, the engineer down on the deck and Scott up on the house, telling him to jump overboard, you were so afraid you would not go to the aid of either of them?"

"Yes, and I believe you would too," replied Sawyer.

"You let Scott walk up and down, and did not go to the assistance of any of those three white men? Were there not plenty of belaying pins, other nearby objects you could use as weapons to bring down Scott?"

"No, sir."

That raised the next question: If Sawyer was afraid to tackle Scott when the three officers were alive and could have helped him, why was he brave enough to do so and take Scott's pistol away from him later, after the three victims had been killed and tossed overboard?

"That was the first opportunity I had," Sawyer insisted. Not all three officers were on the deck at the same time, plus Sawyer and the other sailors were spread out, terrified, confused about what to do. "I didn't have an opportunity to jump on him until he was getting the boat ready" to lower, when all four sailors were gathered close together, and Scott happened to avert his glance long enough for them to act.[4]

Scott also testified, this time in his own defense. And this time, Skinner went at him loaded full bore, insisting Scott was a full participant in the killings. He reminded Scott of how, according to his own testimony, he had witnessed the other three sailors buy pistols and plan the insurrection while they were ashore in Mobile, and yet did not report it to his captain or the police.

"You were on land—could have protected yourself—put those criminals in charge of city authorities and protected the lives of those four white people?" As to why he failed to do so, Scott had no reply except for a vague belief that it would have caused "trouble" if he had reported it.

Skinner hammered Scott about how he claimed to have shot Coakley in self-defense, after Coakley supposedly had fired at Scott as he was chained down to the cabin roof. Captain Stetson had testified there was no bullet damage to the roof. And of all the shots fired during the entire ordeal, how could it be that the only one that failed to hit its mark was the one fired at Scott, from only a few feet away, while he was stationary?

"That was the only missing shot. No other shot missed. Coakley was right over you and could not hit you?" demanded Skinner, incredulously.

Scott answered, with a smirk and perhaps a bit of subconscious pride, "Everybody don't shoot alike."[5]

Once the testimony was over, the counsels went through their closing arguments, hitting the predictable points. Bellamy spoke for an hour and a half, trying to appeal to the jurors' sense of reasonable doubt, hoping that after hearing such a confused mishmash of stories they might be reluctant to convict his client. Most in the gallery, though, would have seen the defense attorney's task as a hopeless one. Even his opponent, Skinner, offered Bellamy some sympathetic praise for his efforts, saying that Scott could not have found a better advocate, "no matter how much wealth he possessed."

As for Skinner, his closing lasted just forty-five minutes. But with his rhetoric, he ranged back to the oldest days of piracy in North Carolina, to the depredations of Blackbeard and Bonnet. He also recalled the legend of Theodosia Burr, the daughter of Aaron Burr, who was travelling to New York in 1813 when her ship disappeared off the Carolina coast, and was long rumored to have been captured by murderous pirates. But none of those crimes compared with the horrific slaughter on board the *Berwind*, according to Skinner. "All the negroes were in the mutiny, blacks against whites," and the intention was murder all along.[6]

The newspapers all seemed to agree that the case against Scott was stronger than that against Adams and Sawyer, and since their jury had taken only a couple of hours to convict the two West Indians, most thought the Scott jury would return soon as well. Surprisingly, it was not to be. The jurors kept at it until 11:30 p.m. on the first night, and, ultimately, they spent forty-eight hours deliberating before they returned with the guilty verdict.

Why would it take so long? The papers claimed to have heard rumors about what was said—and by whom—in the jury room, but they made it a point not to publish such rumors "in justice to the persons whose names were mentioned."[7] Perhaps it had something to do with the jury instructions. Unlike in the trial of Adams and Sawyer, Judge Purnell had given the Scott jury an additional instruction regarding self-defense: that if they found that Scott reasonably believed Coakley was trying to kill him when he killed Coakley, the killing was justified. But even if that gave the jurors an additional point to contemplate, it is hard to imagine why they could have had much doubt about the guilt of Scott, whom virtually everyone by then had come to see as the "archconspirator."

When brought before the judge to receive his death sentence, Scott seemed "nervous, his eyes dancing everywhere." He proclaimed his innocence of killing anyone except Coakley, and while he acknowledged that his trial was fair, Scott believed the public had not been fair to him. As the judge urged Scott to reconcile himself with God before he was hanged, Scott became "visibly affected," and said it was not true, as some witnesses had claimed of him, that he had ever denied belief in God. Scott's voice rose almost to a shout, "half in anger, half in desperation, almost hysterical." He brought his hand down on the court railing, "with a slap that was heard all over the courtroom."[8] The demonstration was quite in contrast to the calm demeanor exhibited by Sawyer and Adams.

Scott's attorney did not file a bill of exceptions, as George Peschau had done for his clients. Bellamy was glad to be relieved of the case, as he saw no apparent grounds for appeal, at least at that time. In a letter that he wrote several months later, Bellamy expressed what he really thought of his client. He believed all along that Scott was insane, and therefore it would be an injustice to hang him. But there had never been any realistic chance of proving insanity to a jury, given the rules of the day.[9]

Adams and Sawyer were going to appeal, and although few people had any illusions that they would succeed in the higher courts, some still felt uneasy about the prospect of hanging all three men. The only people then living who knew for certain what happened on board the *Harry A. Berwind* were the three condemned men themselves, and they had told two versions of the events that were 180 degrees contrary to each other. Yet all three had been judged equally guilty.

Even the Wilmington papers had expressed doubts, and now that the verdicts were pronounced, members of the national press were taking note as well. One account, carried by papers in Chicago and Boston, described it this way:

"Sawyer and Adams were tried jointly and convicted largely on the testimony of Scott. . . . Scott's trial followed, and he was convicted on the evidence of Sawyer and Adams, whose story made him alone the murderer. If either story is correct, either Scott will die innocent, or Sawyer and Adams will die innocent. The two stories cannot be harmonized. If one is right, the other is wrong."[10]

While the appeals were working themselves out, there was the logistical question of where the hangings would take place. In Wilmington, a legal hanging—as opposed to a lynching—would ordinarily be conducted in the county jail, but since this was a federal case, the federal government would have the say. It could be done at the jail or on the Post Office lawn, but no government entity seemed eager to host the event. In fact, the *Morning Star* speculated that "there would be such a clamor to see the executions that hundreds of dollars or property would be destroyed in the crush."[11]

The best option might be to take the three condemned onto the federal revenue cutter, the *Seminole*, which was regularly docked at Wilmington. The 188-foot steel ship, built in 1900, was the federal government's main vessel for pursuing smugglers in the area.[12] The *Seminole* could sail down to the mouth of the Cape Fear and hang the infamous three from yardarms. Not only would it take the executions away from public view, it would avoid a distasteful scene. But since the alleged murderers committed their crime on the ocean wave, it might be most appropriate for them to die "on board a vessel and on the waters of the mighty deep."[13]

CHAPTER ELEVEN

APPEALS BEGIN

lthough Adams and Sawyer were sentenced to hang on January 26, 1906, it was routine for the executions to be stayed for appeals. On January 17, Judge Purnell signed an order to that effect. About the same time, and to the surprise of many, the judge also ordered Scott's execution to be stayed until July 6. Although Scott was not appealing his conviction, and most were skeptical that the U.S. Supreme Court would grant relief to Adams and Sawyer, Judge Purnell thought it prudent to keep Scott alive in case his testimony was needed in a retrial of the other two defendants.

The judge also accepted the petition from Adams and Sawyer, each of whom "humbly pray[ed] this honorable Court for an order that he be allowed to prosecute his writ of error without cost to him." Consequently, the two condemned men did not have to pay court costs. Likely they were granted some assistance with attorney fees, as well. Otherwise, it is hard to imagine how they could have obtained the attorneys.

When it came time to file the formal assignment of errors,

setting forth the grounds for Adams's and Sawyer's appeal, it was
signed by George Peschau, the young attorney who had advocated
for them at trial despite his affiliation with Colonel Waddell, the god-
father of the insurrection. Remarkably, they were also represented on
appeal by George Rountree, the author of the Disenfranchisement
Amendment and legal counsel to the White Government Union,
who had walked the streets of the city with a rifle in hand during the
bloody chaos.

By 1906, Rountree was fifty years old, and with his Ivy
League background, was recognized by many as the most academi-
cally learned attorney in Wilmington. Unlike younger lawyers such as
Peschau or Bellamy, Rountree would not have been assigned a complex—and low-paying—federal appeal if he was unwilling to accept
the task. It seems likely that Rountree took on representation of
Adams and Sawyer voluntarily.

But why would he? Why try to save from execution two
Blacks who had reputedly killed four white men and tossed their
bodies into the waves, denying them even the dignity of a Christian
burial? Chances are that Rountree saw little harm that could come
to him, one way or the other. More than seven years after the insurrection, thanks to the legislation that he personally had written, the
power of the white establishment in North Carolina was so firm
and unassailable that Rountree knew he would keep his wealth and
privilege, whatever the Supreme Court chose to do with Adams and
Sawyer.

Aside from that, Rountree may have thought that if he be-
stowed his legal talents upon the doomed Black sailors—if only
from a sense of *noblesse oblige*—it would raise his hometown's image.
For any Northern reporters who took note, it would show that Black
defendants, even in the most desperate circumstances, could still obtain quality representation.

At the risk of seeming to look back on the past with naiveté,
perhaps Rountree took the case because he thought it was the right
thing to do. Like others in town who had followed the trials, heard
the sailors' conflicting stories and had compared the seeming earnestness of Adams and Sawyer with the narcissism of Scott, Rountree might have concluded the two West Indians really had been convicted wrongly. If so, then it would do no harm to at least try to right

the wrong.

As Rountree and Peschau prepared the appeal, it is clear that they took the case seriously. They brought in two experienced Washington litigators, Corcoran Thom and Henry P. Blair, to help draft the brief.[1] Both men were deeply rooted in the District of Columbia legal establishment, and Thom in particular shared a proud Southern heritage with Rountree. He was the grandnephew of William Wilson Corcoran, a wealthy investment broker who founded the capital city's Corcoran Gallery of Art in 1874, despite having been a personal friend of Robert E. Lee, and having to leave the city for France during the Civil War due to his well-known Confederate sympathies. For those white-shoe D.C. attorneys, the case of Adams and Sawyer was a pro bono project: They could not possibly have received much pay. Yet, they did what they could for their clients.

They focused their arguments on issues that might seem minor, at least from today's perspective. But that was a calculated strategy, as the attorneys knew racial issues would be a nonstarter. They anticipated that if they went into the Supreme Court claiming that their clients had been wrongly indicted because they were Black, or railroaded because there were no sympathetic Blacks on the jury, then they would toss away what little chance they had of winning. The majority of the Supreme Court simply was not yet receptive to such arguments, as was shown by the lamentable case of Alfred Daniels two years earlier.

Indeed, that same year, the Supreme Court would be confronted with two cases in which Black defendants asked the justices to expand their concept of racial discrimination, as Daniels had, with the assistance of both Black and white attorneys. In each case, the defendant came out no better in the end than the alleged assassin on the Trent River.[2]

The first of those test cases arose from Fort Worth, Texas, where a Black farmhand named Rufus Martin was charged with murdering a white farmer for whom he worked. Martin had allegedly shot the man three times in order to rob him. No doubt it would have been a quick trial and execution—if not a lynching—but for the fact that Martin's family appeared to have money. Somehow, his mother retained attorneys to litigate her son's case through the state courts for more than two years, and then appeal to the U.S. Supreme

Court.[3] The crux of the appeal was the jury pool: No African American had even been considered for jury service, even though a quarter of the county population was Black.

It was essentially the same argument raised by Alfred Daniels, and when Justice Harlan issued the court's opinion in Martin's case in February 1906, he was compelled to give the same answer. The court could not conclude that a trial was racially discriminatory unless some state law or procedure expressly allowed discrimination.[4] There may have been no Blacks in the jury pool, but Texas law did not specifically state that no Blacks could serve. Even if there were no Blacks on the voter rolls or the property tax listings, and every attorney in the courtroom was white, it was not the court's concern.

Simply put, it would be several more decades, in the Warren Court era, before the federal courts seriously faced up to the harrowing obstacles that confronted Black defendants in southern courtrooms. Thus it was that Rufus Martin would die on the gallows in July 1906, after, according to newspapers, at least, confessing to the crime and commending his soul to God, "although in the courts of this world I didn't get due justice."[5]

Far more horrific was the second case, which came out of Chattanooga in January 1906. Ed Johnson, a Black man with a fourth-grade education, was accused of raping a young white woman on a dark street at night. At trial, the victim's identification of Johnson was tentative: She "believed" he was the attacker but was not quite certain. Five alibi witnesses testified he was elsewhere at the time. Johnson prayerfully proclaimed his innocence, but the guilty verdict and death sentence were inevitable. His attorneys, hastily appointed beforehand, did not encourage him to appeal, thinking it would only arouse a lynch mob if he did.[6]

In desperation, Johnson's family prevailed upon Noah Parden and Styles L. Hutchins, two of the only Black attorneys in east Tennessee, to try to save their son. They prepared an appeal, focusing on the same issue as in the *Martin* case: no Blacks in the jury pool. They sought an emergency stay of execution from Justice Harlan, which he granted, although it likely would have turned out to be only temporary relief. The stay only allowed Johnson time to bring his case before the full Supreme Court, and there is no reason to believe the outcome would have been different than in *Martin*.

Johnson never got that chance. On the night of March 19, 1906, shortly after news of the stay broke in Chattanooga, a mob forced its way into the Hamilton County Jail, extracted him from his cell, and hanged him from the girders of the nearby Walnut Street Bridge over the Tennessee River. After they also riddled him with rifle fire, one of the lynchers pinned a note to Johnson's body, reading, "To Justice Harlan. Come get your nigger now."[7]

Such was the backdrop against which Rountree and the D.C. law firm composed their appeal for Adams and Sawyer. They knew it would do them no good to try to push the envelope on racial discrimination, as the courageous but overwhelmed Black attorneys from Chattanooga had done. Their clients, after all, were still housed in the New Hanover County Jail, and there was definitely no shortage of rope, rifles, or bullets in town.

The problem was that, if they could not address race, the defense attorneys were left with few issues to work with.

In their brief, the defenders did touch on the issue of jury selection, but they could not point to any specific harm that had resulted to Adams and Sawyer from it. They recalled how prosecutor Skinner had made "conditional" challenges to some of the prospective jurors: he had them to step aside temporarily, excluding them from being considered, without either (1) challenging them for cause or (2) formally dismissing them without having to give cause, by use of a peremptory challenge. Each side, government and defense, was allowed a limited number of peremptory challenges, and if a prosecutor tried to exclude additional prospective jurors without giving a reason, it might be a serious issue. But in this case, the Supreme Court noted that despite Skinner's conditional exclusion of some jurors, both sides were eventually able to select twelve jurors that were acceptable to them, without either side using up all of its allowed peremptory challenges. Therefore, they reasoned, there must not have been any problem.

Interestingly enough, if Scott had been the one making the appeal, he might have had a more credible argument to make. When his second trial began, the attorneys had run through all fifty prospective jurors who had been summoned, so that the marshal and his deputies had to go out on the streets and recruit passersby. The Supreme Court likely would have viewed that as a serious irregularity and might have put its foot down.

Beyond that, Rountree and his colleagues raised a couple of minor points. They recalled how Skinner had questioned Adams about his time serving on another ship prior to the *Berwind*, implying that he had been insubordinate on that vessel as well, getting into arguments with the captain. But Adams had denied it and Skinner had offered no corroboration for his claim.

And in his closing argument, Skinner had spoken indignantly about how Adams and Sawyer claimed they took the time to eat and drink coffee in the galley in the hours after the murders took place, and before they seized their opportunity to tackle and disarm Scott. "A man, under such circumstances, who would drink coffee, ought to be hung on general principle," Skinner had told the jury. The Supreme Court acknowledged that the statement was inflammatory and improper, but since the defense had objected at the time and the judge sustained it, no harm.[8]

Ultimately, the Supreme Court had no grounds upon which to save Sawyer and Adams. They affirmed the convictions and death sentences in an eight-to-one opinion authored by Justice Rufus W. Peckham of New York. Even Justice Harlan went along. The lone dissenter, surprisingly, was Justice Edward Douglass White, a Louisiana Democrat and Confederate veteran.

Once the high court had spoken, the case was remanded back to the Circuit Court in Wilmington, where the only remaining task was to set a new date for Adams and Sawyer to be hanged. On June 19, 1906, the parties gathered before Judge Purnell. The atmosphere in the room was heavy that day, and not just with the gravity that comes with imposing a death sentence. There was the added weight of ambivalence and doubt.

George Rountree attended the hearing with his clients, along with George Peschau, even though Rountree had not represented them at the trial level and technically was not required to be there. Few would have blamed him if he had excused himself and delegated the thankless task to Peschau. Yet, he did not shrink from it.

Before the judge pronounced sentence, Rountree stood and addressed the court. He let the judge know that although he entered into the case late, he had made a "very comprehensive" review of every detail, to satisfy himself that no stone had been left unturned. Based upon that, he sincerely believed that Adams and Sawyer were not guilty and was willing to say so in full view of Wilmington's legal establishment. Rountree knew the judge had no real discretion at that stage, and the attorney's words would have no legal effect. Nor were they likely to win him any votes, although they might not cost him many either. He asked the court only to give his clients adequate time to prepare for death and make peace with God.

Granted the opportunity to speak, Adams and Sawyer both maintained their innocence, as they had at sentencing back in November. Adams, in particular, struck the press as "frail" in demeanor, "pitiful to behold." He "declared before God his hands spotless of human blood," but of course it was all in the hands of the Almighty. "I am weak; God is great," he was quoted as saying.[9]

With that, the judge set the executions for August 17, just under two months away, and just over one month after Scott was set to hang. He pronounced the trial to have been a fair one according to the law, and if Adams and Sawyer were guilty as charged, then the death sentence was certainly warranted.

Surprisingly, Judge Purnell added an unusual postscript, not required by statute. He told the two condemned that if they were not guilty, then unfortunately "the evidence was such as to prove them guilty by false testimony," and the court "could but pray that some means would deliver them from their impending fate." But "what such means could be, the court did not know and could not pretend to say."[10]

It was as if the judge was concluding the case with a prayer, maybe seeking forgiveness for what the law compelled him to do, perhaps hoping for divine intervention.

That is exactly what would come about only a few days later.

Some might have called it the Lord's work, and if it was such, it arrived in a mysterious way.

In the form of an anonymous letter.

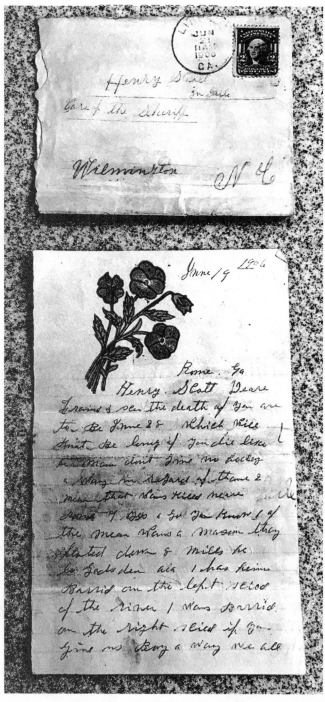

The first of two anonymous letters sent to to the
Wilmington jail, though quite possibly hoaxes,
nonetheless would lead to a startling admission.

CHAPTER TWELVE

OLD
CORRRESPONDENCE

ll through the first half of 1906, as the attorneys did what they could to navigate a barely chart-ed path through the appeals process, the three condemned sailors languished in the pitch-black confines of the New Hanover County Jail. They had no nearby family members to visit them, and the jailors carefully restricted those with access to them.

Any mail sent to the prisoners was scrupulously monitored, not that many people on the outside had interest in contacting them, anyway.

But then in late June 1906, only days before Scott's scheduled July 6 execution, a pair of surprising missives arrived by mail from out of the blue. Two letters, both apparently in the same handwrit-ing, were sent to Henry Scott at the jail. Both were postmarked from Lindale, Georgia, a mill town not far outside of Rome, in the hill country in the northwestern part of the state.

The first was written on a sheet of faintly lined paper, with a printed image of purple pansies at the top. But despite the flowery im-age, there was nothing cheerful about the letter, which read as follows:

Henry Scott, Deare friend I see the death of you are to be June 28 which will knot be long if you die like a man don't give no body away in regard of them 2 mean that was killd near Rome 7 yes a go you know I of the mean was a mason they floted down 8 mills be lo Gadsden a/a I has him barrid on the left side of the river I was barrid on the right seid... die like a man don't give ower clark a way fare all neigrew is deisfrenchise and we are gone in to a clube that we are to killd ever white man at we cand keck if bey his scape what we don't killd we are to burn up if a neigrew can't be a free man and have his right we will put an end to some....

Very similar in style was the second letter:

I will be in Atlanta ga next week to geat men to gurne owlr club; we have got 264 that has gurine ower club and if the US a steate ever gest in trouble... I wan all of us culler people to turn back on the USA and all we cant killd lest us burne.... you have got to die on the gallie die like a mane as we will mak thing deiffernin 10 yes time we have 2 hunden 64 member in Fla 264 Ark 329 Missep 442 Ala 629 Ga 827 Tenesee 476 SC 92 NC 47 Texas 968 we will get all of the culler raices to come to gether....[1]

When the jailers saw the letters, they and the sheriff immediately turned them over to prosecutor Harry Skinner. They all shared the same impression: the intentional misspellings, suggesting a crude attempt to imitate the southern Black dialect of the day, definitely made it look like a hoax. Someone likely was just playing a trick, trying to cast new accusations of murder upon Henry Scott in the days before he was to be hanged.

The details described, in the second letter especially, seemed quite farfetched. It was hard to believe there was some sort of Black insurrectionist conspiracy brewing, with hundreds of participants all over the Southeast, planning a wholesale slaughter of white people. True, white supremacist politicians were not above using the fear of Black crime and conspiracy to their advantage, as they had in 1898 Wilmington. But few really would give credence to rumors of a multistate revolutionary plot.

The town of origin itself cast doubt on the letters: Lindale,

Georgia, consisted almost entirely of one textile mill and its employ-ees. Founded in 1896 by an industrial outfit from Massachusetts, it was a staunchly segregated workplace, staffed by white men, wom-en, and children from the nearby Appalachian hollers. Shortly after it opened, a major strike nearly broke out when an inexperienced manager from up North made the mistake of hiring a Black machine operator. Even though the white workers had no union and virtually no concept of workplace organization, they immediately protested, saying they "did not want their wives and children working along-side of the colored hands." The owners relented, brought in new management, and afterward the color line was strictly enforced. The mill's floor of operations remained white, with only a few Blacks employed as janitors and groundskeepers.[2]

So even if there was some sort of Black revolution in the works, which was unlikely, it seemed even more unlikely that any participant was residing in Lindale. Still, some details mentioned in the letters were unnerving enough to warrant a second look.

The writer suggested that Scott had been involved in a dou-ble murder near Rome several years before, and that the bodies were buried downriver near Gadsden, Alabama. Gadsden is located about sixty miles downstream from Rome, along the Coosa River. In the early 1900s, before the river was dammed to form Weiss Lake in 1961, it was routine for small boats to travel between the two towns. Plus, Adams and Sawyer testified at the trials that Scott had an uncle in Mobile, Alabama, whom he visited while the *Berwind* was docked there. If Scott lived in Philadelphia and had family in south Alabama, might his travels have taken him near Gadsden or Rome, and might he have killed someone there? It surely was not impossible for some-one who apparently had killed five men at sea.

Also, that creatively misspelled word "deisfrenchise" would have struck a chord. During that summer of 1906, Georgia was in the midst of a heated political debate, not too different from what North Carolina had gone through shortly before. Georgia also had flirted with Populism in the 1890s, but now the Democratic Party was back in full control, and as the 1906 Democratic gubernatorial primary campaign was in full swing, the term "disfranchisement" appeared regularly on the front pages throughout the state.

The two leading candidates for governor were the publishers

of Georgia's two largest newspapers. Hoke Smith, owner of the *Atlanta Journal*, was a staunch advocate of what he called the "Disfranchisement Amendment," a combination of poll taxes, literacy tests, and property ownership requirements that would eliminate the black vote in the state. Clark Howell, owner of the *Atlanta Constitution*, was opposed to the provisions, but only insofar as he suspected they would disfranchise many white voters as well.[3]

As one would expect, the campaign waged by the rival newspapers over the summer was vitriolic and vicious, reminiscent of North Carolina in 1898. Smith's expressed purpose, regarding Blacks in Georgia, was to "handle them as they did in Wilmington," where the woods were "black with their hanging carcasses."[4] The papers were filled with overblown stories about Black-on-white crimes of all sorts, occurring throughout Georgia, from murder and rape to theft and everything in between. In September, violence did break out in Atlanta, resulting in at least two dozen deaths. Smith won the primary in early September, taking nearly four times as many votes as Howell.

With all of that in mind, it is no surprise that Harry Skinner, as the prosecutor, wanted to look into any possibility that Henry Scott had killed others in addition to the *Berwind* officers. If the contents of the odd letters turned out to be true, he did not want it said that he had failed to investigate. Skinner wrote to the clerk of court to say, "I am inclined to think that it was written by some crank who perhaps never saw Scott," but at any rate the matter should be investigated before Scott "passes away." Skinner suggested showing the letters to the "colored minister" who had been providing pastoral care to Scott in jail, in the hope that the minister might elicit a death-cell confession.[5]

And so, in what would be the final week and a half in the life of Henry Scott, those crank letters brought about the revelations that would eventually resolve the affair of the *Harry A. Berwind*, even if it took several years for all the pieces to fall into place.

The minister who had been visiting the three sailors was one of the few people to do so during their time in jail. The Reverend Edmund Bennett was the rector of St. Mark's, founded in 1869, and the first African-American Episcopal church to be established in eastern North Carolina. The congregation is still active today in its historic location on the corner of Sixth and Grace streets downtown. Reverend Bennett had gained the men's trust because he shared their backgrounds in some respects. Like Sawyer and Adams, he was a West Indian immigrant, having been born on the island of Antigua. He also had grown up in Baltimore, in the same neighborhood where Scott claimed to have originated.[6]

Bennett had gained the respect of Wilmington's white community as well, since he had served at St. Mark's since 1897, and the church had not only survived but expanded in the tense years since the insurrection. The church remained financially solvent, and the money came not only from the Northern philanthropists who helped establish it after the Civil War, but from white locals as well. In 1901, St. Mark's had hosted a five-act play at Thalian Hall to raise funds for new the church's new windows, pews, and pipe organ. On Labor Day, 1903, the church had chartered steamboats to take hundreds of Black Wilmingtonians on an excursion down the river to Carolina Beach, for a weekend of swimming and sports events.[7]

Surely none of that would have been possible without the good graces of the white establishment. St. Mark's, along with many of the city's Black churches, was the center of community for its parishioners. Not just places of worship, the churches also operated schools and served as a gathering place for Black businessmen and tradesmen of all stripes. They were places of relative safety and security for Blacks, provided, of course, that they remembered their place in the scheme of things.

It appears that Reverend Bennett was approached by someone, likely Harry Skinner, the clerk of court, or the sheriff, and shown the contents of the Lindale letters. Essentially, the reverend was put up to the task of questioning Henry Scott about the wild story from Georgia, using his role as spiritual advisor to gather incriminating information.

It would be fascinating to know how that conversation went, and even more so to know what the reverend said to Scott when they met. But within a few short days, Scott spoke with G.W. Bornemann, who was a justice of the peace and notary public working at the jail. According to Bornemann, Scott "did not desire to die with a lie on his lips." Scott's own attorney, William Bellamy, was also present and urged Scott to put his statement in writing, which the notary agreed to witness.[8] The result was a remarkable written statement signed by Henry Scott on June 30. It was not a confession to murder in Georgia, but it was a partial exoneration of Adams and Sawyer for the *Berwind* killings.

Scott's statement reads a bit like his courtroom testimony, in that it is grandiose, melodramatic, and maddeningly vague. In other words, it seems like a statement that he either wrote or dictated himself.

> With godly truth, this lovely morn of June, to the world at large—I am not shielding Sawyer and Adams—nor trying to save them.... I release Sawyer and Adams to the great community in general, to save the Christian body both white and colored ... as a fallen Christian the world is against me, I am doing my duty at the last hour on earth ... I stands before the law now as a murderer ... therefore I concluded with this release by saying to the Commonwealth that I, H. Scot, release to the world as two innocent men, A.A. and R.S., from the date of this reading to the Commonwealth. The Commonwealth can just do what they like with them, the burden is strictly off my hands, now God bless all on earth ... I am finished ... closed ... Henry Scott.[9]

For anyone in sympathy with Adams and Sawyer, this statement was a mixed bag. Scott did not explicitly confess to killing all four officers and Coakley by himself. But despite all the prevaricating mumbo-jumbo, he did use the word "innocent" regarding the two West Indians. Here, at last, was a real opening to establish the truth of what really happened.

Their attorneys had less than two months remaining in which to save the lives of Adams and Sawyer, and Scott was to hang within the week. The mad scramble began.

CHAPTER THIRTEEN

HENRY SCOTT'S
FINAL ACT

The urgent maneuvers began with a hurried train journey up North, by the attorney who seemingly had been most eager to rid himself of the case.

In that first week of July 1906, in the last days before Henry Scott was set to be hanged on that Friday, the sixth, the Wilmington papers were rife with rumors that Scott had finally come clean and made a full confession to all five murders, and in doing so had exonerated Adams and Sawyer. The same rumors had it that William Bellamy was making an emergency trip to New York, where he hoped to meet with President Theodore Roosevelt. The president was spending part of the summer at his beloved Sagamore Hill estate, just outside Oyster Bay on Long Island, no doubt hoping to avoid Washington's miasmal heat and humidity, as well its politics.[1] It would require a lot to get a personal meeting with, much less convince, the president to take the unusual step of granting clemency in a murder case like this. But a written confession just might do the trick.

The rumors, in fact, were true. Bellamy had a new written confession, signed by Scott and legally attested, which went well beyond the vague statement Scott had made on June 30. On its face, it appeared to set forth a full explanation of what happened aboard the *Berwind*.

Earlier, when Scott's trial had ended, Bellamy did not file an appeal on his behalf, because he did not see any realistic legal grounds for it. But now, though he technically was no longer obligated to act as Scott's appointed counsel, Bellamy went the extra mile on behalf of his client. Just as likely, he was thinking about the codefendants as well. Even if the president would not spare Scott's life, he might be willing later to spare Adams and Sawyer.

On July 5, Bellamy sent a telegraphed message to Claudius Dockery, the United States marshal in Wilmington, informing him of his efforts. He had been granted a personal meeting at Sagamore Hill with both the president and William Loeb, the senior presidential secretary and Roosevelt's all-around "right-hand man" since his days as governor of New York. Roosevelt appeared to take the matter seriously, and, according to Bellamy, had sought input from his attorney general, William H. Moody. But now, unfortunately, the president had declined to intervene with Scott's execution. Barring an extraordinary event, Scott would hang the following day.[2]

At the same time, Bellamy wrote to Reverend Bennett. He enclosed a copy of Scott's written confession, and expressly urged Bennett to relay it to Adams's and Sawyer's attorneys, in hope that it would aid them in seeking clemency. Bellamy said he regretted not being able to save Scott's life. In his mind, the confession only confirmed what the attorney had suspected of his client all along, that Scott was not of sound mind. Bellamy quoted one of Blackstone's most fundamental legal principles, that "no one insane should be executed," although he knew if he had tried to mount an insanity defense in court, it never would have prevailed.[3]

Bennett probably had Scott's confession in hand already, and the marshal, sheriff, prosecutor, and other attorneys for Adams and Sawyer likely did as well. They all, in varying degrees, had worked behind the scenes to arrange the confession and execution. When Henry Scott finally met his death at the end of a rope on July 6, it was anything but a lynching. The execution took place within the walls of the New Hanover County Jail, in the most orderly fashion, with all the trappings of a choreographed media event. Reporters were there to record the details, right down to the prayers offered and the hymns sung. The most critical feature, naturally, would be Henry Scott's verbal proclamation of guilt.

The day began early for the condemned man. After a hearty breakfast of ham and eggs, Scott dressed in a dark blue suit, a black-and-white negligee shirt, and tan shoes. One of the press described him as the "calmest person in the jail," as he "carried himself as though he had no care or worry in the world."

The sheriff had issued a limited number of tickets for those who clamored to be witnesses to the hanging. Many more were gathered outside the jail, even though it was a rainy day. But ultimately only fifty people were admitted inside, likely to crowd together in the cramped basement of the jail where the gallows had been set up. If the press source can be believed, Scott gave away signed photographs of himself—most likely prints of the best-known photo of him, the one that shows him seated with his sailor's cap on his lap, looking quizzically at the camera—to the surprised witnesses.

Before Reverend Bennett led the procession of dignitaries into the "death chamber," Scott was permitted to stop by the cells where Adams and Sawyer were being held, to exchange farewells. There still was much animosity between them: The West Indians blamed Scott for the entire affair, and, as Scott would soon express in his dying confession, he still resented Adams and Sawyer for tackling him and—as Scott saw it—betraying him. But their final parting was civil enough, with Scott urging them to "[b]e good, boys."

After they entered the basement around 2:00 p.m., Scott sat on a chair beside the trap door of the gallows as Reverend Bennett read aloud Scott's final written statement—his confession—to the witnesses. It surprised everyone, not just because Scott seemed willing to admit to all five murders, but because his new account of the killings was so wildly different from every story he had told before. It left everyone wondering: Was this dying declaration the truth, or just another trick being played by a cunning attention-seeker who loved to see people hanging on his every word?

"The fact is that Sawyer, Adams, nor Coakley had nothing to do with the tragic affair," Scott wrote emphatically to begin his statement.

There had been ill will between the officers and sailors nearly

from the beginning of the voyage. Just three days after they departed Philadelphia, Scott claimed, Coakley had complained to both the
cook and Captain Rumill that the crew were not getting enough to
eat, but both officers ignored him. The following Sunday, Sawyer
and the cook had gotten into the well-documented dispute over the
water rations, which led to each calling the other a "son of a bitch"
of differing color. That much was consistent with what all three sailors, plus the logbook, had recounted.

But with this new account, Scott went into previously un-
mentioned details. He claimed that aside from allowing the four
sailors only a small amount of fresh water for drinking, cooking,
and bathing, the captain also added saltwater to their supply, "just
for meanness," and to render their condition more "hellish." It also
meant the captain, whom Scott claimed was a cheapskate as well as
a sadist, would not have to purchase as much freshwater as he might
otherwise have to do when they reached Cuba.

Further, Scott now claimed that along the way, the *Berwind*
had made an unannounced stop on Bimini, one of the small Bahama
islets just ninety miles offshore from Miami. Once there, the captain decided to barter away about one-third of the ship's stores for
virtually nothing except for a few coconuts, sponges, and bananas.
Scott saw that as "a pretty fine way to start trouble on a ship, when
trouble was at hand already." Yet up to this point, no one else had
recalled the ship stopping at Bimini, and it was not mentioned in the
logbook.

They went on, with tempers still smoldering, to Cuba and
then to Alabama. But now Scott claimed that while ashore in Mobile,
first mate Hall and cook Falbe got into trouble, ending up tossed in
jail for drunkenness. These events, too, had never been testified to
by anyone before. But according to Scott, Hall and Falbe now were
angry at the Black sailors, apparently blaming them for their predic-
ament.

Once back at sea, and after battling their way through the
storm near the Tortugas, first mate Hall and engineer Smith approached Scott and Coakley—as Scott now claimed—with a startling revelation. They told Scott and Coakley that the captain was
conspiring with all four white officers to cheat the Black sailors out
of their wages. Captain Rumill intended for one of the officers to

provoke a fight with the sailors, which would give the captain a pretense to arrest all four sailors, and take the ship back to port without having to pay them. Supposedly, the officers planned to carry out the scheme before the ship reached Cape Hatteras.

It was a bizarre claim, and not a very plausible one. If the four white officers were in cahoots to frame the four sailors, why would two of them alert Scott and Coakley to the plot? Why would the officers think it worthwhile to go to the trouble of framing the sailors just to avoid paying them their minuscule wages? And even if they had carried out the plan and put the four sailors in confinement, somehow they would have had to maneuver the undermanned ship into port and hire new crew.

It also seemed too convenient for Scott that Coakley, the only other named witness to this strange conversation, was now deceased and unable to corroborate or deny the story.[4]

In the early morning hours of October 10, Scott maintained, it was true that the altercation started shortly after the changing of the watch. At 4:00 a.m., Scott and Coakley relieved Sawyer and Adams of duty. Coakley took the wheel, Scott manned the bow as lookout, while Sawyer and Adams went to the forecastle to get some sleep, as everyone had agreed all along. But now, Scott said the first mate and engineer had provoked a fight, which Scott took to be the culmination of their plan to subdue and arrest all four Black sailors.

Supposedly, the first mate ordered Scott to saw some wood, for what purpose at that dark hour, he did not say. Scott balked at the command, asking if he could drink some coffee first, since it was so early, and he had just arisen from sleeping. The engineer chimed in and boasted that if *he* were in charge, then he would *make* Scott saw the wood, or else punch him. At that, Scott challenged the engineer to "punch me your own self."

Scott had also made it a point to clarify, in this new statement, that neither Adams, Sawyer, nor Coakley had carried a gun. Earlier, of course, Scott had claimed all three men had bought pistols in Mobile while they considered seizing the ship. But Scott now acknowledged he had lied about that. Scott certainly did have at least one gun of his own. And he now claimed that all the white officers were armed as well, although it would have been unusual for officers on a commercial vessel to carry guns, and no one could seem to account for where the officers' guns had disappeared to, if indeed they possessed them.

In response to his challenge, Scott now claimed that the engineer "drived at me," starting the fight by flailing away at Scott with his fists. The first mate then drew his pistol and was stepping around the two grapplers, looking for a way to get a clear shot at Scott, when suddenly the cook came rushing in from the galley, carrying a pistol in one hand and a hatchet in the other.

Scott boasted that, even though outnumbered three to one, he was prevailing in the fight. "I was winning from all of them, when the mate fired one shot from his revolver at me," but missed. At that point, Scott made use of the gun he had concealed under his coat. "When I drew my revolver, I promptly shot all three of them, and down the galley they went."

Captain Rumill supposedly was watching all his from his cabin, some distance up the deck. But upon seeing all three of his officers fall dead, Scott said the captain then charged in with his own gun, "but before he had any time to shoot me, I shot him twice, and down the cabin he went."

It was all over within minutes, Scott said. He had disposed of all four officers with minimal effort. Coakley was at the wheel, and Sawyer and Adams were in their bunks, and thus had not witnessed the shootings directly.

Scott then tossed all the bodies overboard, although Coakley was the only one to witness that.

Later in the day, Scott had shared with the other sailors his plan to set the yawl boat adrift and concoct the story about the officers drowning in the storm. Scott thought the others were in agreement with him and trusted them, up until the point when they tackled him and chained him down. "These three men spoiled my business to be sure," he said. Scott remained bitterly resentful about it although, as he claimed, he just couldn't bear to let them hang for murders that he alone had committed.

To conclude his statement, Scott thanked his attorney, William Bellamy, whom he called a "great young battler," for his excellent representation at trial. He also commended Reverend Bennett, "the also-coming Christian brigadier" for being so kind to him during the miserable months he spent in jail.

In broad letters at the bottom of his document, Scott scrawled the words, "This Ends the Tragedy."

Once the reverend finished the reading, Scott stood to address the witnesses himself. To the very end, he maintained his characteristic air of command and control.

"**K**eep quiet," Scott demanded of the crowd. "I want to give you gentlemen some good advice. . . . We are all men, and we are all born of women. I am talking to you now, white and colored. The white and the colored are the same to me, and when a man kills another, the best thing to do is to put him out of business. . . . I am not trying to shield Sawyer and Adams. Let them go to the world as traitors and scoundrels. . . . The power I now have, President Roosevelt has not. Nobody could save them but me. I release them to the world as two innocent men, and so is Coakley, but I don't know where he is now.

"The officers of that vessel treated me dirty and violated the laws of God and righteousness. . . . I want to tell you now, I did not kill these men because they were white. . . . I was going to kill Adams, Sawyer, and Coakley and throw them overboard, so I just want to show you that I did not kill them because they were white, but because they were dirty. If they had been colored, I would have killed them the same way."

A last-minute confession and a quick hanging: the day's newspapers told the story.

SCOTT DECLARED THAT HE ALONE WAS GUILTY OF MURDER

Negro Seaman Hanged at Wilmington To-day Made a Statement Exhonorating Sawyer and Adams who were Sentenced to Hang for Mutiny and Murder.

Efforts will be Put Forth at Once to Secure the Release of the Two Negroes Condemned to Die for the Crimes of a Brute of the High Seas.

MUTINEER SCOTT HANGED TODAY

Last Statement Exonerates Adams & Sawyer

THEY MAY BE PARDONED

On October 10 Last Scott Murdered Capt. E. B. Rumill of the Schooner Harry Berwind, the Steward, Mate and Engineer—He Was Calm on the Scaffold.

As with so many hangings, including those of Alfred Daniels and Rufus Martin, the press accounts of Henry Scott's death were steeped in religious solemnity. Reverend Bennet gave a final prayer, and the entire assembled crowd joined in singing "Nearer, My God, to Thee." The marshal tied Scott's wrists and ankles, placed the rope around his neck and the black cap over his head, and then asked the condemned, "Are you ready, Scott?"

From underneath the cap came a clear voice saying, "Let 'er go. Goodbye, all."

Eight minutes later, he was pronounced dead.[5]

Thus ended the young but tumultuous life of the sailor known as Henry Scott, and perhaps no one will ever know if that was his real name, or just a pseudonym adopted by a man who went to sea to escape whatever dark past he left behind on land. He claimed to have been reared in Baltimore and Philadelphia, but the records are sparse, as they are for so many African-American families of that era. He claimed to have a wife and young children in Philadelphia, and an uncle in Alabama, but none of them surfaced, even to claim his body after the execution.

Consequently, the mortal remains of Henry Scott—like those of many hanged convicts—were sent to medical students for dissection. Before the trap was sprung, Scott asked that his body be sent to Jefferson Medical College in his hometown of Philadelphia, or maybe to Johns Hopkins in Baltimore, which had been founded as a philanthropic hospital with an eye towards serving the city's impoverished, both black and white. If neither option could be arranged, Scott asked that his remains go to the Navy, for use in "Uncle Sam's Medical Department." Whatever happened, he did not wish for his body to be buried in North Carolina.

It was not, although his remains would never leave the state. Scott was not informed of it prior to his death, but just days before, the federal court had issued an order that the bodies of himself— and of Adams and Sawyer, too, if it came to that—were to be sent to the medical school at the University of North Carolina. They would not be relinquished to any Yankee institution, whatever Scott may have desired. Before the end of the day on July 6, Scott's body was placed in a pine box for shipment on a night train to Chapel Hill.[6]

No trace of him remains today. Not a bone, not a grave marker, not even a definitive memory of his true name or where he came from. Only some photographs, and a trail of homicidal destruction remain.

One of the execution witnesses was George Peschau, and once the proceedings were concluded in the jail basement, he went upstairs to meet with his clients in their cells. He shared with them the good news that Scott had confessed and fully exonerated them in writing. The papers may have paraphrased their reaction, but the quotes attributed to them are close enough.

Sawyer said, "Thank God, he's told the truth at last," while Adams exclaimed, "I knew God would help us."[7]

God may have helped the two condemned men, but it remained to be seen whether the establishment would. The Wilmington press, at least, seemed to be on their side. The *Messenger* acknowledged that Scott's confession was a "disappointment," and had "muddied the waters." It was entirely different from the testimony Scott had given earlier, and his new account of having shot down all four of the *Berwind*'s officers on his own, while all four also were armed with pistols, strained credulity at the least. But with so much doubt hanging over the culpability of Adams and Sawyer, the paper now openly advocated for the president at least to commute their sentences. They might not be entirely innocent, but "no man should be hanged for any crime when there is the least doubt about his guilt. . . . Better that ninety and nine guilty men should escape punishment than that one innocent man should be punished."[8]

It was the right sentiment, and a difficult one with which to argue. It was also a bit late for the very newspaper which, seven years earlier, had cheered and cajoled the extrajudicial killings of dozens of people in the streets of Wilmington. None of that had been improper, in the view of the *Messenger*'s editorial page. It had all been provoked by the "disgraceful and outrageous conduct of the negroes" in attempting to register their people to vote.[9]

Now, the question on everyone's mind was whether the Rough Rider in the White House would bring himself to share the sentiment.

To the President:-

We, the undersigned citizens of the Eastern District of North Carolina, respectfully ask that you would exercise executive clemency in the case of Robert Sawyer and Arthur Adams, convicted of mutiny and murder on the high seas at the November Term 1905 of the Circuit Court of the United States, sitting in Wilmington, North Carolina, upon the ground that the only testimony against these parties was the testimony of Henry Scott who was tried and convicted at the same term with Adams and Sawyer for the same crime, and who was executed on the 6th. day of July, 1906, but before his execution he made an ante-mortem statement in which he completely and emphatically exonerates Adams and Sawyer from all knowledge of, or participation in, the crime of which they were convicted.

William H. Bellamy,
Attorney appointed
by United States Circuit
Court to defend Henry
Scott, (Mutineer)

B.F. Keith
COLLECTOR OF CUSTOMS.

A.M. Waddell - Mayor of Wilmington
Thos. O. Bunting by Register Deeds
Frank H. Stedman Sheriff New Hanover County
Robert Strange, Bishop of East Carolina,

President
Theodore
Roosevelt and
the petition
for clemency
he received
on behalf of
Arthur Adams
and Rob-
ert Sawyer.
Many of
Wilmington's
elite signed
the peitition,
including some
very unlikely
petitioners.

142

CHAPTER FOURTEEN

A CHANCE
AT JUSTICE

t first blush, a clemency petition from Arthur Adams and Robert Sawyer was not the sort of issue to draw much interest from President Theodore Roosevelt. Although the crime was shocking enough, it was a relatively mundane criminal justice matter, and TR preferred to spend his time on big issues. Even in his own time, he was a man larger than life.

Few personalities in American history have received as much biographical adulation as Roosevelt. And there are not many politicians whose life experiences can be accurately recounted as death-defying, but Roosevelt is one. His experiences in the Spanish-American War, in which he led the Rough Riders—a motley regiment of Ivy Leaguers and cowboys—in its charge up San Juan Hill in Cuba, is well known. But consider also the story of Roosevelt's 1913 exploration of an unknown river in the Amazonian rain forest, during which he and his team braved malaria, river rapids, piranhas, and hostile natives armed with poisoned arrows. Two of the men lost their lives and Roosevelt himself nearly died from fever. Yet he persevered and documented his discovery of the river in a scholarly presentation to the National Geographic Society.

Roosevelt was a man of learning as well as a man of action. He wrote more than twenty books over his lifetime, and while some were self-serving memoirs, others were legitimate works of scholarship. His first book, published when he was twenty-three years old and barely out of Harvard, was *The Naval War of 1812*, a history of the battles fought at sea and on the Great Lakes during America's second war of independence. He wrote biographies of Oliver Cromwell and Gouverneur Morris, one of the lesser known leaders of the Revolutionary War period.

Both as an adventurer and a scholar, Theodore Roosevelt seemed to defy the stereotype of the languid, reactionary patrician some might have expected him to become. He was born into a wealthy landowning and merchant family whose roots in New York state dated back to the 1600s. Why, then, would he feel inclined to risk life and limb exploring South America, or on hunting safaris through Africa? In the political arena, why would a son of privilege embrace progressivism by endorsing land conservation, or supporting antitrust laws that would limit wealthy business monopolies?

Much of the Roosevelt legend is due to his willingness to live contrary to stereotype. Yet, his progressivism has often been overstated. Roosevelt sincerely believed in land conservation, but not so much for the sake of saving beautiful landscapes. He was more interested in the efficient use of resources—like promoting careful forest management, for example—than in preservation. His reputation as a trust buster is exaggerated, too. While Roosevelt's Justice Department did bring antitrust actions in several high-profile cases, he did not think it wise economic policy to persecute corporations.

There is one area in which even Roosevelt's most admiring biographers do not claim that he was progressive at all: that of race relations. The hard truth is that Theodore Roosevelt had little regard for racial minorities, whom he thought inherently inferior and second-class citizens at best. He could be expected to show little concern for the fate of two Black sailors who were implicated in a mutiny and murder of four white officers onboard a ship.

The reasons may lie in his family background. Despite his Dutch name and Manhattan upbringing, half of Roosevelt's ancestral roots lay in the South. His mother, Martha "Mittie" Bulloch, was the quintessential Georgia belle. She grew up at Bulloch Hall, her father's palatial plantation estate on the outskirts of present-day Atlanta. Vivacious, quick-witted, and charmingly attractive, many have speculated that Mittie was Margaret Mitchell's inspiration for Scarlett O'Hara in *Gone With the Wind.*

Mittie remained a proud Southerner all her life, even through the Civil War. She thrilled her children, Teddy in particular, with stories of her home in the red hills of Georgia. Her Bulloch relatives were the masters of their realm, a spacious cotton plantation that not only was worked by Black slaves but was situated on land recently inhabited by the Cherokee tribe before their forced removal west on the Trail of Tears.[1]

For the younger Theodore, the intended lesson would have been clear. He was raised to be part of a class of masters, all of them with white skin and Northern European blood. One of Roosevelt's biographers, Carleton Putnam, summed up Roosevelt's attitude by citing his own words "Teutonic [and] English blood is the source of American greatness: Our American republic, with all its faults, is, together with England, the fine flower of centuries of self-discipline and experience in free government by the English-speaking branch of the white race."[2]

From his maternal uncles, Theodore also inherited a sense of seafaring adventure that was rooted in the Rebel tradition. Irvine Bulloch, his mother's younger brother, served the Confederate Navy as an officer aboard both CSS *Alabama* and CSS *Shenandoah*, two "commerce raiders" that were outfitted in England for the purpose of carrying the Civil War onto the High Seas, by destroying Northern trading vessels. And James D. "Jimmy" Bulloch, Mittie's older half-brother, was responsible for the activities of both ships. He was the Confederacy's leading intelligence agent in Great Britain. He arranged for the proceeds of southern cotton sales, brought in by blockade runners, to be used for building and manning the raiders.

Upon Roosevelt's taking office, he found that raising America's stature as a world power meant promoting national unity at home, which Roosevelt found to be a challenge in the early 1900s. Civil War and Reconstruction were living memories, especially for Southerners. Roosevelt made a sincere effort to reach out to the Solid Democratic South, and he enthusiastically recalled his family's Confederate roots to do so. On one visit through Georgia, he gave a speech at his mother's former home, saying, "It has been my very great good fortune to have the right to claim my blood is half Southern and half Northern, and I would deny the right of any man here to feel a greater pride in the deeds of every Southerner than I feel."[3] Even so, most Southerners still could not see the patrician New Yorker as one of their own.

In 1904, when Roosevelt ran for his full term as president, he won in a landslide, one of the most lopsided in years. The former Confederate South was the only place Roosevelt could not win. The Democrat, Alton B. Parker, still won every state in the region, and it was not close. He carried North Carolina by sixty to forty percent.

If Roosevelt wanted to improve his political standing in the South, and he surely did, he could not do so by antagonizing white voters, who now held all political power there. He had received his first lesson in that regard back in October 1901. Very soon after he moved into the White House following McKinley's assassination, Roosevelt invited Booker T. Washington over for dinner, ostensibly to talk about the status of Black education. It might have seemed an innocuous gesture; Washington was, of course, known to whites as the nonthreatening black conciliator. But the Southern press erupted in near-unanimous outrage at the idea of a Black man eating dinner in the White House. Senator Benjamin Tillman of South Carolina, true to form, opined that now "[w]e shall have to kill a thousand niggers to get them back in their places." His Mississippi colleague, James Vardaman, lamented that Roosevelt's White House was "so saturated with the odor of nigger that the rats have taken refuge in the stable."[4]

Not surprisingly, Roosevelt never hosted another Black dinner guest. When confronted with an act of alleged Black lawlessness, especially in the South, he could be expected to come down hard on the side of law and order. So it was with the infamous Brownsville Affair, a military scandal that was making national headlines in the summer and fall of 1906, about the very time when the attorneys for Arthur Adams and Robert Sawyer were submitting their clemency petition.

In August of that year, a troop of soldiers from the all-Black 25th U.S. Infantry Regiment were stationed at Fort Brown, near the border town of Brownsville, Texas. Many of the soldiers, coming as they did from outside the South, were unaccustomed to Texas segregation laws, and tensions between the soldiers and local police were high. On one hot sultry night, a fight broke out and shots were fired, wounding a police lieutenant and killing a local bartender. The exact circumstances were unclear, but the white commanders at Fort Brown vouched for their men. They swore that all the Black soldiers were accounted for in their barracks when the shooting occurred.

Local officials, assisted by the Texas Rangers, tried to pressure some of the soldiers to inform on each other, but none would do so. The state courts could find no evidence on which to charge any of the soldiers, but the local white population was demanding justice. In frustration, they appealed to the president.

Despite the lack of evidence against them, Roosevelt ordered that 167 Black soldiers be dishonorably discharged from the service, asserting they had created a "conspiracy of silence" contrary to good military order. The vast majority had honorable records, and some were nearing retirement with pension rights, which now were lost. For most, they would never be able to serve in the military or civil service again.

Booker T. Washington was appalled and said so publicly. He was especially offended by Roosevelt's partisan opportunism, which added insult to injury. The president announced his decision just days after the November 1906 midterm elections, so that Black Republican voters would not be discouraged from turning out for his party.[5]

Without question, any presidential decision on clemency would be influenced by political calculations. Therefore, how could George Rountree and George Peschau possibly hope to persuade Roosevelt to show mercy in a case like that of Adams and Sawyer, in which four white men had been shot down in cold blood by Black hands? As they had before the Supreme Court, it was by keeping their plea as simple as possible, focusing on the basic issue of guilt or innocence, not on race.

The attorneys had their clemency petition typed and ready to go on July 7, 1906, the day after Henry Scott was hanged. From the first page, they described Scott's gallows statement as an "exoneration" of Adams and Sawyer. Since Scott's testimony was the only evidence against the two men, and he had now retracted it, the convictions must not stand. Even though Scott's final account of the murders was questionable at best, at least he was emphatic in the end that Adams and Sawyer were fully innocent. In fact, the petition alleged, Scott now "gave as his reason for not having told the truth [earlier] on the trial of [Sawyer and Adams] and in his own trial that he feared lynching should the true state of affairs be known."

Further, Rountree and Peschau pointed out, "The statements of Sawyer and Adams have not varied from the beginning. . . . Whereas Scott never told the same story twice! . . . All the natural evidence—the facts certainly known—points to the innocence of Adams and Sawyer. They overcame and bound Scott, Scott certainly killed Coakley, one of those who helped overpower him; they signaled for help and delivered the vessel, Scott, and themselves to another vessel. If they were guilty, why did they do these things? We submit they are irreconcilable with guilt."

Finally, the defense attorneys noted, "It is suggested that one man could not have killed all those white men," and yet "according to the evidence, the men were killed at different times, in different parts of the ship. It is [not] often that one or two men hold up a train and rob it and its passengers, and the acts of Scott are no more improbable."[6]

The petition was accompanied by four pages of signatures from prominent Wilmington citizens, both white and Black, who urged the president to spare the men's lives. As one might imagine, the whites and Blacks signed on separate sheets of paper.

Most of the African-American signatories, although not all, were clergymen. Reverend Bennett of St. Mark's Episcopal was one. He was joined by sixteen other ministers from the various local churches, including Episcopal, Baptist, Presbyterian, and A.M.E. congregations. The petition also was signed by several men who listed their occupations as druggist, postal clerk, and insurance agent. Then there was J. Luther Telfair, LLB, thirty-five years old, and the son of a prominent minister and Masonic leader in town. The younger Telfair was a practicing attorney, the first African American to be admitted to the North Carolina Bar in the years following the insurrection.[7]

And on the white signature pages, one finds a remarkable Who's Who of Wilmington leadership, including attorneys, bankers, and other assorted businessmen. Among the highlights:

- William J. Bellamy, who in addition to signing his name, identified himself for President Roosevelt as the "Attorney appointed by United States Circuit Court to defend Henry Scott, (Mutineer)." Now that his client was confessed and hanged, Bellamy had no problem with freely acknowledging his guilt in writing.

- Benjamin F. Keith, the former Populist who recalled white men being shamed and coerced into joining the White Government Union prior to the insurrection and had briefly fled from Wilmington after the violence.[8] Now he was the appointed collector of customs for the port.

- The Reverend Robert Strange, formerly the rector at St. James Episcopal, and who is believed to have assisted Alex Manly in fleeing the city. He also was the grandson and namesake of one of North Carolina's pre-Civil War United States senators, and in 1906 he was the presiding bishop of the Diocese of East Carolina.

- James Iredell Meares, an attorney who, as everyone knew, was one of the leading lights of the White Government Union. He also wrote an article with the grand title, *The Wilmington Revolution*. The revolution, he claimed, was a necessary corrective to return the city's government to "law-abiding" citizens, and "make the great mass of ignorant negro voters realize the deep-seated purpose of the white man to control in the future."[9]

- Frank Stedman, the Democratic sheriff of New Hanover County. Stedman had been in the streets during the insurrection and was a well-known cohort of Alfred Waddell. But he had personally intervened when the mob was on the verge of lynching George French, a white Republican deputy sheriff. A group of Red Shirts were in the process of hanging French from a telephone pole on Front Street

when Stedman spoke up, threatening them with prosecution. He and some friends were able to hustle French
away, and Stedman told him, "I will protect your life with
my life, if necessary, but only on condition that you leave
town and agree to remain away from Wilmington for the
rest of your life." That very evening, French was on a
train leaving town.[10]

- J. Allan Taylor, now president of Wilmington's Chamber
of Commerce. Six years earlier, he was a member of
the Secret Nine and, along with Hugh MacRae, led the
white shock troops sweeping through the Black neighborhoods. He was on the scene when Daniel Wright fell
dead with thirteen bullets in his body. Days later, Taylor
was installed as one of the new drumhead aldermen, and
was instrumental in rounding up the Black and white Fusionist leaders who had been marked for banishment and
escorted to the train station.[11]

And then there was the most surprising signatory of all. It
takes a bit of rudimentary handwriting comparison to confirm it,
because it seems so unbelievable. But fortunately, "Colonel" Alfred
Moore Waddell was a prolific letter-writer, and many of his documents are preserved in the Southern Historical Collection in the Wilson Library at UNC Chapel Hill. The coup-installed mayor of Wilmington, who once spoke of filling the Cape Fear with Black corpses,
who once publicly urged his supporters to shoot down Black voters
in the streets, did in fact sign the clemency petition for Adams and
Sawyer.

Why? Perhaps Waddell did it as a favor to his younger law
partner, George Peschau. Or maybe for the same reason that George
Rountree felt comfortable taking their case. Men who feel secure in
their positions of power may, under the right conditions, be willing to distribute some measure of Christian charity to those they
deem inferior, weak, and helpless. In the case of the *Berwind* murders, Scott had already confessed and paid the price of the crime in
due course. If Adams and Sawyer really were less culpable, as now
seemed apparent, then it would do no harm to extend them a little
mercy.

Recall the Wilmington Declaration of Independence, which Waddell had circulated in the days after the insurrection, setting forth rules by which he and the other coup leaders would govern the city. Blacks would absolutely have to remain in their place, and never utter another word about anything like social equality or voting rights. But if they did so, they would be treated "with justice and consideration." Perhaps this was Waddell's idea of justice: If the one guilty mutineer had been hanged, then one hanging was enough.

Apart from that, Waddell might have suspected that his surname on the petition might strike a chord with President Roosevelt, the scholar of seafaring history. His first cousin, James Iredell Waddell, had been a Confederate Navy man. He was the commanding officer of the *Shenandoah* during its global commerce-raiding voyage that one of Roosevelt's uncles had commissioned, and on which another of his uncles had served

When Roosevelt first put his eyes on the petition, he issued a brief stay of execution, postponing the hangings from August 17 to November 1, 1906. It was to allow time for him to consider its merits, and toward that end, he instructed Peyton Gordon, a pardon attorney working for the Justice Department, to interview Sawyer and Adams.

Gordon was a thirty-six-year-old attorney beginning a long public service career; from 1928 to 1946, he would be a judge on the U.S. District Court for the District of Columbia. He travelled to Wilmington, staying at the Orton Hotel uptown, and met with Harry Skinner as well as the two defendants, whom the press was now describing as "model prisoners."[12]

Gordon met with both Sawyer and Adams at the jail, and took a new deposition from Adams, witnessed by both himself and Skinner. It did not break any new ground and was notable only for its consistency with what he and Sawyer had claimed all along. Coakley had awoken them at around 5:00 a.m., with the alarming word that Scott was shooting. Apparently, he had just killed the captain. Then Scott appeared at the forecastle door, saying, "I will shoot every son of a bitch on board." The wording was slightly different from what Adams had testified to earlier, but not significantly so.

Over the next five hours, Gordon was told, Scott had methodically killed the engineer, then the first mate, and then went in search of the cook. He shot them all and threw them over the ship's rail. Adams mentioned another detail that would cause trouble for him. During one of the intervals, between the killings of the first mate and cook, Adams went to the galley and made a pot of coffee, which he and Sawyer shared. Where was the cook at that point? Had Adams and Sawyer made no attempt to locate or warn him?

When asked what he thought of Scott's final statement from the gallows, Adams said he was not entirely clear about how Scott claimed the killings had taken place, but "From what I know of it, it is true." Apparently, Adams was not aware of the details of Scott's final story. Scott had claimed he shot all four officers within minutes, not hours, and there was no way to square that account with the one Adams and Sawyer had told all along. But at least they agreed on the relevant point: Scott did it all alone.[13]

It came as a devastating blow to both defendants on October 15, when the president issued his decision. He would not grant clemency, and the executions would proceed on November 1.

Public reaction in Wilmington was mixed. The *Morning Star* thought it came as a "distinct surprise" to many, who "generally believed that if the prisoners were not pardoned outright their sentence would be commuted at least to life imprisonment." The less sympathetic *Messenger* concluded that after a full Justice Department inquiry, there were "no extenuating circumstances," and no reason to think Adams and Sawyer were not "equally guilty" with Scott. There was "nothing now for them but to prepare for death."[14]

Perhaps Roosevelt was dissuaded by the thought of the murders taking place over so many hours, and especially the image of Sawyer and Adams drinking coffee in the midst of it all.[15] If they felt so at ease amidst the bloodshed, then they likely had some culpability in it. Also, at that very time in October, the press was focusing on the more publicized Brownsville affair, and Roosevelt did not want to hand them additional fodder.

All seemed lost for the two forlorn sailors, but on October 22, the president received a visit on their behalf from two Episcopal priests, James Carmichael of Wilmington and Hubert H. Barber of Fredericksburg, Virginia. It is not known what the two ministers said to Roosevelt, nor is it clear what motivated them to make the trip to Washington to plead for Adams' and Sawyer's lives.[16] It remains one of the most persistent puzzles in the entire case. Reverend Carmichael, in particular, was an unlikely advocate. At age 72, he was Virginia-born and a Confederate veteran. He had served as chaplain to the Virginia 30th Infantry Regiment during the war and remained a loyal adherent to the Lost Cause afterward. His obituary, six years later, noted his allegiance to the Cape Fear Camp of the United Confederate Veterans.[17]

Although he served white congregations throughout his career, Reverend Carmichael seems to have had good rapport with African Americans as well. When he died, the parishioners at St. Mark's, the Black Episcopal church led by Reverend Bennett, met and decided to place a memorial window in their sanctuary in Carmichael's honor. "For over twenty-five years, he was a devoted friend to the best interests of that parish."[18]

Perhaps the Black churches in Wilmington, remembering so well the fiasco after Booker T. Washington visited the White House in 1901, thought it safer for two white emissaries to go there on their behalf.

Somehow, those two seemingly disinterested priests prevailed upon Roosevelt to grant Adams and Sawyer another reprieve, this time until December 15, 1906. That additional time allowed an opportunity for Judge Purnell and Harry Skinner to confer with the president, as well as Attorney General Moody. Both men were now openly advocating for Roosevelt to commute the sentences, and Skinner made a special trip himself to Washington to plead the case.[19]

When the presiding judge and the prosecutor both stated they were willing to have the death sentences set aside, that was the clincher. On December 5, Roosevelt formally commuted the sentences of Adams and Sawyer from death to lifetime imprisonment at hard labor. In the declaration, the president did not elaborate on

THEY WILL NOT HANG

Death Sentence of Adams and Sawyer Commuted to Life Imprisonment.

PRESIDENT INTERFERRED

Announcement Made From Washington Yesterday Afternoon—Prisoners Strongly Relied Upon Appeals In Their Behalf

(Special Sta

ROOSEVELT GRANTS RESPITE TO SLAYERS

Stays Execution of Negroes Convicted of Mutiny and Murder on High Seas.

STORY OF CRIME LIKE NOVEL

Captain and Other White Men on Schooner Murdered.

IN PRISON FOR LIFE

Sentence of Adams and Sawyer Commuted.

BY PRESIDENT OF THE U. S.

Decision Gives Almost Universal Satisfaction Here.

Action of the President was Announced Yesterday—Prisoners Had Almost Given up Hope of any Further Action Being Taken—Short History of the Notable Case and the Earnest Efforts to Save the Lives of the two Men.

"Almost Universal Satisfaction."
Clockwise from top: The Wilmington *Morning Star*, the *Semi Weekly Messenger*, the *Indianapolis Star*

154

his reasons; he likely did not want to draw too much attention to the case. But the Wilmington press speculated that Roosevelt had personal doubts about the *degree* of their guilt and was impressed by the wide diversity of people advocating on their behalf. The *Morning Star* reported, "It has been a long time since as many petitions have been received at the Department of Justice asking for clemency. They came from all over the country, but the majority from Wilmington."[20]

Naturally Adams and Sawyer were relieved for their lives to be spared, but a life in prison was nothing to look forward to. They both were still determined to establish their full innocence. The case was not over.

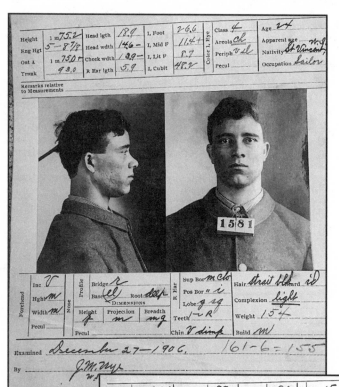

Arthur Adams (above) and Robert Sawyer in the federal penitentiary in Atlanta.

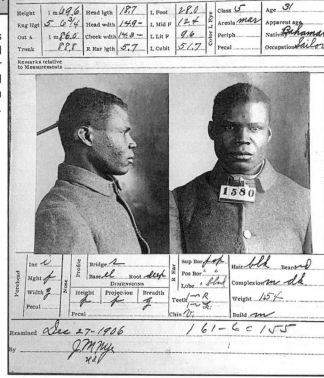

CHAPTER FIFTEEN

THE GATES
OF HELL

hrough the latter part of 1906, as public sympathy for them grew, Arthur Adams and Robert Sawyer may have believed they had a realistic chance of not only winning presidential clemency, but of being fully exonerated. In December, now that the president had spared their lives, they dared to hope that the Supreme Court would follow his lead by granting them a new trial.

Within days of Roosevelt's decision to commute their sentences, the unthinkable actually happened. The high court, which in April rejected their first appeal without much discussion and with little controversy, now issued a new order permitting the two defendants to file a motion for a new trial in the Wilmington circuit court. In light of Scott's confession, it may have seemed the only proper course. But given the judicial tenor of the times, it was unusual. Even the Washington D.C., press, to say nothing of the Wilmington papers, seemed astounded by the "unprecedented action" by the Supreme Court.[1]

Adams and Sawyer may have felt optimistic they could win a

not-guilty verdict with another jury. Virtually all the evidence against them had come from the lips of Henry Scott, and Scott had retracted his claims in his written dying declaration. With Scott now dead and dissected, there was no chance he could retract his retraction.

George Rountree spoke with the reporters and sounded eager for the chance to get his clients acquitted. He said he could not imagine what new evidence the government might try to bring, unless it came from the *Berwind*'s logbook. But Rountree scoffed at the prospect that such evidence would do his clients any harm. Most of the logbook's contents, after all, had been ruled inadmissible in the first trial.[2]

The court file reflects that Rountree and Peschau had prepared a motion for a new trial back in October, should the Supreme Court eventually allow them to present it. The motion asked the Circuit Court to vacate its previous guilty verdict on the grounds that the jury's decision was "predicated upon perjury." Scott had lied, plain and simple, as revealed later by his new statements, which could not have been obtained any earlier by "due diligence" on the part of the defendants. Their motion also was accompanied by affidavits from the notary public and others who heard Scott give his confession, who stated that he seemed to be of sound mind. Scott had told them he was afraid to confess prior to the trials, for fear that a mob would storm the jail and drag him out, far more afraid of a lynching that might involve burning or mutilation than of the relatively humane hanging that he eventually received.[3]

Even today, it is hard to imagine how any defendant could have more ideal grounds upon which to seek a new trial. But if Adams and Sawyer thought they were going to sail into court and win a resounding acquittal, they were mistaken.

It appears that while the Supreme Court's order did permit the defendants leave to seek a new trial, it did not allow them to proceed *in forma pauperis*, as Adams and Sawyer had done until this point. If they wanted a new trial, they would have to pay their attorneys on their own.

Adams and Sawyer had no money, and apparently none of their families back in the islands—nor extended family in the United States—had any resources to contribute. Rountree and Peschau, having expended so much time and effort for minimal if any pay, were not willing to continue their representation without being paid. They had pulled off a minor miracle by saving the lives of their clients, and that surely was enough.

Consequently, there would be no retrial for Adams and Sawyer at the Wilmington Post Office. By the end of December, they were on their way by train to the Federal Penitentiary in Atlanta to serve their life sentences. If the two men had heard even vague rumors about their destination, it must have seemed like the gates of hell were opening up before them.

The penitentiary was new, only having opened in 1902. But already it had acquired the ominous nickname of "The Big A." It was needed because the entire country, and the federal system especially, was facing a major increase in crime. The 1890s and 1900s were the heyday for European immigration to the United States, and cities in particular were bursting at the seams. Urbanization brought a new host of law enforcement headaches, such as gangsterism and racketeering, which the federal government took an increasingly aggressive role in combatting. As a result, the federal prison population was a tempestuous mix of everything from white-collar fraudsters to smugglers to violent extortionists from gangs such as the Black Hand, a forerunner of the modern Mafia. It also included those who committed murders and robberies in the federal territories such as Oklahoma, New Mexico, and Arizona, which had not yet been admitted as states, as well as crimes on the high seas.

The prison cell house was designed to be both majestic and intimidating. Built from granite quarried at Georgia's nearby Stone Mountain, it had a sixty-foot-high façade decorated with Corinthian columns and topped by a Roman dome. Naturally it was built with the labor of convicts, who lived in temporary housing until its completion in 1902. Once that was finished, they set about constructing the outer stone wall that encircled the twenty-seven acres of prison grounds. Four feet thick and thirty-nine feet high, it took seven years to complete.

Labor was an integral part of the inmates' existence, as was harsh discipline. The first warden, William Moyer, instituted a program of strict isolation known as the Auburn System, named after one of the first modern penitentiaries established in upstate New York in the 1820s. The inmates wore the stereotypical black-and-white "prison stripes" and usually had their heads shaved upon entry. No outside visitation was allowed, and inmate mail was strictly censored. At least as onerous was the rule of silence. Inmates were not allowed to speak to each other, not even when working or eating together. In the mess hall, they were instructed to communicate only with hand gestures; for example, raising a right hand if they needed a fork, or a left hand for a spoon.

Cells were spare and cramped. There was no running water; buckets were used for toilets. There was no heating in winter, and air conditioning had not yet been invented to relieve the hot Georgia summers.[4]

In an interesting sidenote, Warden Moyer would serve at Atlanta until 1915, when he was commanded to resign by the attorney general in the wake of allegations made by an eccentric celebrity inmate, Julian Hawthorne. The son of author Nathaniel Hawthorne, of *The Scarlet Letter* and *The House of Seven Gables* fame, Julian was able to parlay his family name into some success as an author himself, although his works were mostly dime store detective novels and newspaper pieces. In 1908, an old friend persuaded him to use his family name to assist in promoting a western silver-mining venture to investors. The mine apparently did not exist, and in 1913 Hawthorne ended up with a short prison sentence for mail fraud.

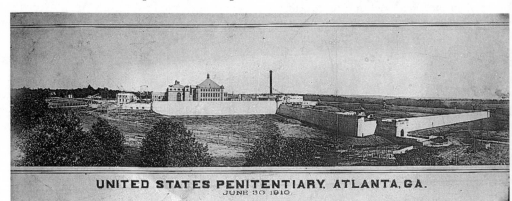

UNITED STATES PENITENTIARY, ATLANTA, GA.
JUNE 30 1910.

The federal penitentiary in Atlanta, photographed not long after Adams and Sawyer arrrived. The prison, though new, was notorious enough to be dubbed "The Big A."

Hawthorne served his time in Atlanta, and within a day of his release in October 1913, he gave an interview to reporter Sidney Ormund of the *Atlanta Constitution*. Calling Moyer an "oily, comfortable rogue," he alleged that the warden was running the penitentiary to profit off of inmate labor, "starving men in the name of economy," attempting to "feed strong men on nine cents a day." For even slight infractions, Hawthorne claimed, prisoners might be sent to solitary confinement in "The Hole," where they were "chained by their wrists and held with arms outstretched for hours," closely surrounded by "walls slimy and covered with crawling things."[5] His resulted in both an investigation and the warden's replacement.

Unfortunately, that was the nature of the penal system at the time, federal as well as state. Prisons were expected to be self-sustaining, to maintain their own facilities with convict labor. Prisoners had to work, under the supervision of officers who did not hesitate to enforce the rules with whips and billy clubs. There is no way to sugarcoat the environment into which Adams and Sawyer found themselves cast.

The only thing that Adams and Sawyer had going for them was that they were in the federal system, rather than the state one. If the *Berwind* murders had occurred while the ship was docked at Southport or Wilmington, rather than on the High Seas, they likely would have been hanged with due dispatch. Had they been sentenced to prison in a North Carolina state court, they would have ended up as the vast majority of African-American convicts did at the time: working on a prison farm or a chain gang.

In Atlanta, Sawyer and Adams had beds on which to sleep, and they had medical care, as surviving records show. When an inmate had a health complaint, it was logged. The federal prison system maintained such records because it was subject to oversight from Washington. Adams and Sawyer each had numerous medical issues noted, such as migraines, constipation, and influenza. For each instance, the record also notes the treatment provided. For "chapped hands," it was "Vaseline," and for "grippe" (i.e., cold or flu), the medical staff provided "tablets." It was not sophisticated, but at least it was consistent with the medical knowledge at the time. On November 30, 1909, Adams noted that he was suffering from swelling in his face, due to a faulty tooth filling he had received from the prison dentist some months before. Prison dental care was not perfect, but it was a cut above what any chain gang prisoner would have received.[6]

During and after their trial, Adams and Sawyer had their lives spared because their case was a federal one. Now that they were in prison, the layers of federal bureaucracy—plus an unexpected hand from international power brokers—would provide them with a second salvation. But it would take time for it all to come together.

At first, they tried with little success to keep interest in their case alive from behind prison walls. They maintained correspondence with some supporters, such as Warren Spaulding, president of the Massachusetts Prison Association and a major voice for prison reform, and Thomas H. Knight, an officer with the Atlantic Seaboard Railroad in Wilmington, one of the city's most influential companies. At the sailors' request, both men exchanged letters with Warden Moyer, asking if there was any way to arrange a new pardon or parole hearing for Adams and Sawyer.[7]

Knight, in particular, would prove an important ally. He was one of the most highly positioned African Americans in Wilmington's business community, operating his own tour company. An active member at St. Mark's Episcopal, he very likely had been involved in gathering signatures for the sailors' first clemency petition. Moreover, Knight and his wife Mary—an arts and music teacher—had Northern connections. Both were New York natives, and Mary conducted musical programs in New York City as well as Wilmington.[8] It is not clear from existing records, but it is possible that she had show-business connections that would soon—and very unexpectedly—enter into the case.

Still, the warden could offer no encouragement to Adams or Sawyer. Parole officials were in no hurry to offer a hearing to two men serving life sentences for murder. The two sailors' lives had been spared, and even if Scott had done the actual killing himself, they might not have been entirely uninvolved in planning the murders. They should not have been dissatisfied to be serving life.

In June 1908, a desperate Sawyer put together a handwritten letter addressed to a much higher authority. A duplicate remains in the prison file today, neatly preserved, with elegant, almost calligraphic handwriting. Presumably Sawyer made a special effort for his appeal to look as neat as possible, properly befitting its recipient.

"To His Majesty My Lord the King," Sawyer began his letter to King Edward VII of Great Britain and Ireland, Emperor of India, amid many other titles. Sawyer introduced himself and Adams as loyal British subjects who had been ensnared into the murderous designs of Henry Scott and were now languishing in an American prison hellhole.

Sawyer gave his exalted reader a brief rundown of events, which once again was entirely consistent with every account he had given thus far. He described how he and Adams had been surprised in the forecastle by the gunshots fired by Scott, how Scott had threatened them and killed off the officers one by one, all the time holding Adams and Sawyer under the gun. Not until much later, when they were attempting to lower the "big boat," could they seize the opportunity to subdue Scott and signal the passing ship.

Although the "Supreme Court granted us privilege to motion for new trial, we was not able to raise fund." Despite the commutation of their sentences, Sawyer described how he and Adams were kept "shackled and chained in cell from October 17 1905 to

Part of Robert Sawyer's letter to King Edward VII of Great Britain.

December 21 1906. Some months of that time we both been very sick," and "only the mercy of God kept us alive."

"Therefore," Sawyer concluded, "I humbly beseech My Lord the King, in the name of God, to have pity and compassion on us. . . . And intercede on our behalf with His Excellency the President of the United States . . . and for the sake of my dear old widowed mother," who was dependent on him.[9]

There was no official reply from the king or from his government. That would come later, and only through the intercession of another, very different British public figure.

It happened in April 1910, after nearly two more long years in which Adams and Sawyer must have nearly abandoned all hope.

Somehow, the imprisoned sailors must have seen—or been told of by some sympathetic friend—an article in the *New York Times* that could be of help, even if it was a long shot. A popular stage actor of the day, Henry Byron Warner, had announced that he would contribute the proceeds from one of his performances to a social cause that he held dear. He would use the money, in whatever way possible, to aid the conditions of men who were serving life prison terms.

Prison charity, at first glance, would not seem a likely mission for Warner to take on. He was upper-crust British all the way. At age thirty-four, he had grown up in London, immersed in the theater circles in which his father, Charles Warner, also excelled as an actor. The son attended Bedford Grammar School and was a rugby standout at Oxford. His father would have preferred that he become a barrister or a financier, but the allure of the stage apparently was too strong. In his youth, Henry understudied for his father in stage roles like d'Artagnan in *The Three Musketeers*. He first ventured to the United States for the 1905-06 theater season, where he took on increasingly important roles, gaining fans as he went. But he suffered a personal tragedy in April 1909, when his father took his own life by hanging in a fit of "insanity," as it was called in the jargon of the day.[10]

Warner's interest in prison conditions likely came from the very role he was performing in 1910, and his preparation for it. Part of it was set in prison, and it dealt with themes of punishment and redemption, and how men try to rebuild their lives in society after time behind bars. As Warner told it, he studied for the role by "acquaint[ing] himself at firsthand with the life and conditions he expected to portray on stage. He read prison reports from all parts of the world, met wardens and prison officials both in America and in England, as well as convicts and ex-convicts."[11]

The source material for the popular play was written by an ex-con. "Alias Jimmy Valentine" was based on *A Retrieved Reformation*, one of the short stories of William Sydney Porter, better known by his *nom-de-plume* O. Henry and published in 1903. Porter, a Greensboro, North Carolina, native, served three years in prison in the 1890s for embezzlement while working as a bookkeeper in an Austin, Texas, bank. There is still some question about whether the theft was intentional, or just careless record-keeping, or possibly both. But Porter served his time and seemed to maintain his creativity and good humor in spite of it.

Jimmy Valentine, the title character played by Henry Warner, is an experienced safecracker who is released from prison. He intends to stay clean, but temptation leads him back into the trade. But when two young girls accidentally become trapped in a bank vault with the air supply running out, Jimmy, though knowing that it will incriminate him, takes out his safecracking tools and opens the vault to save their lives. Afterward, he walks up to a bank detective, intending to turn himself in, but the detective recognizes the "retrieved reformation" and says nothing, letting Jimmy walk on by.

Henry Warner

Warner's offer to assist men serving life prison terms was genuine. In 1910, and over the next several years, he spoke about it publicly and often. He urged prison officials to do away with the harsher sides of prison life, such as corporal punishment and solitary confinement, which were in abundance in Atlanta. He also said,

Governors and other executives would do well to exercise
the pardoning power wherever by doing so a moral life
can be saved. The majority of those who go to jail are not
necessarily criminals in the true sense. They are the unfortunates of the world. Show them the error of their ways,
correct them, help them to help themselves.[12]

Arthur Adams, not knowing whether it would do any good,
but desperate to try anything, wrote to Warner in follow-up to the
Times article in April 1910. Interestingly the letter is typewritten, suggesting some sympathetic party in the prison administration assisted
him.

Much as in Sawyer's letter to the king, Adams summarized
the plight of them both. They were serving aboard ship with Scott
when he "ran amuck" and killed all the officers and would have killed
them as well if he had not needed them to help man the vessel. Scott
lied in court to convict them, but later "confessed all" on the gallows.
He was not sure how much money Warner had available, but since
he and Sawyer had "no funds whatever," Adams pleaded with him
to use some of the proceeds from the benefit play for their cause,
predicting that "if we can get someone to help us get this matter of
his confession properly before the president we will no doubt be set
free.

"The disposition upon the part of a public man to be friendly and generous to we poor devils, is so unusual and delightful to
our minds that I cannot refrain from imposing myself upon you,"
Adams wrote. If it was possible for Warner to help, Adams asked
him to please contact Thomas Knight in Wilmington, their friend
and contact person throughout their ordeal.[13]

Within days, Adams and Sawyer had their reply.

Warner was going to put his personal attorney on the
case.

CHAPTER SIXTEEN

FREEDOM
BECKONS

A s soon as he received the letter from Adams and Sawyer, Henry B. Warner had become captivated by their case, and thought it was well worth some of his resources. An attorney in New York, Joseph S. Buhler, apparently had worked for him on show-business related issues. Warner now enlisted him in what would turn into a full-court press to obtain a second presidential clemency for the two imprisoned sailors.

At twenty-nine, Buhler was a promising young talent in entertainment law, a field that grew increasingly important as more and more theaters were built in the big cities, and would continue to grow as the new motion picture industry got off the ground in the 1910s. He was a partner in the firm of Dennis & Buhler, located on Nassau Street at the foot of Manhattan, a stone's throw from the Stock Exchange and New York's City Hall. He was an officer in The Lambs club, the country's oldest theatrical organization, which was founded in the 1860s and reflected the growing professionalization of the acting community.

Among Buhler's clients was Greta Garbo, the sultry Swedish

actress who rose to fame with her melancholy romantic roles in the 1920s. He also represented Irvin S. Cobb, a Kentucky-born journalist who found success in Hollywood as his books and magazine stories were made into films in the 1930s.

Yet Buhler did not have any particular background in criminal law, and for his work on the Adams and Sawyer case, he was going to have to familiarize himself with the nuts and bolts of crime investigation. Essentially, he would become a bit of a detective, something like the characters whom his clients wrote about and portrayed on stage. Later, Buhler would serve as a U.S. Army Captain in military intelligence during World War I.[1]

In fact, considering the amount of time and expense that Warner and Buhler put into advocating Adams's and Sawyer's case, one might speculate that they considered turning it into a media production of their own. A story of multiple murder at sea, with two men wrongly accused and then saved in the end with a surprise confession, would have made a compelling storyline for a stage play, based upon an entirely true story.

The story eventually would be dramatized for film, but it was not until decades later, and the film took such drastic liberties with the facts that it was hard to claim it was even "based" on the true story. Neither Warner nor Buhler was involved with the production. So if Warner did not use the shipboard murder case as a theatrical

opportunity for himself, it may be that he was sincerely moved by the plight of Adams and Sawyer, and wanted to help them right the wrong done to them.

First, attorney Buhler had to determine that Warner, as his client, was not being exploited by two guilty men trying to con their way into a pardon. He contacted Warden Moyer in Atlanta, to make sure that the facts of the case were as Adams and Sawyer described them: that they had been found guilty but later exonerated by the confession of the true murderer. Moyer wrote back that he was

Joseph Buhler

not familiar with the procedural history of their case and was not certain why President Roosevelt decided to commute their sentences, but he imagined that the reasons must have been "ample" in the president's mind. Further, he could attest that Adams and Sawyer were model prisoners; their conduct at the Atlanta Pen was "absolutely free from criticism."[2]

With those encouraging words, Buhler hit the road. His travels would take him to Wilmington, where he would meet with various people who were involved in the case, as well as to Atlanta to meet in person with his new clients. Through the latter part of 1910, Buhler's activities were well-documented in the North Carolina press, and it is notable to see how candid Buhler was in describing them. He had little fear that his presence in the case, as a well-to-do New York litigator, would arouse any new prejudice against Adams and Sawyer, not even when the papers revealed that he was working with Thomas Knight, the Black railroad official, to prepare the case,[3] nor even when they carried headlines such as "Strange Story of How a Noted Actor Is Working For Freedom of Two Men."[4]

In Wilmington, Buhler stayed at the Orton Hotel uptown, and quickly found many who were willing not only to talk with him, but to sign affidavits in support of a pardon. Not only George Peschau but also Iredell Meares, the attorney who had praised the insurrection in his writings, were involved. They gathered signatures from G.W. Bornemann, the notary who had witnessed Scott's confession, as well as the jailer, and from eight of the twelve trial jurors who had convicted and condemned Adams and Sawyer four years earlier.

For the jurors, especially, it was a potentially powerful statement to let it be known publicly that they supported clemency. Although jury service is *supposed* to remain confidential, and the papers had made it a point not to reveal the jurors' identities during the trial, word surely would have gotten around. These people easily could have suffered social ostracism, if not violence, if the public in Wilmington were still insistent that Adams and Sawyer be hanged. But by 1910, those eight jurors were among the "many people in Wilmington who believe the negroes are innocent and will gladly aid any effort to secure their freedom."[5]

One newspaper reported that when Buhler contacted William Bellamy, Henry Scott's attorney, and asked him to provide Scott's original confession to include with their new pardon petition, Bellamy asked for five hundred dollars in exchange for the document, since he had spent so much time defending Scott for "gratis," and now thought "he should have something out of the case."[6] It makes for interesting gossip, although it may not have been true. By 1910, the contents of Scott's confession were well known, and Bellamy had provided the document to Reverend Bennett—and maybe others—back in 1906, apparently with no expectation of pay.

In Washington, meanwhile, the case was now in the hands of James Finch, the new pardon attorney working in the Justice Department of President William Howard Taft, who had succeeded Roosevelt after the 1908 election. He was aware of Buhler's activities, and knew the clemency petition would first be submitted to him after it was completed. With that in mind, Finch undertook some inquiry of his own.

In June 1911, Finch wrote to Warden Moyer, asking that he allow Adams and Sawyer to correspond with him, and answer a particular question that had vexed him in his review of the case. Obviously, Adams and Sawyer's account of the murders differed from *all* the various stories told by Scott, even the final one that Scott had read from the gallows. Adams and Sawyer claimed Scott had killed the four officers at intervals, hours apart, and in different areas of the ship. But Scott, in his dying declaration, said that he shot all four men within a matter of minutes, in or near the galley, and only after they attacked him with pistols of their own.

If the officers were carrying guns, as Scott claimed, then what was done with them after the killings were over? In the end, only two guns had been recovered, one black-handled and one ivory-handled, which Adams and Sawyer claimed both belonged to Scott. Further, if Adams and Sawyer's story was true, and the officers had each been carrying pistols, how had none of them been able to defend himself as Scott stalked and killed them individually?[7]

Within days, Adams and Sawyer wrote back to Attorney Finch with a simple reply. To their knowledge, none of the officers had been armed. In fact, it would have been very unusual—and contrary to maritime convention—for the officers to carry guns. The *Berwind* was a commercial vessel, not a military one. While there were sure to be disagreements and bad feeling among the crew on occasion—which might well turn into cursing or fisticuffs—such things didn't require deadly force to resolve.

If one of the officers had been armed and had fired the first shot—and it would be a stretch to assume so—Adams and Sawyer thought perhaps Scott had killed him, taken his gun and then used it himself, or thrown it overboard along with the bodies.[8]

That explanation may have been satisfactory enough for Finch, at least on the issue of pistols. But at about the time as that correspondence took place, a new problem arose. And like several instances before, it would threaten to derail Adams and Sawyer's bid for freedom. These two men had to brace for yet another dip on their six-year roller coaster ride.

It appears that the company that owned the *Berwind*, D.S. Stetson and Company of Philadelphia, had been monitoring the pardon proceedings. Now in July 1911, Mr. Stetson took it upon himself to write to James Finch and express his grave concerns about the two sailors possibly being exonerated. He told a detailed—and disturbing—story about Adams and Sawyer. It also was corroborated by Captain John Taylor of the *Blanche H. King*, who scrawled across the bottom margin of the letter, "I hereby agree to the correctness of the above and I concur in Mr. Stetson's opinion."

Some must have been struck by the fact that Stetson and Taylor had waited nearly six years to voice the accusations that they now hurled at Adams and Sawyer. Neither of them had mentioned them when they testified either at Southport or Wilmington.

Stetson now claimed there was "not the slightest doubt in my mind" that Scott, Sawyer, Adams, and Coakley each had shot one of the white officers, and they did so in collusion and almost simultaneously. Stetson claimed he had seen blood in too many places on board the ship—in the galley, just forward of the cabin, on the lumber pile, on the starboard rail, and on the engine room door—for Scott to have done the shootings alone. He also claimed some insight into the pistols. According to Stetson, Captain Rumill had owned two pistols: he carried one at the time of the shootings but had hidden the other behind a sofa in the cabin, where Stetson now claimed to have found it, fully loaded. Apparently, Stetson thought, Rumill had been anticipating a confrontation.

Further, Stetson said in his letter that when he met with the three surviving sailors in the Southport jail, he was struck by the deviousness of them all. This was the meeting in which Scott supposedly confessed that all three participated in the killings, and said he knew he would be hanged and did not care, since he did not believe in God anyway. That much, at least, Stetson *did* mention when he testified at Scott's trial.

But now, he added a surprising new detail. Stetson claimed Adams and Sawyer had threatened the lives of both himself and Taylor, promising to kill them if they ever were set free.

That left Stetson certain that Adams and Sawyer were full participants in the murders. He was sure that Scott's claim on the gallows to have done all the killing was a lie, only a ploy to help Adams and Sawyer defeat justice. It was "just deviltry prompted him to make the confession."[9]

The problems with Stetson's new claims were multiple. At no time previously had he mentioned finding a gun in the cabin. When he testified at Scott's trial, he said he found blood only on the starboard and port rails, not near the galley or engine room. And Stetson did not testify at all in the trial of Adams and Sawyer, though he was there in Wilmington and easily could have done so. If the two West Indians really had threatened him, it seems he would have insisted on testifying to that point. But he did not, nor did Taylor mention any such threat when he did testify in the trial of Adams and Sawyer.

If Stetson and Taylor were fabricating new dirt to cast upon Adams and Sawyer, why do so at this late date, when they may have been on the verge of gaining their freedom?

The answer may lie in a remark that Stetson made in closing his letter. He recalled how the damage and seizure of the *Berwind* "cost me largely in salvage, I cannot afford to spend more on the case." If Adams and Sawyer were to receive a presidential pardon— as opposed to merely having their sentences commuted, as Roosevelt had already done—it could have meant a financial loss for Stetson's company. A pardon would have established that the two sailors were legally innocent of murder and mutiny, and therefore would have been owed back wages for their service on the ship. In fact, in late

October 1905, just as the trial for their lives was about to begin in federal criminal court, George Peschau made a point to file a lien in civil court for $188. The idea was for the men to be able to collect their wages if they were to be found not guilty.

Peschau served the lien on the attorneys for Stetson's company, who happened to be John D. Bellamy and Sons, the uncle and cousins of William J. Bellamy, who was representing Scott. Those gentlemen did not challenge the lien, apparently feeling confident that Adams and Sawyer would be convicted. At any rate, $188 was a relatively small matter, equivalent to approximately $5,600 in present-day dollars, perhaps not enough to trouble with at the time.[10]

But perhaps it was enough to justify sending a letter, even one bearing false witness, if the prospect of having to pay now seemed more realistic. If Stetson's company was on the line, Taylor and the owners of the *King* had far more at stake. Back in March 1906, the salvage court had awarded them seven thousand dollars in prize money for their success in recovering the *Berwind* . But that finding was dependent on the legal fact that the ship had been abandoned, due to the guilty involvement of *all* of its crew in the mutiny and murders. If two of those crew were now to be declared not guilty, then that judgment would be cast into doubt, and the equivalent of more than $200,000 present-day dollars might have to be recouped.[11]

On seeing Stetson's letter, James Finch wrote to Adams and Sawyer through Warden Moyer, asking them to respond to the allegations. Both replied that they were malicious lies. They had never threatened Stetson or Taylor in any way, and now the two prisoners had the warden to vouch for them. Moyer himself wrote back to Finch saying that Adams and Sawyer "had absolutely no chance to frame up a story regarding their relations with Mr. Stetson and Captain Taylor, and I am inclined to believe that they have correctly represented their attitude in this respect. . . . Both of these men have declared that they are entirely free from any desire for revenge against any living person and . . . I do not believe they have misrepresented their attitude."[12]

Joseph Buhler now prepared the mother of all petitions for executive clemency on behalf of Adams and Sawyer. It was signed not only by the men's current prison warden, William Moyer, but also by nine of the twelve trial jurors who had convicted them; prosecutor Harry Skinner who had convinced the jurors to do so; Judge Purnell, who had imposed the death sentence; and two United States senators.[13]

One of those senators, Republican Frank Flint of California, had left office earlier that year. It is not clear how he was involved in the case or how he first became aware of it. However, he was involved in real estate development in Southern California, the new frontier for urban expansion at the time. It is at least possible that he knew Warner or Buhler through show-business connections.

But the second senatorial signatory came as a shock. Lee Slater Overman, North Carolina's junior senator, had taken office in 1902, shortly after Furnifold Simmons had. He had not spearheaded the White Supremacy Campaign, as Simmons had, but he was a loyal lieutenant. Overman would serve in the Senate until his death in 1930, always opposing anything that hinted of anti-lynching legislation or women's suffrage. If white women were allowed to vote, he and Simmons argued, it would open the door to Black women voting. There was nothing in Overman's political background thus far to predict that he would ever show leniency to an accused black murderer.

Yet, in the case of Adams and Sawyer, Overman did so, because the evidence to show their innocence had become too persuasive to justify keeping them in prison. That persuasion would soon come to bear upon the current president, William Howard Taft. The question was, would he have the forthrightness to follow his predecessor, the great Roosevelt, in showing mercy where it was warranted?

CHAPTER SEVENTEEN

A FINAL
PLEA

illiam Howard Taft is often remembered as the president who later served
as chief justice of the Supreme Court,
the only president to do so. Comparing
his one term in the White House with
his nine years on the high court, few
would doubt which position was more personally fulfilling. By tem-
perament, Taft was more suited to the life of a jurist than to the
rough-and-tumble of elected politics. He came from a prominent
family of attorneys in Ohio and was himself appointed to a local
judgeship before the age of thirty. Later, he served as solicitor general, as well as a federal Court of Appeals judge.

History remembers Taft as a sedate, contemplative sort of
politician, at least in contrast with Roosevelt, who had seemed to
thrive on publicity and controversy. When he was faced with the
petition in which Arthur Adams and Robert Sawyer were seeking a
full pardon, one might imagine Taft sitting back and weighing the
decision carefully.

From a legal standpoint, Taft might have been inclined to focus on the simple justice of the matter: if it now was evident that the two men were wrongly convicted and imprisoned for six years, then they should be set free. But looking at the matter through a political lens, Taft knew he was running for reelection in 1912 for the job he did not particularly like but felt honor-bound to defend. Furthermore, he was being challenged for renomination by Roosevelt, the very man who had arranged for Taft to succeed him in 1908 but had grown impatient with Taft's perceived reluctance to carry on Roosevelt's progressive reforms. Since Roosevelt had already seen fit to grant clemency to the sailors once by sparing their lives, Taft might have preferred just to ignore the case. If he gave Adams and Sawyer further relief, it might have been perceived as weakness on his part, as if he were following Roosevelt's lead.

Of course, there was also the ever-present factor of race. Taft's background was nearly as patrician as Roosevelt's, and his biography provides no reason to think he was more progressive on cultural issues than his predecessor. Both men had similar views on the proper role of white Europeans as the natural governing class.

In 1901, Taft found himself appointed to the thankless position of civilian governor of the Philippines. Filipino insurgents were no more willing to live under the American style of colonialism than the Spanish. While the Army tried to subjugate the islands through tactics that ranged from the burning of villages to the internment of civilians in concentration camps, to outright torture—including the method now known as "waterboarding"—Taft claimed it was all necessary for the greater good. He wanted to assimilate America's "little brown brothers" into the family, although it would be difficult. Of the Filipinos, Taft said, "These people are the greatest liars it has been my fortune to meet, in many respects nothing but grownup children. . . . They need the training of fifty or a hundred years before they shall even realize what Anglo-Saxon liberty is."[1]

As president, Taft seemed to express little more sympathy for African Americans. In his 1909 inaugural address, he spoke platitudes about how Blacks, even in the South, had made such strides since the Civil War through their own thrift and industriousness, "as well as upon the aid and comfort and sympathy which they may receive from their white neighbors of the South." But political rights for Blacks were not a priority. Taft said that the Fifteenth Amendment, which ostensibly guaranteed the right to vote, could be restricted by state laws "which shall exclude from voting both negroes and whites not having education or other qualifications thought to be necessary for a proper electorate."

Anyone listening in North Carolina would have grasped the president's meaning. Taft was perfectly willing to acquiesce as Southern states imposed racial discrimination, as North Carolina did with its disenfranchisement amendment of 1900.

Taft would concede an occasional gesture of friendship toward the African-American community. But like Roosevelt before him, he grew careful not to let personal gestures turn into policy commitments. In 1910, Taft appointed William H. Lewis, a son of freed Virginia slaves—as well as a Harvard graduate and football star—to serve as an assistant attorney general. No African American had ever been appointed to such a high position in the executive branch, and while no one seriously questioned Lewis's credentials, the appointment caused a ruckus.[2] Taft stood by his nominee, and Lewis eventually was confirmed by the Senate. But while he served in the Justice Department, Lewis had little opportunity to pursue civil rights causes. He was relegated to handling land claims on Native American reservations.

Even aside from Taft's reluctance to take up the cause of racial justice, he was not enthusiastic about granting clemency in general. During his four years in office, he received 1,913 requests for clemency in criminal cases. Of those, he granted only 319 commutations of sentence and 391 pardons.[3] Where the president did choose to act, most requests dealt with lesser federal crimes such as fraud or smuggling. They were not sensational, bloody murder cases.

What eventually won the day for Adams and Sawyer? In addition to the disinterested generosity of Henry B. Warner and his attorney, it would be the personal connections of two men with roots in the British Isles: James Sprunt, the British consul in Wilmington, and Sir James Bryce, the British ambassador in Washington. Neither had anything to gain personally by advocating for the sailors' pardon, and like so many others in this long narrative, they acted against type in doing so.

Deep within Robert Sawyer's prison file, there is a list of people to whom he wrote letters and from whom he received them in return. It shows that Sawyer, the lowly convict, corresponded personally with both Sprunt and Bryce.[4] Yet the letters are not to be found, or at least not in the penitentiary records. It remains unclear how Sprunt or Bryce first took notice of the case, or what assurances of help they may have given Sawyer. It is possible that Adams's earlier letter to King Edward, while it did not receive a personal reply from the sovereign, was forwarded to the attention of the Foreign Office.

Consul James Sprunt was the last man whom anyone would expect to show sympathy toward a mutineer of any skin color, much less a Black one. His family built their wealth through ocean-going commerce, after his parents brought him with them from Glasgow to North Carolina in 1854. Only fifteen when the Civil War broke out, James gained his first nautical experience on Confederate blockade runners. When one was captured by a federal gunboat, James found himself thrown into prison at Fortress Monroe in Norfolk, and yet he managed to escape and make his way back home, an adventure he wrote about in his book. After the war, he and his father expanded their cotton exporting business into Wilmington's largest, with foreign agencies in France, Belgium, Holland, Italy, and the United Kingdom.

No doubt, Sprunt was disturbed by the 1898 Insurrection and the bloodshed that accompanied it. Not only did it threaten his business, as shown by his attempt to face down the rebels at his warehouse gate. He also recognized it as a shameful blot on the history of his hometown, and since—as the city's wealthiest plutocrat—he did not want to criticize openly the conservative segregationist order that the insurrection created, the best he could do as a historian was to gloss it over. In his lengthy *Chronicles*, in which Sprunt devoted many of its six hundred-plus pages to such things as his blockade running voyages; the legends of Stede Bonnet, Rose Greenhow; and Theodosia Burr, he dispensed with the "Revolution of 1898" in exactly *one* brief page of shameless obfuscation. Calling it "the quietest and most orderly riot . . . ever seen or heard of," Sprunt described it this way:

A negro printing office was destroyed by a procession of perfectly sober men, but no person was injured until a negro deliberately and without provocation shot a white man, while others, armed and defiant, occupied the streets, and the result was that about twenty of them were killed and the rest scattered. It constituted an interesting chapter in the public history of the country, and therefore I will not enlarge upon it further than to say that it was the spontaneous and unanimous act of all the white people, and was prompted solely by an overwhelming sense of its absolute necessity in behalf of civilization and decency.[5]

Yet the propagandist also had a social conscience. It may have arisen partly from a sense of guilt, or from the tribulations of James Sprunt's own life. He and his wife had three children, but only one son survived to adulthood; both their daughters died of scarlet fever as teenagers. And in 1882, Sprunt himself endured a tragic injury that altered the course of his life. While driving toward the beach in a horse-drawn wagon, his foot became entangled in the reins when the horse bolted. His foot was crushed so badly that his lower leg had to be amputated in a crude surgery carried out on the kitchen table of a nearby house, a procedure illuminated with a kerosene lantern.

After that, Sprunt seems to have taken on the mantle of Wilmington's Andrew Carnegie, another business magnate who came to America from Scotland in his youth, rose to great wealth by his own pluck and determination, and then gave much of it away. Sprunt became the city's leading philanthropist, donating untold amounts of money to the University of North Carolina and other colleges. He built several churches, including the huge neo-Gothic St. Andrew's Presbyterian near downtown Wilmington. He also established the Marion Sprunt Hospital for women and children as a memorial to one of his daughters, where special attention was given to "crippled" children, young people who had sustained debilitating injuries like Sprunt's own.[6]

While it requires speculation, it is not hard to see how James Sprunt, who was semiretired and focusing most of his time on charitable pursuits by 1911, might have thought it worthwhile to speak up for Adams and Sawyer. The two sailors had been dealt a tragically unlucky set of cards. Now, after six years in prison, they had suffered enough. Sprunt might easily have taken up their case with the attorney general, or with President Taft, whom he knew personally. When Taft travelled through Wilmington in November 1909 and was honored with ceremonies and a military parade in downtown, he stayed overnight at the stately Dudley Mansion. Although originally built by the family of Judge Purnell, by that time the mansion was owned by Sprunt, who had spearheaded the festivities for the presidential visit.[7]

Even if Sprunt did not correspond personally with Taft about the Adams and Sawyer case, the British Embassy is known to have done so, and Sprunt's connections with the embassy were well established. He had served as the British consul in Wilmington since 1884, a position for which he was well suited due to his Scottish heritage and the wealth he had gained through international trade.

Sprunt had a kindred spirit in the Washington embassy with whom he could confer on the case. Sir James Bryce, the son of an Ulster Irish family with Scottish Presbyterian roots, had been ambassador to the United States since 1907.

Bryce was one of the few politicians of that era, on either side of the Atlantic, who could legitimately be called a Renaissance Man. He was a scholar and a world traveler from an early age, with a special aptitude for mountaineering. In 1876, he was one of the first men to climb more than sixteen thousand feet on Mount Ararat in Turkey, where he reported finding a length of hand-hewn wood that might—although he did not claim proof—have come from Noah's Ark. Among his climbing conquests were all the hills on Mount Desert Island, Maine, the same island where Captain Rumill's family made their home.

Everywhere he traveled, Bryce made it a point to converse with locals, from waiters to rail conductors, and incorporate his observations in his writings. It was said that "No travelling American citizen could hope to escape the thrust of his keen and pleasant inquisition."[8] And so, out of several trips and many months spent journeying through the United States, came his most famous work, *The American Commonwealth*. Published in 1888, the three-volume

President William Howard Taft, center, with British Ambassador James Bryce (right, in top hat) on porch of the White House. Bryce supported clemency for Adams and Sawyer, the convicted sailors.
Also with them is Robert Baden-Powell, who had recently formed what became the international Scouting movement for boys and girls.

tome was an exhaustive study of the political history of the US, touching on all its aspects, from the social and religious to the intellectual. He examined not only the federal government, but also the history of every state government and constitution, as well as those of cities. It made Bryce a household name in American academic and journalistic circles, with many comparing his work with Alexis de Tocqueville's seminal work of the 1830s, *Democracy in America.*

Theodore Roosevelt, in particular, was a fan. He wrote to Bryce in 1889, commenting that his work "has all of de Tocqueville's really great merits, and has not got, as his book has, two or three serious faults." Roosevelt was pleased with Bryce's optimism about the American experiment, for Bryce believed that Americans' widespread religious beliefs, and their love of education and philanthropy, would ensure the stability of constitutional government. Bryce was not fearful, as de Tocqueville was, of the "tyranny of the majority;" partly because Bryce was more confident than de Tocqueville in America's ability to assimilate immigrant groups and other minorities, such as black and Native Americans.[9]

For Bryce and Roosevelt, assimilation of minorities was to occur gradually, and only after they had proven their worthiness and conformed to the Anglo-Saxon model of government. Bryce always opposed giving women the right to vote, and as he travelled throughout the southern United States as ambassador, he took a decidedly paternalistic view of Black people as well. Visiting Tuskegee, he enthusiastically praised Booker T. Washington's model of "economic education" and "economic labour," but thought it was a grave mistake to allow Blacks to vote. "Political ambition," where Blacks were concerned, "could only lead to bitterness and strife."[10]

Another such admirer was James Sprunt himself, who quoted Bryce in his 1916 book as "a brilliant observer of American affairs." Sprunt recalled how, in the 1880s, Bryce had criticized American city governments as hotbeds of corruption and mismanagement. The solution, as Sprunt saw it, was to limit the power of popularly elected city councils, and place authority in the hands of appointed, professional city managers. Naturally, Sprunt was speaking in praise of the changes enacted in Wilmington's city charter after the insurrection, and the "corruption" he criticized was that of the Black Fusionist government that preceded it.[11]

Back in Washington, Bryce was one of President Taft's favorite foreign dignitaries, and the door to the White House was always open to him. In 1915, after both men had left office, they worked together as co-authors of a series of articles about the history of the District of Columbia, published by the National Geographic Society.[12] James Bryce even has a public park in Washington named after him, located on Embassy Row, just across Massachusetts Avenue from the National Cathedral. Very few foreign nationals—the Marquis de Lafayette may be the only other—can claim such distinction.

Thus, when Joseph Buhler completed his 188-page clemency petition, and prepared to submit it to Pardon Attorney Finch in mid-1911—for consideration by the attorney general and the president—he also sent it along to the British Embassy. His Majesty's Government was reluctant to get involved at first, as they had other pressing diplomatic issues on their plate.

But once the story was brought to the ambassador's attention, he became "enthusiastic" in support of Sawyer and Adams. In fact, after the president issued his decision, Bryce wrote personally to Henry Warner—on behalf of Foreign Secretary Sir Edward Grey—to thank him for his extraordinary efforts. The embassy staff also took up a collection and sent two hundred dollars to Buhler to present to his two clients, to help them make a new start on their release from prison.[13]

Procedurally, the case reached its final act on August 12, 1911, when Finch issued his formal report, endorsed by Attorney General George Wickersham. It officially recommended that the president grant clemency to Adams and Sawyer. Taft did not act immediately, however, and so Buhler met with him at the White House on December 22.

As Buhler recalled it later, the president had reviewed the petition and was familiar with the case details, agreeing in principle that Sawyer and Adams had been unjustly dealt with. Taft made no firm commitment during the meeting, but toward the end, he shook hands with the attorney and said, "I'll do my best."[14]

How exactly Ambassador Bryce communicated with the president on the sailors' behalf is not clear, but on January 2, 1912, Taft signed the clemency order, releasing Sawyer and Adams from prison. Virtually all the press coverage from the United States and Canada mentioned, without elaborating, that "the British ambassador intervened to secure consideration of the pleas for executive clemency." The international implications of the case were emphasized with headlines such as "British Negroes Pardoned by Taft."[15]

But it was not accurate to describe the president's action as a pardon. He simply issued a second commutation of Sawyer's and Adams's sentence, this time reducing it from life in prison to time served, thus allowing them to be released immediately. In his order, Taft took pains to express that he was not exonerating the two men, nor was he proclaiming them innocent, at least not of the mutiny, as opposed to the murders. He said,

> I do not find Adams and Sawyer free from fault, and I do not think that their conviction, insofar as it has led to their present imprisonment, is an injustice; but I do think that the confession of Scott and the other circumstances are enough to relieve them from active complicity in the murders and to justify their now being freed." Even if Scott carried out all the shootings on his own, Taft still had doubts about whether Sawyer and Adams would have stood by for several hours before subduing Scott, if they really were "brave and determined to save their fellow shipmates.[16]

It was, in essence, a legal settlement—not a case of justice tempered with mercy, but rather of mercy tempered with politics. The two sailors needed to be released from prison because they quite clearly were not murderers. Yet the president did not think it politically wise to let them off entirely, and so he let the convictions stand as a matter of record, —even though one might argue that if they really were guilty of *any* crime resulting in the deaths of five people, they probably should have served more time than six years in prison. As with many legal settlements, it was all about the end result, not the logic behind it.

Two months after President Taft ordered Adams and Sawyers
released, *The New York Times* published this full-page telling
of the story. The headline, however, may have overstated
actor Henry Warner's authority.

Within a day of the president's decision, Adams and Sawyer had gathered up their meager belongings and were escorted out of the Atlanta Penitentiary gate. Immediately, they hopped on a train to New York, where they planned to rendezvous with their liberators. The travel plans had to be kept secret, because Atlanta was part of the South, and one never knew when resentful vigilantes might appear.

CHAPTER EIGHTEEN

THE
REASON WHY

T he legal proceedings surrounding the *Harry A. Berwind* had continued far longer than anyone could have anticipated. The affair lasted more than six years, and included two jury trials, a Supreme Court appeal, and two presidential clemency proceedings. It was an exhausting odyssey, especially for the two men who finally were released from prison. In the end, few would have argued with the result. There was more than reasonable doubt as to whether Robert Sawyer or Arthur Adams were complicit in any of the five murders. All available evidence, though it took so long to be revealed, pointed clearly toward the guilt of one man.

Yet there is an element of mystery that lingers still. It concerns not so much the "who" or the "what," but rather the "how" and the "why?" Henry Scott killed five men in a brutal, terrifying fashion, and it looks as if he was plotting trouble before he set foot on the vessel. He brought at least two guns, ammunition, and a black-jack on board, when the captain and officers likely had no weapons at all. What motivated him to go on the rampage? And how could he ever have expected to pull it off and escape with his own life?

On the surface, the logistics of the crime posed a tremendous problem to contend with. When Scott began shooting, he was more than thirty miles offshore, on a sailing vessel manned by a total of eight people: four officers and four crew. Shipping company owners were not in the habit of over-staffing their vessels; all eight men were needed to perform the essential tasks that kept the ship running. At all hours, someone had to man the wheel, stand watch, maintain the sails and rigging, swab the decks, and cook the food, among plenty of other chores. They served on a schedule of four-man watches: while four worked, the others rested. Otherwise, no one would have had the stamina to keep going. There was no way the ship could operate for long with only four men on board.

At minimum, it appears that Scott intended to kill four. Even if he did not plan to kill John Coakley at the outset, Scott clearly targeted the four white officers. That is apparent from the methodical way in which he hunted them down, one by one. If he intended all along to murder half of the men on board, including the only ones who had the navigational skill to steer the vessel, then one certainly must wonder: What did Scott intend to do with that ship?

Adams and Sawyer gave their own answer to that question, and they were remarkably consistent with it all along. They maintained that Scott tried to enlist them in his salvage scheme, perhaps thinking they would go along with his plan because they *all* had been pushed and abused by the racist white officers. They would cast the yawl boat adrift, claim that all four officers had drowned in the storm, and direct the ship into port. For good measure, Scott also intended to partially disable the ship, by opening the scuppers and flooding the cargo hold. That, in addition to the fractured rudder and sails that actually had been torn away in the storm, would make the damage look even more convincing. Then they could claim the legal prize money.

Perhaps Scott thought that if he could not sway Adams, Sawyer, and Coakley over to his plan, then he could kill all of them as well. In his dying declaration from the gallows, Scott definitely implied as much when he denounced Adams and Sawyer as "traitors and scoundrels" for not going along with him. Or maybe Scott planned from the beginning to kill all seven of the other men on board, disable the ship, and guide it aground by himself, so he would not have to share the prize money with anyone. That farfetched scenario was seized upon by David Murrell, who wrote a highly embellished account of the case in *True Detective Mysteries* magazine in the 1930s. According to Murrell, Scott's scheme for mass murder "represented one of the best plans for a perfect crime that the mind of any man ever conceived... There would be no witnesses. . . . And the decks of the water-logged ship would be washed by the sea of every trace of human blood."[1]

Either case would require someone—either the four sailors working together, even though none of them were navigators, or Scott alone—to steer the ship safely into port. That in itself would have been a remarkable feat. Even if it succeeded, the next task would have been still more formidable. They would have to convince the authorities in some southern port, whether Wilmington, Charleston, Norfolk, or some other, to accept their story that all four white officers had drowned in the storm, and all four of the lower-rank sailors—Black, no less—managed to swim back to the ship. They would have to swear to the story before a federal court and convince a judge to put the prize money into their hands, essentially with few questions asked.

Perhaps Scott had it in his mind to steal the ship and use it for some other purpose, perhaps to go into the smuggling business. Illicit commerce, although not as common on the North Carolina coast as it was around the larger ports, was a real concern at the time.

Recall how the crew of the *King*, as they boarded and searched through the *Berwind*, made it a special point to look for "bay rum" or any other liquors that might have been stowed aboard. They knew the vessel had come in from the Caribbean, where rum distilled from sugar molasses was one of the few profitable local products. Just two years earlier, in 1903, the North Carolina General Assembly had passed a sweeping series of statewide and local ordinances to limit alcohol production. White Supremacist politicians, who loved to play upon the worst stereotypes of Black licentiousness, claimed they needed the laws to keep Blacks sober and docile. The U.S. Revenue Cutter Service, forerunner of the Coast Guard, was always on the lookout for smugglers. They had one vessel, the *Boutwell*, stationed at New Bern, and the *Seminole*, which was briefly considered as a location for the hangings in the *Berwind* case, was docked at Wilmington. The *Boutwell*, in particular, had to respond to a noteworthy situation on the Outer Banks in May 1903, just a couple of years earlier. It was an egregious case that reeked of the earlier days of slavery, and what today could only be called human trafficking.

A mysterious Portuguese sailing bark, the *Vera Cruz*, dropped anchor in Ocracoke Inlet. It had sailed from the Cape Verde Islands off the west coast of Africa, supposedly bound for New Bedford, Massachusetts, but as it approached the North Carolina shore the heavily laden ship appeared to be taking on water and running short of supplies. The ship carried a large quantity of "Holland gin" in tall stone jugs, and the alcohol alone would have raised the suspicions of revenuers in the Cutter Service. But crowded aboard also were more than three hundred African people, many of them suffering from tropical diseases such as the eye infection trachoma.

The master of the vessel, a certain Captain Fernandez, managed to abscond across Pamlico Sound after ditching his ship and passengers. He caught a train heading north, carrying with him all of his passengers' travel documents and a large quantity of cash. Clearly, he was attempting to smuggle those unfortunate souls illegally into the United States, the purported land of opportunity. The crew of the *Boutwell* had the task of picking up the refugees at Ocracoke and then accompanying them to Massachusetts, although some of them later returned to North Carolina to find work after being legally patriated. The first mate of the *Vera Cruz*, Anile Fernandez—brother of the fleeing captain—was later prosecuted for smuggling in New Bern's federal court by Harry Skinner, presided over by Judge Purnell.

The Wilmington papers, reporting the incident at the time, were careful to report that "[s]muggling is a very rare offense in North Carolina." Maybe so, but for those who were criminally inclined, and had the nerve to make the attempt, it might seem profitably alluring.

Perhaps Henry Scott was brazen enough to consider embarking on a career as a smuggler. He might have had it in his head to find a secret cove in the Bahamas or elsewhere and set up base as a sort of latter-day Blackbeard, shipping bootleg rum into the States. It is possible, but he could not have done it by himself. If he intended to seize a ship and turn it into a smuggling vessel, he would at least have to win over his fellow crewmen, Adams, Sawyer, and Coakley. And even after doing so, they all would have to recruit additional crew to sail the ship, all the while concealing the ship's identity and staying one step ahead of the law. Ships always need to return to port for repairs. And by the 1900s, unlike two centuries before, legal authority was well established throughout the region, and it was well backed up by the United States and British navies. There just were not that many places left for a pirate to hide, so it would not have been easy.

Try as one might, it is hard to come up with any *rational* way that Henry Scott could have thought a shipboard murder spree would turn out well for him. Reason, therefore, to focus attention instead on his state of mind. No one attempted to evaluate Scott psychologically during his life, and of course it is impossible for even a psychiatrist to do a conclusive analysis of a man who is more than a century deceased. But historical record reveals quite a bit about Scott's actions, mannerisms, and personality. From those, several things are readily apparent.

First, Scott was not insane, at least not in the legal sense. His attorney William Bellamy described Scott in his correspondence as "insane" in a general sense, probably just to say that Scott's actions seemed irrational. Yet Bellamy did not try to mount an insanity defense, knowing the deck would be heavily stacked against him.

In federal court at that time, Scott's sanity would have been judged according to the original M'Naghten Rule, an English concept that only had developed over the past half-century. A man was not insane unless he was unable to distinguish right from wrong, or, as the House of Lords first expressed it, was "labouring under such a defect of reason, from a disease of the mind, as not to know the nature and quality of the act he was doing; or, if he did know it, that he did not know he was doing what was wrong."[2]

Henry Scott gave a very different presentation, especially

with his lengthy testimony in court. While many ultimately concluded he was lying, his demeanor on the witness stand was not disorganized or delusional at all. From his very first appearance in the Southport courtroom, viewers were struck by how calm he seemed, how confident he was in his facts, how clearly he recalled details of who struck whom and when.

William Bellamy would have recognized early on that an insanity defense was not the right fit for his client. It was, and still is today, a very difficult legal hurdle to clear, and that is to say nothing of the racial dynamics involved in the Wilmington trial. Moreover, the defense had seen few tests in federal court by 1905, and those few were not encouraging for an accused.

Likely, the lucid and coherent Henry Scott was no madman. But he very likely was a psychopath and a narcissist. In the words of Dr. Robert D. Hare, a professor of psychology at the University of British Columbia who has done the most in-depth studies of the psychopathic mind, such people commit crimes "not from a deranged mind, but from a cold, calculating rationality combined with a chilling inability to treat others as thinking, feeling, human beings."[3]

A rudimentary analysis of the *Berwind* case reveals that Henry Scott displayed quite a few of the items on the psychopathy checklist. They include:

• Pathological lying. Henry Scott was able to testify meticulously and—to some people's minds, at least at first—convincingly, in three different public hearings: the initial Southport hearing, his own trial, and the trial of Adams and Sawyer. His story changed several times, and ultimately most people came to see through the lies. But when testifying, he always maintained his self-control, and stood up well to cross-examination. Lying came easily to him.

• Glibness and superficial charm. Many spectators at the trials noticed how Scott kept up his breezy, conversational demeanor when he testified. He made friendly gestures towards the attorneys and judge, trying to be helpful with the stenographer who was taking down the testimony. At times, he cracked jokes. But all that was revealed to be a shallow façade, when the jury delivered its verdict, and Scott shouted out angrily in court.

• Grandiose sense of self-worth; i.e. narcissism. That was apparent throughout the trials, as Scott described his testimony as a "wide statement to the world." He knew some people were being swayed by his storytelling, although he over-estimated how many. And even as Scott stood on the gallows with the rope about to be placed around his neck, he kept the rapt attention of the spectators, clearly enjoying the attention. He claimed credit for ultimately saving the lives of Sawyer and Adams when he confessed, despite previously doing everything he could to convict them. Scott even claimed the right of presidential clemency for himself, saying, "The power I now have, President Roosevelt has not." For a lowly Black sailor, it could not get more grandiose than that.

• Lack of remorse. Scott never showed the slightest trace of contrition for the five murders he committed, preferring in his gallows speech to blame it all on those who treated him "dirty." Even as he exonerated Sawyer and Adams with his confession, he still called them "traitors and scoundrels."

• Cunning and manipulation. That was evident throughout the entire affair, even when Scott gave his final confession. Although he seemed to let Sawyer and Adams off the hook, his final account of the murders did not ring true. No one seriously believed that Scott was able to shoot down all four officers all at once, while all of them were armed with pistols. It was the narcissist in Scott, trying to add one last twist to the story before he was hanged.

• Impulsivity, irresponsibility, lack of realistic long-term goals. Scott may have acted impulsively, on the spur of the moment, when he started the killing spree. But if instead he had thought out the crimes in advance—and he probably did, as he came aboard armed with guns—he had not thought out a realistic plan for what to do with the vessel afterward. He certainly overestimated his ability to persuade Sawyer, Adams, and Coakley to go along with his plans, whatever they were. The other three sailors, like Scott, may have borne some resentment towards the white officers, who may well have been racially insensitive in running their ship. But even if so, there appears to have been only one psychopath on board.

Just as psychopaths use many criminal techniques, they also act from a variety of motives. Henry Scott may have thought, in some convoluted way, that he had a chance to make money by seizing the *Berwind*. Maybe Captain Rumill and the other officers were racists and heavy-handed in the way they ran their ship, where working conditions were harsh under the best of circumstances. Or maybe Scott was exactly what white people ordinarily would have assumed about him from the beginning: a mad-dog killer who wanted to exterminate everyone in his path because he hated the officers, whom he called "white SOBs," hated white people in general, or just hated the world at large.

But this much is abundantly clear. The *Harry A. Berwind*, which eventually literally would wreck at sea, had gone down in a human tempest well before that—and the tempest had arisen in the fevered imagination of one man.

CHAPTER NINETEEN

ENDINGS

hen Sawyer and Adams left the Atlanta Penitentiary, their travel arrangements had been planned well in advance. They both would go to New York, where Henry Warner and his attorney Buhler had offered them jobs. In fact, Buhler had made the offer to them several months previously.

In August 1911, just after he received word that Pardon Attorney Finch was going to recommend clemency to the president, Buhler confidently wrote his clients and asked them to consider what they planned to do after their release. With a bit of condescension, he strongly suggested they come to New York and allow him and Warner to ease their adjustment into free society. "I think it would be good for both of you," Buhler said, "if I could see you and supervise to some extent your life for the next year or two." Buhler also urged Adams and Sawyer, whatever they chose to do, to keep striving for self-improvement, hinting that he knew their involvement in the shipboard affair had not been entirely innocent. "I believe that while the imprisonment has been very hard to bear, that you both have benefitted a great deal, and that your life from now on will be absolutely upright and straightforward."[1]

Sawyer and Adams, having few options, accepted the offer. Adams became Henry Warner's personal valet, and Sawyer went to work as a "general utility man" at Buhler's law firm, which amounted to serving as an office helper. His tasks included answering the phone and running errands, putting him "in sole charge of his master's apartment," as the *New York Times* described it in cringe-worthy terms. "He's sworn to be faithful to me forever," Buhler said, "and he's really an excellent fellow. I'd trust him anywhere." Sawyer's first assigned errand was to take a five-hundred-dollar cash deposit to the bank. "And he was back in a few minutes with the receipt."[2]

The two former sailors, now manservants, knew they were expected to be grateful and to display it publicly. Sawyer gave a statement published in the Wilmington papers, thanking everyone in the city who had stood by him and expressed faith in his innocence through their affidavits. The gratitude may have been real, but the words definitely come across as contrived. "I will make good!" Sawyer promised. "I will endeavor to make them [his supporters] continue in their belief by living a straightforward, honest, and upright life."

In the same article, Buhler emphasized how he and his client had spent thousands of their own dollars in researching the case and obtaining clemency for Adams and Sawyer, that "the case was taken up by Mr. Warner and me from a purely charitable point of view."[3] Perhaps they did so, or perhaps they were looking to develop a stage script based upon the story. It is hard to know precisely where their motives lay.

It also is hard to pinpoint exactly what became of the two leading players in the drama, how long they continued working for Warner and Buhler, or whether they even stayed in the United States for the rest of their lives. While one can find a wealth of genealogical information, from sources such as hospital lists, property and tax records, the sad fact is that Black families are not nearly as well-documented as white ones.

The one thing known for certain is that Robert Sawyer was living in Brooklyn, New York, in February 1918, when he submitted a "declaration of intention" to the U.S. Naturalization Service, seeking to become a United States citizen. In his mid-forties by that time, he attested that he was unmarried and working as a "porter," which sounds very much like the work he was doing for Buhler in 1912. To become a legal American, Sawyer had to "renounce forever all fidelity and allegiance . . . to George V, King of Great Britain and Ireland, of whom I am now a subject." Apparently, he was confident that if he got into any new legal difficulties, they would not be serious enough to require help from the British government again.

The declaration of intention itself makes for interesting reading. To qualify, the applicant only needed to state, "I am not an anarchist; not a polygamist nor a believer in the practice of polygamy," and swear that he intended to be loyal and reside permanently in the United States.[4] Apparently, a conviction for murder, which still stood on Sawyer's record, was not a disqualifier. Whether Sawyer stayed in New York, or for how long, is uncertain.

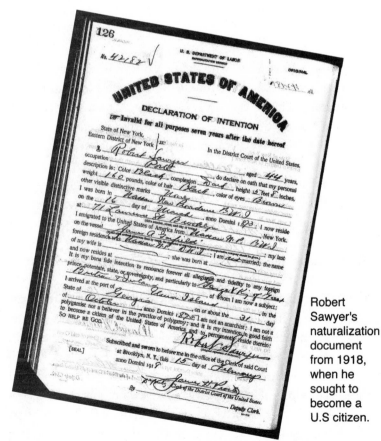

Robert Sawyer's naturalization document from 1918, when he sought to become a U.S citizen.

There is no such naturalization record for his shipmate, Arthur Adams, so it is not clear whether he decided to stay in the U.S. According to his prison correspondence records, Adams had an uncle in Philadelphia, but both his parents and several other family members were still living on Bequia. He may well have returned to the island as soon as he made enough money to book passage.

There was little commercial activity taking place on Bequia, with a notable exception. Many locals were experienced shipbuilders who specialized in working with the white cedar timber that used to grow abundantly on the island. Local historians recall how many of the beaches and coves on the island were used as shipyards for turning out wooden vessels, ranging from twenty-seven-foot whaleboats to larger island schooners.[5] Whaling was still a viable trade in those days, which may have given rise to Adams's testimony in court about his experience with the guns used to kill whales. Perhaps he moved back home and got into that business.

As for the four officers who died on board the *Harry A. Berwind*, Captain Edwin Rumill is the only one who is not lost to history. That is due, in no small part, to his deep family roots in Pretty Marsh, the village in Maine where he grew up. His son George joined the Navy as a young man and moved many times during his life, to stations such as Charleston and Pensacola. But his daughter Edna Rumill Hysom maintained the family home—with its many collectibles gathered from all her father's global travels—throughout her long life. She died in 1998, just having passed her hundredth birthday.

Edna's daughter, Gail Reiber, spoke about her grandparents in an interview with the local historical society in 2019. When she got to the mutiny, she could recount only what she knew from her mother, and in turn, from her grandmother. The captain, as she understood, sometimes had to scrounge around to hire crewmembers prior a voyage, and often the pickings were slim and undesirable. She remembered the name of Scott, the ringleader who plotted to wreck the ship and claim salvage rights, supposedly telling his two cohorts, "We will be all set." Adams and Sawyer, she believed, had no particular issue with her grandfather, "but they were dominated by this par-

Captain Edwin B. Rumill's double headstone, shared with his wife Lettie. The captain, it says, was "Lost at Sea."

ticular man named Scott." After Scott met his well-deserved death, Ms. Reiber recalled, "The two that had been coerced were pardoned by the president, and kept in jail for 13 more years because they were black, and then finally set free."[6] She overestimated the number of years, and maybe the extent of their culpability. But she was mindful of the racial factor.

Captain Rumill's wife, Lettie, outlived him by more than thirty years, passing away in 1936. She lies buried in the Pretty Marsh village cemetery, and appropriately enough, shares a double headstone with her husband, though his remains are not there. Along with his name and the dates of his birth and death, one sees the inscription, "Lost at Sea." An accurate statement as far as it goes, although hardly the full story. If a stranger were to come upon the grave while browsing through the cemetery, he would assume that the captain's ship went down in a naturally occurring storm.

The *Harry A. Berwind* did not literally sink in the human storm that engulfed it on that early morning in October 1905, but she had less than a year to remain afloat. On October 3, 1906, papers reported that the *Berwind* had wrecked on the shore of the Isle of Pines, a small island off the south coast of Cuba. Although the crew evacuated safely and made its way to Havana, the ship was a total loss. With the wreck coming as soon as it did after the murders, and while Adams and Sawyer were still fighting for their lives in court, newspapers could not refrain from rehashing the story. They called the *Berwind* "a bad luck ship, the history of which is probably known to every English-speaking sailorman in the world." The ship, they said, "never had a day's luck from the hour that she slid down the ways at Millbridge, Me."[7]

The *Blanche H. King*, the other wooden schooner that featured in the story by intercepting the *Berwind* off of Cape Fear, likewise did not meet with a natural ending. In December 1920, while carrying a load of coal from Norfolk, Virginia, to Bermuda, she had almost reached her destination when she struck a reef just off the southwest shore of the island. The hull settled in about thirty-five feet of water, within easy reach of modern scuba equipment. A century later, some iron portions of the ship remain, and the *King* is one of Bermuda's most popular dive sites.[8] One can find any number of online videos of the wreckage, showing fish as they snap at tiny crustaceans that live among the corals that now encrust the old engine parts. Few divers are aware of the drama that once unfolded on the wooden decks, which long ago rotted away.

Henry B. Warner continued with his stage career, and successfully transitioned into film work in the 1910s. He appeared in plenty of silent films through the next couple of decades, the most prominent being his starring role of Jesus Christ in *The King of Kings*, Cecil B. DeMille's 1927 biblical epic. Later, Warner transitioned again into sound films, and his most recognizable role was in *It's a Wonderful Life*, the Frank Capra Christmas classic produced in 1946. Warner played Mr. Gower, the inebriated druggist who came close to poisoning a child's prescription through drunken negligence and was saved from going to prison only through the divine intervention of young George Bailey—Jimmy Stewart's character—who later is talked out of suicide by his guardian angel. That plot twist may have had a meaning for Warner, who once had played the role of an intervening angel in real life, releasing two men from a very real prison.

B
ack in Wilmington, life went on through the first half of
the twentieth century as it did elsewhere in the South. White
people and Black people lived in neighboring, yet strictly
separated, spheres. Political influence tended to remain centered in
the same conservative Democratic circles, often within the same
families. The attorneys who defended Sawyer and Adams—George
Rountree, George Peschau, and William J. Bellamy—all lived into
their eighties and retired as esteemed pillars of Wilmington's legal
establishment. Each served as a local judge during his career.

Harry Skinner, the formerly Fusionist prosecutor, was part
of that establishment as well, even though he made it a point not to
rejoin the Democrats. His memories of the White Supremacy Campaign and insurrection were too vivid, and he never got over the
viciousness of the Democrats' tactics. After he left office as U.S.
attorney in 1910, he remained in private practice, and served as president of the North Carolina Bar Association for a year beginning in
1915. Yet while he maintained his partisan independence, he did not
use that platform, or any other, to advocate civil rights for Blacks.
By that time, only white people were voting, and racial equality was a
political nonstarter.[9]

Black people in Wilmington were expected to be seen, be pro-
ductive, make few sounds, and certainly never make political waves.
The city's white leaders liked to make speeches about how race relations had grown so harmonious since the destructive "chaos" and
"disorder" of 1898, and how Blacks were prospering through dili-
gent effort and lawfulness. Underlying all the happy talk, of course,
was the subtle threat of prosecution for those who stepped out of
line, and occasionally when rumors of protest arose, the threat was
made explicit.

To cite one of many examples, Governor J. Melville Broughton gave a speech on the Cape Fear riverfront in July 1943, ostensibly
to dedicate one of the liberty ships that were being mass-produced
there for the war effort in Europe. But labor unrest was growing,
brought about by the strain of Blacks and whites having to work
together in new, unfamiliar industries. Just days before Broughton's
speech, thirty-eight people died in a race riot in Detroit. The governor urged all his listeners to disregard "radical black agitators . . .

seeking to use the war emergency to advance theories and philoso-
phies, which if carried to their ultimate conclusion would result only
in a mongrel race." "Forty-five years ago," Broughton reminded everyone, "blood flowed freely in the streets of this city."[10] As far as the
governor was concerned, it was all the fault of the rabble-rousers,
none of whom were white.

Change began in the 1960s with new federal laws and school
integration, a much more painful, prolonged endeavor than many
would like to acknowledge. The full reckoning did not come about
until the 1990s. The city, in conjunction with the local church congregations, Black and white, formed an 1898 Centennial Foundation, which hosted a number of public forums to discuss the events
surrounding the insurrection. One of them was on November 10,
1998—the exact anniversary of the coup—held at Thalian Hall, the
site of Colonel Waddell's infamous speech. There, more than a thousand people gathered to sign a "People's Declaration of Racial Inter-
dependence," a pointed contrast to Waddell's White Declaration of
Independence. The 1998 declaration called upon the city's leaders to
"declare openly their common commitment to the path of interracial dialogue, inclusion, and reconciliation."[11]

The city's leaders were listening, as was the state government
in Raleigh. In 2000, the General Assembly established a state commission to study the events of 1898. Six years later, their 480-page
report confirmed what many had known all along. The violence of
1898 was not the spontaneous act of an enraged mob, but a calculated conspiracy of the city's white business and political establishment. By the commission's estimate, at least sixty Blacks were killed
and more than two thousand fled Wilmington in the aftermath. Two
years later, the 1898 Memorial Park was dedicated near the corner
of Fourth and Harnett streets, where the first shots were fired. The
dedication plaque reads, in part:

> *Wilmington's 1898 racial violence was not accidental. It began
> a successful statewide Democratic campaign to regain control of
> state government, disenfranchise African Americans, and create
> a system of legal segregation which persisted into the second half
> of the 20th Century.*[12]

Wilmington's 1898 Memorial Park. A plaque notes
that the six tall paddles are decidated to those who
suffered during the violence. "The paddles refer
symbolically to water, an important element in the
spiritual belief system of people from the African
continent. They believed water to be the medium for
moving from this life to the next."

Not everyone would have agreed. One of the speakers at the 1998 forums was George Rountree III, a prominent Wilmington attorney in the field of admiralty law, and the grandson of George Rountree, Sr. While some gave the younger Rountree credit for having the courage to defend publicly his grandfather's role in the insurrection, his words disappointed those who were hoping for an apology, an acknowledgment that the insurrection in itself was wrong. Rountree III did not go there. While he regretted the bloodshed, he maintained—in 1998 and since—that his grandfather was a man of "moderation" whose goal was to place the city's government in the hands of the commercial class, those best able to manage it. As for addressing society's inequities, racial and otherwise, he urged everyone to do as his family had always done: contribute to private causes supporting schools, hospitals, and women's shelters. "At what point will I have done enough?" to make amends, Rountree asked.[13]

It is a bit surprising, if Rountree III wanted to defend his family's legacy, that he did not mention the work that Rountree, Sr. did to secure the freedom of Arthur Adams and Robert Sawyer. Surely that story would have shown that the grandfather had some interest in making amends. In fact, it may have inspired the grandson in his own career. One story that George Rountree III has recounted publicly is a case that he took on as a young attorney in 1962. He defended a Black man, James Fuller, who was convicted of vehicular manslaughter in the death of a white woman. In a remarkable parallel with the *Berwind* case, Rountree III appealed Fuller's case to the state supreme court and had the conviction overturned, even though the client was unable to pay.[14] Yet, for whatever reason, the case of Adams and Sawyer does not seem to come up.

Nor does one find the *Berwind* case on the minds of many in Wilmington's Black community today. Even though the release of Adams and Sawyer from prison was a stunning legal event for its time, few today can recall hearing of it, and written sources make little mention of the case. One result of the 1998 centennial was the publication of a remarkable book by William M. Reaves, distributed by the New Hanover County Library, entitled *Strength Through Struggle: The Chronological and Historical Record of the African-American Community in Wilmington, North Carolina, 1856–1950*. Just as the title suggests, the five-hundred-plus-page book is a long overdue collection of the life stories of people, churches, schools, and other institutions in Wilmington's Black population. It tells of how they persevered and thrived through such difficult times, because of the efforts of so many leaders like Thomas H. Knight and the Reverend Edmund Bennett. Both men were personally involved with the *Berwind* defendants, and both are proudly described in the book. Yet it contains no mention of Adams or Sawyer, their trial, or their hard-won freedom.

Why has the *Berwind* case been seemingly cast aside?

The answer may lie partly in another story that still clings tightly to the heart of Wilmington's Black community, and not just because it is more recent in time nor because it involved Wilmington locals (as opposed to foreigners like Adams and Sawyer). It is the infamous case of the Wilmington Ten.

In 1969, after far too much political delay, court-ordered school integration finally came to New Hanover County. It was much anticipated, but it also caused hard feelings among those it was intended to help. The school board decided to close Williston Industrial, Wilmington's primary Black high school and one with a proud history, and reassign its students to largely white schools. The decision aroused widespread anger, and local Black students called a school boycott. Occurring as it did against the backdrop of anti-Vietnam War protests and anger over the King assassination, the boycott drew many activists to Wilmington, many openly espousing Leninist and Maoist sentiments, and some brandishing weapons. Street demonstrations led to fights between Black activists and whites who were friendly with the Ku Klux Klan. One night in February 1971, a white-owned grocery store was firebombed, and when firefighters responded, they were beset with sniper fire coming from the direction of a church next door where a number of the Black activists had taken up residence.

Nearly a year later, ten people were rounded up and charged with arson and conspiracy. Eight were high-school-aged Blacks. In October 1972, all were found guilty in a trial that was marked with egregious prosecutorial misconduct. Recantations and contradictory statements made by state witnesses were withheld from the defense, and the prosecutor's notes from the jury selection showed that he intentionally placed Klan-affiliated whites on the panel. All of the

Wilmington Ten received prison sentences between twenty-nine and thirty-four years, unusually severe for the charges alleged.

The national media did not let the story die away. Following an expose on "60 Minutes" in 1977, Governor Jim Hunt reduced the Ten's prison sentences in a gesture reminiscent of Roosevelt and Taft. Hunt maintained that the defendants were guilty, and their trial was fair, but he thought the sentences were too harsh. They were not released from prison until 1980, when the federal Fourth Circuit Court of Appeals overturned the convictions on glaringly obvious legal grounds. On New Year's Eve 2012, Governor Beverly Perdue finally granted all ten a full pardon, in one of her final acts in office.

The odyssey of the Wilmington Ten is well remembered in the city today. Like the 1898 insurrection itself, the case now has a memorial marker of its own, dedicated in 2016 on the site of the old grocery store and church. And like the *Berwind* case, it has a happy ending. Justice prevailed, although it was far too long in coming.

So why do Adams and Sawyer, whose freedom was an even more extraordinary legal victory given the times, warrant barely a footnote in the local consciousness? Partly, perhaps, for this reason: Adams and Sawyer eventually won their case through some unusual strokes of luck, but most of all through the good graces of some well-disposed white men. That makes it a stereotypical "white savior" narrative; for many a less satisfying story than that of the Wilmington Ten, in which mostly Black attorneys and activists carried the day. The legal counsels for the Ten, both at trial and on appeal, were James Ferguson and Irving Joyner, two of North Carolina's first Black civil rights litigators. The activists who kept the case in the public eye were a mix of Blacks and liberal whites, such as the Commission for Racial Justice (CRJ), which enlisted the support of black Congressional representatives like John Conyers and Barbara Jordan. Ultimately, that made the difference.[15]

Also, in the 2020s' environment of Black Lives Matter, political discourse places a priority upon being "woke" to the history of white racism in the South. The harsh aspects of that history are more real—far more real—than many would admit, but in their zeal to recognize long-neglected injustices, some activists may find it hard to concede that two Black men could ever have obtained *any* kind of justice in the courts of Wilmington in the early 1900s, or that men like Alfred M. Waddell or George Rountree, Sr. could *ever* have shown a generous impulse toward any African American.

Then, of course, there is the stubborn fact of guilt itself. Whoever may have done what at that burning grocery store in February 1971, it has always been clear what happened on the decks of the *Harry A. Berwind* in October 1905. Five men—four of them white—were sadistically gunned down in cold blood by at least one Black man. Therein lies the rub, and the uncomfortable truth.

CHAPTER TWENTY

THE
HOLLYWOOD TREATMENT

ventually there was bound to be a media adaptation of the story. There was a seagoing adventure, a multiple murder, complex legal intrigues, and eventually a happy ending, for the survivors, at least. The *Berwind* case had so many of the features that one looks for in a good novel, film, or stage play that it was inconceivable no one would ever find use for it. It took more than forty years for it to come together, however.

So much occurred in the more-than-six-year ordeal—and so much of it unexpected—that a novelist or screenwriter of that period may have found it difficult to bring the full story into a coherent piece. One could easily write a novel about a mutiny at sea. That was the stuff of Jack London's fiction, after all. It would not have to be a high-brow piece of literature; there was plenty of mass-produced pulp fiction written in the mid-twentieth century that centered on science fiction, lurid crimes, and steamy romance. But how to incorporate the legal drama? The last-minute confession from Henry Scott would have made a fine plot point, but what about the intricate appeals in court, the back-room political maneuvering, and the surprising change of heart that so many Wilmington people felt toward Sawyer and Adams?

By the 1950s, when the *Berwind* story finally made its way to the big screen, there definitely was an audience for at least one part of the story—the shipboard murders themselves. Film noir was all the rage in Hollywood during World War II and afterward. Not all film historians agree on how the genre is defined, but generally it revolved around the concept of the sultry crime drama. Usually shot in black-and-white—appropriate for their bleak moral settings—those films typically have a lead character who is drawn into a desperate situation, either by the criminal plotting or sexual manipulation of someone else. Many were based on pulp-fiction novels that were popular at the time, such as *The Maltese Falcon* and *The Glass Key*, both from novels by Dashiell Hammett. In keeping with that norm, the filmmakers who produced the *Berwind* story focused just on the crime adventure drama, rather than the more complex legal and political events that followed.

There also was the ever-complicating factor of race, which, as it turned out, the filmmakers did not want to emphasize.

In earlier years, it would have been tempting, and easy, to make a film about Black murderers preying on innocent whites in the confines of an oceangoing vessel. Hollywood, reflecting American culture at large, was rife with the worst racial stereotyping from the 1910s through the 1930s. D.W. Griffith's *The Birth of a Nation*, released in 1915 as America's first true epic film, was deservedly hailed as groundbreaking cine-magic. Yet it also was grotesquely racist, depicting Blacks in the post-Civil War South as corrupt, drunken, lecherous rapists and the Ku Klux Klan as noble defenders of white female virtue. *Gone With the Wind*, which came out in 1939, is well known for its cartoonish depiction of simple-minded slaves, as well as the scene in which Scarlett O'Hara is menaced by a Black ruffian in the shantytown outside of Atlanta. Those are only two of many examples.

Things started to change in the post-war era of the late 1940s. Segregation was still law in the South, and there was plenty of racism yet to be found. But the shared national ordeal of World War II had altered the way that Blacks and whites saw each other. Although they served in segregated units, they had fought together in a common cause at the battlefront. They worked together in factories to produce the massive quantities of material needed. At the very least, people of different races began to know each other better, to be more familiar with the other's styles, fashions, and manners of speaking.

The transformation could be seen in the films noir that came out in the 1950s, which began to show at least a measure of empathy, although not camaraderie, between Blacks and whites. In *No Way Out* (1950), Sidney Poitier played a young black doctor who treats a very bigoted white gangster who is injured in a robbery, and later wins the grudging respect of the gangster's family during an ensuing race riot. *Odds Against Tomorrow* (1959), an extremely dark crime drama, starred Harry Belafonte as a black nightclub singer who teams up with a white partner for a robbery.

By the late 1950s, as the Civil Rights movement gained steam and desegregation was becoming reality in some parts of the country, overt racism was gradually going out of style in Hollywood.

Thus, the film depiction of the *Berwind* murders could not take a form that depicted Black men as stereotypical brutes. It was thought better, in fact, to re-structure the story to eliminate race, at least as a motive for the killings and mutiny. However good the intentions may have been, they led to a film that transformed the story into something utterly unrecognizable from the true events. It was a disaster, from both a critical and commercial standpoint.

The Decks Ran Red—the title says it all—was released in 1958. It showed some promise in the beginning. Produced by MGM Studios, it was directed by Andrew Stone. At age fifty-six, Stone had amassed a major body of work in the noir category over thirty years. Most of his films were low-budget, high-impact affairs that were all about shock value. Not all of them achieved mainstream success, but by 1958 Stone was coming off a major win with *Julie* (1956), for which he received an Academy Award nomination for Best Original Screenplay. That one was a "damsel-in-distress melodrama" set on an airplane, in which a former stewardess played by Doris Day is terrorized by her jealous ex-husband, Louis Jourdan.[1]

From that, it was not much of a leap to make a new film about terror onboard a ship. Stone brought in James Mason—by then a well-known box-office draw—to play an English-accented

Captain Ed Rumill. Using the real captain's name was fully intentional, because the story was presented to the audience as a true one. Similar to real life, the ship in the film was called the SS *Berwind*. And in the trailer, the voice-over proclaimed the adventure was unlike anything else to be found on all the Seven Seas, "the more exciting because it actually happened!"

But the action depicted in the film bore little resemblance to what occurred on board the *Harry A. Berwind*. The film was set not in 1905, but in the present-day late 1950s. Not off the coast of the Carolinas, but in the Pacific near New Zealand. The wooden sailing schooner was transformed into a fully modern steel cargo vessel, of the Liberty Ship class used in World War II. It was double the size of the actual ship, completely mechanized and electrified, and manned by a crew of at least thirty men.

The villain was still named Henry Scott, but in the film he was not the wiry young Black desperado of real life. He was played by Broderick Crawford—best known as Willie Stark in *All the King's Men* (1949)—as a portly, balding, middle-aged white desperado. In

MGM lobby card for *The Decks Ran Red*, explaining that—in the movie, anyway— "Broderick Crawford and Stuart Whitman heave overboard one of the crew members they suspect of betraying their plan for mutiny."

fact, all of the crew shown in the film are white. Crawford's Scott has a motive similar to his real-life counterpart, in that he tried to incite a mutiny, kill the officers, and then take the ship to port to claim as a prize. Yet it was not about race. And in the film, Scott and his one cohort are seen plodding from deck to deck, armed with single-shot rifles, picking off a few men one by one and holding all the rest of them in paralyzed fear. It looks ridiculous, and moviegoers at the time may have thought the plot was as implausible as any of the stories the real Henry Scott had told fifty years earlier.

Once the murder scenes in the film begin, melodrama is heaped upon melodrama. Captain Rumill eventually leads the surviving crew to evacuate in the lifeboat, but he then swims back to the ship in a feat reminiscent of London's Wolf Larsen. Just as Scott is steering the massive ship towards the lifeboat, intending to crush it, Rumill confronts him and stabs him to death, of course saving the lives of the men in the lifeboat. They cheer as Scott is dead, and Rumill is alive and back in command of his vessel.

All that would have seemed absurd to anyone who knew the true story, as few moviegoers of the 1950s would have. In fact, one might ask why the filmmakers bothered to use the real names of the ship, Rumill, and Scott if they intended to distort the facts so radically. It may be that they wanted James Mason's character to have the name "Rumill" because it sounded like "Rommel," as in the German World War II general whom Mason had played, to great acclaim in *The Desert Fox* several years earlier.[2] It is hard to imagine any other reason.

Yet the greatest absurdity is the added love interest. Of course there were no women on board the real-life *Berwind*, but the film version just had to have at least one. Here again, the trailer voice-over provides the general idea. She was "a dangerously beautiful native woman ... the exotic Mahia!" A dark-skinned New Zealand Maori, Mahia is the wife of the ship's cook, whom Captain Rumill reluctantly allows aboard, soon to his regret. She cavorts shamelessly around the ship, wearing skin-tight tops, her nipples nearly exposed, tempting the supposedly love-starved crew, loyal and mutineer alike. Eventually, Mahia joins forces with Rumill and incapacitates Scott's accomplice. She does it by grabbing him, kissing him passionately, and lifting his handgun from his back pocket, shooting him twice in the head.

The cringe-worthy role of Mahia was played by Dorothy Dandridge, a wonderful actress who, not long before, had been the first woman of color to be nominated for the Best Actress Oscar in 1954 for *Carmen Jones*. In 1959, just a year after *The Decks Ran Red*, Dandridge was nominated for a Golden Globe for *Porgy and Bess*. For Dandridge, Mahia was a demeaning low point in a groundbreaking career that showed how much things had changed for African Americans in film, and yet how some things stayed the same. Black actors were gaining respect, and the stereotype of the violent Black killer was not as widespread as it once was. But other forms of "blaxploitation"—like the over-sexualization of "exotic" black women— were alive and well.

The Decks Ran Red was a flop at the box office, its $800,000 in worldwide receipts failing to cover its nearly $1.3 million cost. The press reviews were almost entirely negative, with the *New York Times* critic speaking for many when he said the film showed a profound "indifference to plausibility." The story was too silly even for moviegoers who thrived on pulp fiction. Director Stone, said the critic, had asked his viewers to believe that just two miscast thugs, armed with only a few guns, "could terrify a crew of officers and seamen and put them to an ignominious rout." It was insulting to the audience's intelligence for the director and writers to assume they would "lack perception of ways the mutineers might well be foiled."[3]

Everyone agrees that the film was terrible, and a sad injustice to the history of the events. With today's insight, a far better film version could be made, taking account of all the political and social realities involved as well as the dramatic crime story.

The *Times* critic may have spoken too broadly, in that there are any number of ways that a shipboard argument could turn into an ignominious rout, and it might be more difficult than one assumes to foil a mutiny. On a wave-tossed ship in the darkness of early morning, it is not always so easy to pick up a belaying pin and subdue a gun-wielding attacker. Many years after the fact, it would have been challenging—but fascinating—to untangle the truth behind the real events that inspired the film. Even at the time, it took two jury trials, two presidential clemency appeals, a gallows confession, and much behind-the-scenes negotiation over six years to sort it all out. The whole process, in just its documented facts, is quite a story.

As is frequently said about the Hollywood creative process: Sometimes it pays to tell a lie, even when the truth is good enough.

But where history is concerned, truth comes better late than never.

ACKNOWLEDGMENTS

When my brother and I were very young—four and two years old, maybe—our grandmother once took us treasure hunting in Southport. It was on the narrow beach just below the seawall at the foot of Howe Street, near Whittlers Bench. She showed us where to dig with our plastic toy shovels, and, after we managed to move aside a few inches of damp sand, we would scream with delight as we came upon a piece of costume jewelry, or a few links of brass chain . . . that our grandmother had secretly buried there beforehand.

It looked like pirate treasure, for sure. And I was hooked. What young boy doesn't think pirates are cool?

As I grew older, I became acquainted with the story of Stede Bonnet, the very real pirate captain who had his final battle with the colonial Navy just a mile up the Cape Fear River from Southport. I understood it to have been a bloody shootout, with several men killed on both sides, and with the surviving pirates captured and taken to Charles Town for hanging. That was just the law of the sea.

But actually, even in those hardscrabble days, the iron hand of justice did not crush indiscriminately. We know now that against all odds, four of Bonnet's crew were found not guilty and released. Somehow they managed to prove they were captives who were forced into piracy against their will, and had not taken part in the plunder or murders.

I was even more surprised to come across the story now told within this book of no less a miraculous escape, made nearly two centuries later by Arthur Adams and Robert Sawyer after being captured on a ship near that same famous river and cape. They, too, were caught up in events not of their own making. Researching this story has been rewarding; it is good to know that, even in some of the darkest days of the Southern past, justice could still prevail, even in the most improbable ways. Yet the case of the *Harry A. Berwind*, as much as any ancient pirate yarn, does not come wrapped up in a neat package. It has taken much research, by many people building upon the work of those coming before, to sort it all out. I'm certainly a beneficiary, and so my first words of thanks must go to those who laid the groundwork for me.

Most especially, I am grateful to Dr. Vann R. Newkirk, Sr., for "Washed Down in Blood: Murder on the Schooner *Harry A. Berwind*," his excellent 2014 article for *The North Carolina Historical Review*. Without it, I never would have heard of the case. Dr. Newkirk's article lit a fire of curiosity within me.

Like so many others my age who grew up in North Carolina, I managed to get through high school knowing shamefully little about the true history of the Wilmington insurrection or the White Supremacy Campaign. Today the full story is far better known, and visitors who come to admire the reminders of the Old South–like the Bellamy Mansion–also see memorials to the victims of the 1898 atrocities. For that, we can thank historians like Timothy Tyson and David Cecelski. Back in the 1990s, they led the way into unearthing those long-buried chapters. I also thank writers who have followed up and expounded on their work, such as Philip Gerard, Rob Christensen, and David Zucchino, whose recent book, *Wilmington's Lie*, may be the best account yet of the insurrection, its origins, and aftermath. It would be impossible to grasp how remarkable the *Berwind* story is, but for the events that preceded it.

For a case more than a century old, I found a wonderful trove of records from the federal court trial and clemency proceedings. It's hard to describe how exciting it was to put my hands on Captain Rumill's original Logbook, worn and stained, and yet still preserved after all these years, as well as on the trial transcripts and documents like Henry Scott's handwritten confession. My deepest appreciation goes to the staff of the National Archives and Records Administration, especially Sara Brewer in Atlanta and Haley Maynard in College Park, Maryland, for assisting me with these invaluable sources.

In Southport, Nancy Christensen and Bob Surridge of the town's Historical Society also are deserving of appreciation. Nancy gave me a tour of the Old Jail where the *Berwind* sailors spent their first days of nervous incarceration, and shared her own valuable insights. Bob kindly permitted use of some of the Society's collection of photos. Far up the Atlantic coast, Tim Garrity of the Mount Desert Historical Society put me on the right path to discover the history of the Rumill family in Pretty Marsh, Maine.

In Wilmington, I regret not finding many familiar with the *Berwind* story, not only because of the passage of time but because none of the defendants or victims were locals, and none have descendants in Wilmington today. Nevertheless, I am grateful to several people who tried to point me in the right direction, including Rhonda Bellamy of the Arts Council of Wilmington and New Hanover County, Beverly Smalls, Beverly Tetterton, Barbara Smith-Walker, and Deborah Maxwell. To Travis Souther of the New Hanover County Library, my thanks for guiding me through the library's remarkable collection of sources, photographic and otherwise.

Naturally, this book could never have made it to paper without the support and guidance of its publisher, Ray McAllister of Beach Glass Books. Ray is not only a writer of prodigious talent, but a master organizer as well. As he did with my first book, Ray guided me through all the motions of preparing and editing the manuscript. He has been a friend and unfailing resource for all of his authors—even through the past year while every business in America has struggled with the chaos of Covid-19—and for that he has my eternal thanks. And I cannot forget Karen Owen, the lead editor on this project. She took my too-long narrative, trimming the redundant and the irrelevant, smoothing the rough spots, and forwarding a manuscript that best tells the story that needed to be told. I am grateful beyond words. Proofreader Vicki McAllister caught many slipups—after we thought we had caught all the slipups.

Finally, I must thank my family. My parents, Charles and Martha, aunt Pamolu, brother Eric, and nephew Hemingway. I love you all, and I love our time together, especially the days on the Brunswick County shore. I'm glad I was raised by the people that I was, and in the places that I was. Maybe this book goes a little of the way in showing it.

NOTES

INTRODUCTION

1   Philip Gerard, *Down the Wild Cape Fear: A River Journey through the Heart of North Carolina* (Chapel Hill, N.C.: University of North Carolina Press, 2013), pp. 27-31.

2   James Sprunt, *Chronicles of the Cape Fear River, 1660–1916* (Raleigh, N.C.: Edwards & Broughton Printing Co., 1916), pp. 6-7.

3   David S. Cecelski and Timothy B. Tyson, eds., *Democracy Betrayed: The Wilmington Race Riot of 1898 and Its Legacy* (Chapel Hill, N.C.: University of North Carolina Press, 1998), p. 4.

CHAPTER ONE

1   Weronika Laszkiewicz, "Jack London: A Writing Sailor, a Sailing Writer," *Crossroads: A Journal of English Studies*, vol. 6, March 2014, pp. 16-27

2   Ibid.

3   www.penobscotmarinemuseum.org

4   Don Carten, "Schooner Trash," www.patch.com, August 6, 2011.

5   Ibid.

6   Testimony of John W. Taylor, transcripts, Scott trial and Adams/Sawyer trial.

7   "Launching at Milbridge," *Bangor Daily Whig and Courier*, p. 3, October 24, 1895; http://shipbuildinghistory.com; www.milbridge-historicalsociety.org.

8   "Launching at Milbridge," *Bangor Daily Whig and Courier*, p. 3,

October 24, 1895.

9   Testimony of John W. Taylor; "*Berwind* Is In Port," *Wilmington Morning Star*, p. 1, October 17, 1905.

10   Testimony of Theodore Simmons, transcript, Scott trial; "*Berwind* Is In Port," *Wilmington Morning Star*, p. 1, October 17, 1905; "Story of Bloodshed," *Wilmington Morning Star*, p. 1, October 13, 1905; "Washed Down in Blood: Murder on the Schooner *Harry A. Berwind*," *The North Carolina Historical Review*, by Vann Newkirk.

CHAPTER TWO

1   Testimony of Theodore Simmons, transcripts, Adams/Sawyer trial and Scott trial.

2   Testimony of John W. Taylor, transcripts, Adams/Sawyer trial and Scott trial.

3   "Story of Bloodshed," *Wilmington Morning Star*, p. 1, October 13, 1905.

4   Testimony of John W. Taylor and Theodore Simmons, transcripts, Scott trial.

5   Official Log-Book, Mercantile Marine of the United States, *Schr. Harry A. Berwind*.

6   "Story of Bloodshed," *Wilmington Morning Star*, p. 1, October 13, 1905.

7   "Mutiny on the *Harry A. Berwind*," *The Bar Harbor Times*, p. C1, October 12, 1989.

8   Ibid.

9   Testimony of Robert Sawyer, transcript, Adams/Sawyer trial.

10   Mail records, Atlanta Federal Penitentiary.

11   Testimony of Robert Sawyer.

12   Robert Sawyer, Declaration of Intention, US Naturalization Service, filed February 15, 1918; *Early Days of the Georgia Tidewater*, Sullivan, 1990.

13   Testimony of Arthur Adams, transcript, Adams/Sawyer trial.

14   Mail records, Atlanta Federal Penitentiary.

15   Virginia Heyer Young, *Becoming West Indian; Culture, Self, and Nation in St. Vincent (Washington, D.C.: Smithsonian Institution Press, 1993)*, pp. 60-61.

16   Testimony of Henry Scott, Scott trial.

CHAPTER THREE

1   Lawrence Lee, *The History of Brunswick County North Carolina*, (Charlotte, N.C.: Heritage Press, 1980), pp. 179-80.

2   Larry Maisel, *Before We Were Quaint: The Southport Few Remember . . . and Others Can't Imagine* (Southport, N.C.: Southport Historical Society/Years of Yore Books, LLC, 2009), p. 104.

3   "Smith Cemetery Research Reveals More Than 750 Unmarked Graves," *The State Port Pilot* online, Southport, December 6, 2017.

4   Sharon Claudette Smith and Sherry Monahan, *Southport: Images of America*, (Charleston, S.C., Arcadia Publishing, 2012), pp. 26-27.

5   Letter to Harry Skinner from U.S. Commissioner, October 13, 1905.

6   "Murder and Lynching," *Wilmington Morning Star*, p. 1, November 28, 1897; "A Negro Burned to Death, *Greensboro Telegram*, p. 1, November 29, 1897; "A Human Holocaust," *News and Observer*, Raleigh, p. 1. November 28, 1897.

7   Gerard, *Down the Wild Cape Fear*, pp. 167-70; www.waywelivednc.com/before-1770/plantations.

8   Ibid. at pp. 170-74; Fred R. David and Vern J. Bender, *The History of Ocean Isle Beach*, (Virginia Beach, Va.: The Donning Co. Publishers, 2009), pp. 24-25.

9   David and Bender, *The History of Ocean Isle Beach*, pp. 50-51.

10   David Zucchino, *Wilmington's Lie: The Murderous Coup of 1898 and the Rise of White Supremacy*, (New York: Atlantic Monthly Press, 2020), p. 67; Lee A. Craig, *Josephus Daniels: His Life and Times*, (Chapel Hill, N.C., University of North Carolina Press, 2013) pp. 149-50.

11   Christensen, *The Paradox of Tar Heel Politics*, pp. 10-11.

12   Ibid at pp. 11, 14; Zucchino, *Wilmington's Lie*, pp. 81, 92.

13   Craig, *Josephus Daniels*, p. 13.

14   Ibid at pp. 181-82.

15   Zucchino, *Wilmington's Lie*, p. 76.

16   Rob Christensen, *The Paradox of Tar Heel Politics: The Personalities, Elections, and Events That Shaped Modern North Carolina* (Chapel Hill, N.C., University of North Carolina Press, 2008), pp. 14-15.

17   Ibid at p. 19, citing Josephus Daniels, *Editor in Politics*, (Chapel Hill, N.C.: University of North Carolina Press, 1941), p. 293.

18   Ibid at p. 7.

19   Ibid at pp. 17-18.

20   Gerard, *Down the Wild Cape Fear*, pp. 132-133; Zucchino, *Wilmington's Lie*, pp. 48-49.

21   "How Many African-Americans Were Lynched in North Carolina? Curious NC Reveals Our Brutal Past," *News and Observer* online, January 29, 2019.

22   "Willis Not Burned Alive," *Charlotte Observer*, p. 8, November 30, 1897; "Nathan Willis Hanged," *The Lancaster* (S.C.) *News*, p. 1, April 6, 1898.

CHAPTER FOUR

1   "*Berwind* Is In Port," *Wilmington Morning Star*, October 17, 1905, p. 1.

2   *U.S. v. Klintock*, 18 U.S. 144, 5 L.Ed. 55, 5 Wheat. 144 (1820).

3   US Register of Historic Places, Inventory-Nomination form for Southport Historic District, 1979.

4   "Tale of Bloodshed: A Complete Story of the Mutiny and Murder on Schooner *Harry A. Berwind*," *The Southport Herald*, October 18, 1905, p. 1.

5   Ibid.

6   Ibid.; "*Berwind* Is In Port," *Wilmington Morning Star*, October 17, 1905, p. 1.

7   "Tale of Bloodshed: A Complete Story of the Mutiny and Murder on Schooner *Harry A. Berwind*," *The Southport Herald*, October 18, 1905, p. 1.

8   "*Berwind* Is In Port," *Wilmington Morning Star*, October 17, 1905, p. 1.

9   "Tale of Bloodshed: A Complete Story of the Mutiny and Murder on Schooner *Harry A. Berwind*," *The Southport Herald*, October 18, 1905, p. 1.

10   Ibid.

11   All accounts of testimony given by Adams, Sawyer, and Scott at the Commissioners' hearing in Southport come from the following

newspaper sources: "Tale of Bloodshed: A Complete Story of the Mutiny and Murder on Schooner *Harry A. Berwind*," *The Southport Herald*, October 18, 1905, p. 1.; "*Berwind* Is In Port," *Wilmington Morning Star*, October 17, 1905, p. 1.; "Story of Bloodshed," *Wilmington Morning Star*, October 13, 1905, p. 1.

12   "Tale of Bloodshed: A Complete Story of the Mutiny and Murder on Schooner *Harry A. Berwind*," *The Southport Herald*, October 18, 1905, p. 1.

13   Ibid.

14   Newkirk, "Washed Down in Blood," citing "Scott Confesses: Admits Having Helped To Kill All But Captain," *Wilmington Messenger*, October 20, 1905, p. 1.

CHAPTER FIVE

1   Sprunt, *Chronicles of the Cape Fear*, p. 535.

2   "Washed Down in Blood," *The North Carolina Historical Review*, Newkirk, citing "The Day of Doom for the Condemned Mutineers Is Not Far Off," *Wilmington Messenger*, June 10, 1906.

3   Christensen, *The Paradox of Tar Heel Politics*, pp. 8-9, 23.

4   Zucchino, *Wilmington's Lie*, p. 54.

5   Ibid. at p. xix.

6   Ibid. at pp. xvii, 55-59.

7   Christensen, *The Paradox of Tar Heel Politics*, pp. 23-24.

8   Zucchino, *Wilmington's Lie*, p. xvii.

9   Ibid. at p. 336.

10   Ibid. at p. 96; H. Leon Prather Sr., "We Have Taken a City: A Centennial Essay," from *Democracy Betrayed*, pp. 22-23.

11   Ibid. at pp. 97-98, citing George Rountree, "Memorandum of My Personal Recollection of the Election of 1898" (Chapel Hill, N.C.: Henry G. Connor Papers, University of North Carolina), p. 2.

12   Ibid. at pp. 103, 169.

13   Ibid. at p. 104.

14   Ibid. at p. 105.

15   Ibid at pp. 118-120; Prather, *We Have Taken a City*, p. 91.

16   Glenda Gilmore, "Murder, Memory, and the Flight of the Incu-

bus," from *Democracy Betrayed*, p. 79.

17   Christensen, *The Paradox of Tar Heel Politics*, p. 20.

18   Prather, "We Have Taken a City," from *Democracy Betrayed*, pp. 26-27; Zucchino, *Wilmington's Lie*, pp. 140-48.

19   Zucchino, *Wilmington's Lie*, p, 148, citing *Washington Post* article reprinted in *Wilmington Semi-Weekly Messenger*, November 4, 1898.

20   Ibid. at p. 161.

21   Ibid. at p. 163.

22   Ibid. at pp. 167-68.

23   Christensen, *The Paradox of Tar Heel Politics*, p. 23; Prather, "We Have Taken a City," from *Democracy Betrayed*, pp. 28-29.

24   Prather, "We Have Taken a City," from *Democracy Betrayed*, pp. 29-30; Zucchino, *Wilmington's Lie*, pp. 175-78.

25   Zucchino, *Wilmington's Lie*, pp. 165-66.

26   Ibid. at pp. 179-85; Prather, "We Have Taken a City," from *Democracy Betrayed*, pp. 30-31.

27   Ibid. at pp. 189-94, 31-32.

28   Ibid. at pp. 195-98.

29   Gerard, *Down the Wild Cape Fear*, pp. 139-41.

30   Prather, "We Have Taken a City," from *Democracy Betrayed*, pp. 31-34.

31   Zucchino, *Wilmington's Lie*, p. 209.

32   Ibid. at p. 228.

33   Prather, "We Have Taken a City," from *Democracy Betrayed*, p. 35.

34   Zucchino, *Wilmington's Lie*, pp. 216-17, 254-55.

35   Ibid. at pp. 330-31.

CHAPTER SIX

1   John Haley, "Race, Rhetoric, and Revolution," from *Democracy Betrayed*, pp. 212-13, 216.

2   Zucchino, *Wilmington's Lie*, pp. 282-83.

3   Christensen, *The Paradox of Tar Heel Politics*, pp. 27-29.

4   Ibid at p. 30.

5   Ibid at p. 39.

6   Regular Venire for the Fall Term of the United States Courts, Petit Juries, Nos. 1 and 2.

7   Gerard, *Down the Wild Cape Fear*, p. 136.

8   Benjamin R. Justesen, "Black Tip, White Iceberg" (*The North Carolina Historical Review*, April 2005), pp. 222-23.

9   "The Latest Act in the A&NCRR Receivership Matter," *News and Observer*, May 29, 1904, p. 12; "Josephus Daniels In Contempt, Judge Purnell So Decrees It," The Charlotte News, May 30, 1904, p. 1.

10   James M. Beeby, *Revolt of the Tar Heels: The North Carolina Populist Movement, 1890-1901* (Jackson, Miss.: University Press of Mississippi, 2008) pp. 166-71.

11   LaRae Sikes Umfleet, *A Day of Blood: The 1898 Race Riot* (Raleigh, N.C.: N.C. Office of Archives and History, 200), pp. 102-03.

12   "E. Peschau," *Wilmington Semi-Weekly Messenger*, June 3, 1904, p. 5.

13   North Carolina Journal of Law, Vol. 1, 1904, University of North Carolina Department of Law.

CHAPTER SEVEN

1   Philip Dray, *At the Hands of Persons Unknown: The lynching of Black America* (New York: Random House: 2002), pp. 14-15.

2   "Two Sent To Jail For Disturbing Booker Washington's Meeting," The Broad Ax newspaper, Chicago, October 24, 1903, p. 1.

3   Kerri K. Greenidge, *Black Radical: The Life and Times of William Monroe Trotter* (New York: Liveright Publishing Corp., 2020), pp. 78-88; "Munroe Rogers," The Colored American Magazine, Vol. 6, No. 1, November 1902, pp. 20-25.

4   "Death First: That Before Return to North Carolina," *Boston Globe*, August 7, 1902, p. 5; "Rogers Case: Hearing Before Attorney General Parker," Boston Globe, August 21, 1902, p. 7.

5   Ibid; "The Case of Monroe Rogers," *Wilmington Messenger*, August 30, 1902, p. 2

6   "Ten Years For Monroe Rogers," *The Morning Post*, Raleigh, December 4, 1902, p. 7.

7   Christensen, *The Paradox of Tar Heel Politics*, pp. 43-44.

8   Greenidge, Black Radical, pp. 78-88, citing *Boston Guardian*, September 6, 1902, pp. 1-2.

9   110 U.S. 516 (1884).

10   *Jamison v. Wimbish*, 130 Fed. 351 (1904), reversed as *Wimbish v. Jamison*, 199 U.S. 599 (1905).

11   Brent J. AuCoin, Thomas Goode Jones: *Race, Politics, and Justice in the New South* (Tuscaloosa, Ala.: University of Alabama Press, 2016), pp. 143-44; *U.S. v. Hodges*, 203 U.S. 1 (1906).

12   David S. Cecelski, *A Historian's Coast: Adventures Into the Tidewater Past* (Winston-Salem, N.C.: John F. Blair, Publisher, 2000), p. 154-55.

13   "Murdered: Senator Simmons's Father Shot To Death By a Negro," *Wilmington Semi-Weekly Messenger*, September 18, 1903, p. 2; "F.M. Simmons's Father Killed," *Charlotte Observer*, September 14, 1903, p. 1; "Foul Murder of Mr. F.G. Simmons," The North Carolinian (Raleigh), September 17, 1903, p. 1;

14   Ibid.

15   "The Murderer of Simmons," *Wilmington Semi-Weekly Messenger*, November 6, 1903, p. 7; "Taken to Trenton," The Morning Post (Raleigh), November 3, 1903, p. 1

16   "Trial of Alfred Daniels," The Daily Free Press (Kinston, N.C.), November 5, 1903, p. 1; "Daniels Trial at Trenton," New Berne Weekly Journal, November 6, 1903, p. 4; "Found Guilty at Trenton," New Berne Daily Journal, November 8, 1903, p. 4.

17   Ibid.

18   *Patapsco Guano Co. v. Board of Agriculture of N.C.*, 171 U.S. 345 (1898).

19   "Appeal of Slayer of Simmons's Father," The Morning Post (Raleigh), February 26, 1904, p. 5.

20   "Condemned Murderer Appeals to U.S. Court," The Morning Post (Raleigh), March 17, 1904, p. 6.

21   "Writ of Error Denied," The Farmer & Mechanic (Raleigh), April 26, 1904, p. 8.

22   "Under the Black Cap Two Meet Death," The Farmer & Mechanic (Raleigh), May 24, 1904, p. 3.

CHAPTER EIGHT

1   Vann R. Newkirk Sr., "Washed Down in Blood: Murder on the
Schooner *Harry A. Berwind*," (*The North Carolina Historical Review*,
January 2014), p. 6; Lewis Philip Hall, *Land of the Golden River: His-
torical Events and Stories of Southeastern North Carolina and the Lower
Cape Fear*, (Wilmington, N.C.: Hall's Enterprises, 1980) pp. 168-71.

2   "Two of the Berwind Mutineers Placed on Trial For Their
Lives," *Wilmington Semi-Weekly Messenger*, November 7, 1905, p. 8.

3   "Trial of Mutineers," *Wilmington Morning Star*, November 2,
1905, p. 1.

4   Ibid.

5   Ibid.

6   Ibid.; "Two of the Berwind Mutineers Placed on Trial For
Their Lives," *Wilmington Semi-Weekly Messenger*, November 7, 1905, p.
8.

7   Trial Transcript, *U.S. v. Robert Sawyer and Arthur Adams*.

8   Ibid.; "Two of the Berwind Mutineers Placed on Trial For
Their Lives," *Wilmington Semi-Weekly Messenger*, November 7, 1905, p.
8.

9   "Scott Confesses," *Wilmington Messenger*, October 17, 1905, p.
8.

10   Newkirk, "Washed Down in Blood," citing *International Encyclopedia of Comparative Law*, vol. 12, by Konrad Zweigert and Ulrich
Drobnig (New York: Oceana, 1973-), 95.

11   All accounts of testimony by Taylor and Simmons come from:
Trial Transcript, *U.S. v. Robert Sawyer and Arthur Adams*, and "Two of
the Berwind Mutineers Placed on Trial For Their Lives," *Wilmington
Semi-Weekly Messenger*, November 7, 1905, p. 8.

12   To anyone who knew Mobile's harbor district, those street
names would have sounded familiar. The area was well populated with
merchant businesses. Mobile, like many Southern port cities, also had
a well-established Jewish community. The city elected a Jewish mayor,
Lazarus Schwarz, in 1911.

13   All accounts of testimony by Scott come from: Trial Transcript,
U.S. v. Robert Sawyer and Arthur Adams, and "Two of the Berwind
Mutineers Placed on Trial For Their Lives," *Wilmington Semi-Weekly
Messenger*, November 7, 1905, p. 8.

14   "Two of the Berwind Mutineers Placed on Trial For Their Lives," *Wilmington Semi-Weekly Messenger*, November 7, 1905, p. 8.

15   "The Mutiny Horror," *Wilmington Morning Star*, November 5, 1905, p. 1.

16   "Two of the Berwind Mutineers Placed on Trial For Their Lives," *Wilmington Semi-Weekly Messenger*, November 7, 1905, p. 8.

CHAPTER NINE

1   "Prisoners Testify," *Wilmington Morning Star*, November 7, 1905, p. 1.

2   All accounts of trial testimony set forth above come from: Trial Transcript, *U.S. v. Robert Sawyer and Arthur Adams*.

3   Ibid.; Newkirk, "Washed Down In Blood."

4   "'Guilty,' Says Jury," *Wilmington Morning Star*, November 8, 1905, p. 1; "'Guilty,' Says Jury," *Wilmington Semi-Weekly Messenger*, November 10, 1905, p. 8.

5   "Stick to Story," *The North Carolinian*, "Special to *The News and Observer*," November 9, 1905, p. 1.

6   "Doubt as to Guilt," *Wilmington Semi-Weekly Messenger*, November 10, 1905, p. 7.

7   Zucchino, *Wilmington's Lie*, pp. 265-66.

8   Trial Transcript, *U.S. v. Robert Sawyer and Arthur Adams*.

9   " 'Guilty,' Says Jury," *Wilmington Morning Star*, November 8, 1905, p. 1; "'Guilty,' Says Jury," *Wilmington Semi-Weekly Messenger*, November 10, 1905, p. 8.

10   Trial Transcript, *U.S. v. Robert Sawyer and Arthur Adams*.

CHAPTER TEN

1   " 'Guilty' Says Jury," *Wilmington Morning Star*, November 8, 1905, p. 1.

2   Testimonies of Stetson, Taylor, Simmons, and Dosher, Trial Transcript, *U.S. v. Henry Scott*, ; "Scott on Trial," *Wilmington Semi-Weekly Messenger*, November 10, 1905, p. 8.

3   "Scott on Trial," *Wilmington Semi-Weekly Messenger*, November 10, 1905, p. 8; "Jury Can't Agree," *Wilmington Messenger*, November 10, 1905, p. 8.

4   Testimony of Sawyer, Trial Transcript, *U.S. v. Henry Scott*, .

5   Testimony of Scott, Trial Transcript, *U.S. v. Henry Scott*; Newkirk, "Washed Down in Blood."

6   "Jury Can't Agree," *Wilmington Messenger*, November 10, 1905, p. 8; "Henry Scott To Die," *Wilmington Morning Star*, November 12, 1905, p. 1.

7   Ibid.

8   Ibid.

9   William J. Bellamy, letter to Reverend E.R. Bennett, July 5, 1906.

10   "Berwind Mutineers to Hang January 2, 1906," *The Inter Ocean* (Chicago), December 10, 1905, p. 29; "Mutineers Will Hang, *Boston Daily Globe*, November 26, 1905, p. 46.

11   "Henry Scott To Die," *Wilmington Morning Star*, November 12, 1905, p. 1.

12   Bland Simpson, *Ghost Ship of Diamond Shoals: The Mystery of the* Carroll A. Deering (Chapel Hill, N.C.: University of North Carolina Press, 2002), p. 14.

13   "Jury Can't Agree," *Wilmington Messenger*, November 10, 1905, p. 8.

CHAPTER ELEVEN

1   *Sawyer v. U.S.*, 202 U.S. 150 (1906).

2   Newkirk, "Washed Down In Blood."

3   "Rufe Martin Hanged," *Houston Post*, July 13, 1906, p. 5; "Martin Dies on the Scaffold," *Fort Worth Star-Telegram*, July 12, 1906, p. 1.

4   *Martin v. Texas*, 200 U.S. 316 (1906).

5   "Martin Dies on the Scaffold," *Fort Worth Star-Telegram*, July 12, 1906, p. 1.

6   "Chattanooga Versus the Supreme Court," by Meredith Hindley, *Humanities*, November/December 2014, Vol. 35, No. 6.

7   *Contempt of Court*, Curriden and Phillips, pp. 213-14.

8   *Sawyer v. U.S.*, 202 U.S. 150 (1906).

9   "To Hang In August," *Wilmington Morning Star*, June 20, 1906, pp. 1 & 4.

10   Ibid.

CHAPTER TWELVE

1   Letters received, New Hanover County Jail, June 23, 1906.

2   Michelle Brattain, *The Politics of Whiteness: Race, Workers, and Culture in the Modern South*, (Princeton, N.J.: Princeton University Press, 2001), pp. 33-36.

3   Russell Korobkin, "The Politics of Disfranchisement," *The Georgia Historical Quarterly*, Vol. LXXIV, No. 1, Spring 1990, pp. 20-58.

4   Zucchino, *Wilmington's Lie*, pp. 329-30, citing John Dittmer, *Black Georgia in the Progressive Era, 1900-1920*, (Urbana: Ill: University of Illinois Press, 1977), p. 100.

5   U.S. Attorney Harry Skinner, letter to Clerk of Court Samuel P. Collier, June 28, 1906.

6   Newkirk, "Washed Down In Blood."

7   William M. Reaves, *Strength Through Struggle: The Chronological and Historical Record of the African-American Community in Wilmington, North Carolina, 1865-1950* (Wilmington, N.C.: New Hanover County Public Library, 1998). pp. 127-33.

8   G.W. Bornemann, affidavit attached to Adams and Sawyer Motion for New Trial, October 26, 1906.

9   Henry Scott written statement, June 30, 1906.

CHAPTER THIRTEEN

1   "Scott Dies Today," *Wilmington Messenger*, July 7, 1906, p. 4.

2   William J. Bellamy, letter to Claudius Dockery, July 5, 1906.

3   William J. Bellamy, letter to Rev. E.R. Bennett, July 5, 1906.

4   Newkirk, "Washed Down In Blood." .

5   All accounts of Scott's execution come from Scott's written and notarized statement, dated July 3, 1906; and "Henry Scott, With Life, Pays Penalty For Crime, *Wilmington Messenger*, July 7, 1906, pp. 1, 4, 5.

6   "To Hang In August," *Wilmington Morning Star*, June 20, 1906, pp. 1 & 4.

7   "Henry Scott, With Life, Pays Penalty For Crime, *Wilmington Messenger*, July 7, 1906, pp. 1, 4, 5.

8 "The Mutiny Case," *Wilmington Messenger*, July 8, 1906, p. 1.

9 Zucchino, *Wilmington's Lie*, p. 129.

CHAPTER FOURTEEN

1 James Bradley, *The Imperial Cruise: A Secret History of Empire and War* (New York: Little, Brown, and Company, 2009), pp. 39-40.

2 Id. at pp. 332-22, citing Carleton Putnam, *Race and Reason: A Yankee View*, (Washington, D.C.: Public Affairs Press, 1961).

3 "Teddy Roosevelt Tours Old Dixie," *The Washington Times*, February 17, 2006.

4 Robert J. Norrell, "When Teddy Roosevelt Invited Booker T. Washington to Dine at the White House," *The Journal of Blacks in Higher Education*, Spring 2009, p. 63.

5 Frank N. Schubert, "The 25.th Infantry at Brownsville, Texas: Buffalo Soldiers, the 'Brownsville Six,' and the Medal of Honor," *Journal of Military History*, October 2011, pp. 1217.

6 Petition for Executive Clemency, dated July 7, 1906.

7 "A Guide to Wilmington's African-American Heritage," published by City of Wilmington, 2013.

8 Zucchino, *Wilmington's Lie*, p. 223.

9 John Haley, "Race, Rhetoric, and Revolution," from *Democracy Betrayed*, p. 208.

10 Zucchino, *Wilmington's Lie*, pp. 232-33.

11 Id. at pp. 209-10, 249-50.

12 "Interviewed the Mutineers," *Wilmington Messenger*, September 26, 1906, p. 5.

13 Deposition of Arthur Adams, dated September 25, 1906.

14 "Adams and Sawyer Must Hang," *Wilmington Messenger*, October 17, 1906, p. 2; "Sawyer and Adams Must Hang Nov. 1," *Wilmington Morning Star*, October 16, 1906, p. 1.

15 Newkirk, "Washed Down In Blood." .

16 Ibid. Incidentally, Dr. Newkirk stated in his journal article that Revs. Carmichael and Barber (Parker, as named in the article) were African-American ministers, when in fact they were white. Newspaper coverage from the time identifies them clearly.

17 "Dr. James Carmichael Dead," *Wilmington Morning Star*, No-

vember 26, 1911, p. 5.

18   "Funeral Today," *Wilmington Dispatch*, November 27, 1911, p. 5.

19   "The Cause of the Negro Mutineers," *The North Carolinian* (Raleigh, N.C.), December 12, 1906, p. 11.

20   "In Prison for Life," *Wilmington Messenger*, December 6, 1906, p. 1; "They Will Not Hang," *Wilmington Morning Star*, December 6, 1906, p. 1.

CHAPTER FIFTEEN

1   "Convicts Get New Trial," *The Washington* (D.C.) *Herald*, December 11, 1906, p. 8.

2   "To Atlanta Prison," *Wilmington Morning Star*, December 22, 1906, p. 1.

3   Motion for New Trial, dated October 26, 1906.

4   "The Big House," History Channel documentary series, 1998. One episode focuses specifically on Atlanta Penitentiary.

5   Gary Scharnhorst, *Julian Hawthorne: The Life of a Prodigal Son* (Urbana, Ill: University of Illinois Press, 2014), pp. 1-7.

6   Physician's Office Sick Call Records, Federal Penitentiary, Atlanta.

7   Newkirk, "Washed Down in Blood," citing letters to William Moyer by Spaulding (dated May 31, 1907) and Knight (dated April 13, 1908).

8   Reaves, *Strength Through Struggle*, pp. 426-27.

9   Robert Sawyer, letter to King Edward VII, dated June 7, 1908.

10   "Let's Talk It Over," *The National Magazine*, Vol. XXXVIII, No. 38, Apr.-Sept. 1913, pp. 1113-18.

11   Ibid.

12   "Prison Reform: Helping the World's Unfortunates, An Interview with H.B. Warner," *The National Magazine*, Vol. XXXIX, No. 39, Oct. 1913-March 1914, pp. 19-21.

13   Arthur Adams, letter to H.B. Warner, April 27, 1910.

CHAPTER SIXTEEN

1   "Joseph S. Buhler," obituary, *New York Daily News*, May 19,

1961, p. 87.

2   Letters exchanged between Joseph S. Buhler and William Moyer, May 2, 1910 and May 5, 1910.

3   "Letter Received," *Wilmington Dispatch*, May 20, 1910, p. 5.

4   *Charlotte News*, May 16, 1910, p. 3.

5   Ibid.; Newkirk, "Washed Down With Blood" ; "Re-Open Adams-Sawyer Case," *Wilmington Morning Star*, June 25, 1910, p. 5; "Case of Adams and Sawyer, " *Wilmington Morning Star*, June 17, 1910, p. 5.

6   "Have Shadow of a Chance," *Wilmington Morning Star*, May 22, 1910, p. 5.

7   James Finch, letter to Warden Moyer, June 19, 1911.

8   Adams and Sawyer, letter to James Finch, date uncertain.

9   David S. Stetson, letter to James Finch, July 10, 1911.

10   "Mutineers Attach Ship," *Wilmington Morning Star*, October 27, 1905, p. 1; www.measuringworth.com.

11   Ibid.; Newkirk, "Washed Down in Blood," citing "A Strange Coincidence," *Wilmington Messenger*, March 30, 1906.

12   Ibid.; Warden William Moyer, letter to James Finch, July 17, 1911.

13   "Adams and Sawyer," *Wilmington Dispatch*, August 15, 1911, p. 5; "May Get Pardon," *Wilmington Morning Star*, August 16, 1911, p. 4.

CHAPTER SEVENTEEN

1   Bradley, *The Imperial Cruise*, p. 115.

2   "Want Negro's Resignation," *The Evening Telegram* (Lakeland, FL), September 13, 1911.

3   P.S. Ruckman Jr., "Executive Clemency In the United States: Origins, Development and Analysis (1900-1993)," *Presidential Studies Quarterly*, Spring 1997.

4   Inmate Mail Records, Adams and Sawyer prison file, Atlanta Federal Penitentiary.

5   Sprunt, *Chronicles of the Cape Fear River*, pp. 558-59.

6   Gerard, *Down the Wild Cape Fear*, pp. 138-39.

7   Hall, *Land of the Golden River*, vol. 2, pp. 273-75.

8   H.A.L. Fisher, *James Bryce (Viscount Bryce of Dechmont, O.M.)*,

(New York: The MacMillan Company, 1927), vol. 1, p. 224.

9   Id. at pp. 235-36.

10   Id., vol. 2, pp. 296-97.

11   Sprunt, *Chronicles of the Cape Fear River*, pp. 514-17.

12   James Bryce and William Howard Taft, "Washington, the Nation's Capital," *National Geographic Society*, March 1915.

13   "Sailors Convicted of Murder at Sea Freed By Actor," *New York Times*, March 3, 1912, p. 44.

14   Ibid.; Newkirk, "Washed Down In Blood." .

15   "Pardons Negro Sailors," *Semi-Weekly Spokesman Review* (Spokane, Wash.), January 3, 1912; "An Actor Rescues Innocent Prisoners," *The Vancouver* (B.C.) *Daily World*, March 29, 1912, p. 32; "British Negroes Pardoned By Taft," *The Decatur* (Ill.) *Herald*, January 3, 1912, p. 1; "British Negroes Pardoned," *The Gazette* (Montreal), January 3, 1912, p. 4.

16   "Why Taft Saved Two Men From Prison," *Brooklyn Daily Eagle*, February 4, 1912, p. 55; "Two Pardoned By Taft," *The Washington Post*, January 3, 1912, p. 4.

CHAPTER EIGHTEEN

1   "Murder on the High Seas: The Tragedy of the *S.S. Berwind*," Murrell, *True Detective Mysteries*, April 1935.

2   Candice Millard, *Destiny of the Republic: A Tale of Madness, Medicine, and the Murder of a President* (New York: First Anchor Books, 2011), pp. 273-74.

3   Dick Lehr and Mitchell Zuckoff, *Judgment Ridge: The True Story Behind the Dartmouth Murders* (New York: Harper Collins, 2003), pp. 334-36, citing Robert D. Hare, *Without Conscience: The Disturbing World of Psychopaths Among Us* (New York: The Guilford Press, 1993).

CHAPTER NINETEEN

1   Joseph Buhler, letter to Adams and Sawyer (through Warden Moyer), August 10, 1911.

2   "Sailors Convicted of Murder at Sea Freed By Actor," *New York Times*, March 3, 1912, p. 44.

3   "Express Their Thanks," *Wilmington Morning Star*, January 9,

1912, p. 5.

4   Declaration of Intention, US Department of Labor, Naturalization Service, executed February 15, 1918.

5   "A Brief History of Bequia," Bequia Tourism Association, www.bequiatourism.com.

6   Gail Reiber, interview by Tim Garrity, Mount Desert Island Historical Society, June 10, 2019.

7   "Hard Luck Boat Found Grave on Isle of Pines," The Philadelphia Inquirer, October 3, 1906, p. 1.

8   http://bermuda100.ucsd.edu/blanche-king/

9   Beeby, *Revolt of the Tar Heels*, pp. 175-76.

10   Timothy B. Tyson, "Wars for Democracy: African-American Militancy and Interracial Violence in North Carolina During World War II," from *Democracy Betrayed*, pp. 253-54.

11   Zucchino, *Wilmington's Lie*, pp. 337, 340.

12   Ibid at pp. 340-42.

13   Ibid at pp. 338-39; "Coastline: George Rountree III on Confederate Family History, Healing Old Wounds," WHQR Public Radio, November 17, 2017.

14   "George Rountree III, Lifetime Achievement Award for 2016," *Wilmington StarNews* Online, June 7, 2016.

15   For an excellent synopsis of the case, see Kenneth R. Janken, "Remembering the Wilmington Ten: African-American Politics and Judicial Misconduct in the 1970s," *The North Carolina Historical Review*, Vol. 92, No. 1 (January 2015), pp. 1-48.

CHAPTER TWENTY

1   Gary Deane, "Andrew and Virginia Stone: Noir To the Bone," *Bright Lights Film Journal*, August 10, 2018.

2   Fred Blosser, "Reviews: Two James Mason Titles From the Warner Archive: *The Decks Ran Red* (1958) and *The Sea Gull* (1968), www.cinemaretro.com

3   Bosley Crowther, "Loew's State Offers *The Decks Ran Red*; Film About Mutiny on a Freighter Arrives; Broderick Crawford, James Mason In Cast," *New York Times*, October 11, 1958.

BIBLIOGRAPHY

BOOKS

AuCoin, Brent J. *Thomas Goode Jones: Race, Politics, and Justice in the New South*. Tuscaloosa, Ala.: University of Alabama Press, 2016.

Beeby, James M. *Revolt of the Tar Heels: The North Carolina Populist Movement, 1890-1901*. Jackson, Miss.: University Press of Mississippi, 2008.

Bradley, James. *The Imperial Cruise: A Secret History of Empire and War*. New York: Little, Brown, and Company, 2009.

Brattain, Michelle. *The Politics of Whiteness: Race, Workers, and Culture in the Modern South*. Princeton, N.J.: Princeton University Press, 2001.

Butler, Lindley S. *Pirates, Privateers, and Rebel Raiders of the Carolina Coast*. Chapel Hill, N.C.: University of North Carolina Press, 2000.

Cecelski, David S. *A Historian's Coast: Adventures Into the Tidewater Past*. Winston-Salem, N.C.: John F. Blair Publishers, 2000.

Cecelski, David S. and Timothy B. Tyson, eds. *Democracy Betrayed: The Wilmington Race Riot of 1898 and Its Legacy*. Chapel Hill, N.C.: University of North Carolina Press, 1998.

Chaffin, Tom. *Sea of Gray: The Around-the-World Odyssey of the Confederate Raider* Shenandoah. New York: Hill and Wang, 2006.

Christensen, Rob. *The Paradox of Tar Heel Politics: The Personalities, Elections, and Events That Shaped Modern North Carolina*. Chapel Hill, N.C.: University of North Carolina Press, 2008.

Craig, Lee A. *Josephus Daniels: His Life and Times*. Chapel Hill, N.C.: University of North Carolina Press, 2013.

Curriden, Mark and Leroy Phillips. *Contempt of Court: The Turn of the Century Lynching That Launched a Hundred Years of Federalism*. New York: Faber and Faber, 1999.

Daniels, Josephus. *Editor in Politics*. Chapel Hill, N.C.: University of North Carolina Press, 1941.

David, Fred R. and Vern J. Bender. *The History of Ocean Isle Beach*. Virginia Beach, Va.: The Donning Co. Publishers, 2009.

Dittmer, John. *Black Georgia in the Progressive Era, 1900-1920*. Urbana, Ill.: University of Illonois Press, 1977.

Dray, Philip. *At the Hands of Persons Unknown: The Lynching of Black America*. New York: Random House, 2002.

Fisher, H.A.L. *James Bryce (Viscount Bryce of Dechmont, O.M.)*. New York: The MacMillan Company, 1927.

Gerard, Philip. *Down the Wild Cape Fear: A River Journey Through the Heart of North Carolina*. Chapel Hill, N.C.: University of North Carolina Press, 2013.

Greenidge, Kerri K. *Black Radical: The Life and Times of William Monroe Trotter*. New York: Liveright Publishing Corp., 2020.

Hall, Lewis Philip. *Land of the Golden River: Historical Events and Stories of Southeastern North Carolina and the Lower Cape Fear*. Wilmington, N.C.: Hall's Enterprises, 1980.

Harden, John. *The Devil's Tramping Ground and Other North Carolina Mystery Stories*. Chapel Hill, N.C.: University of North Carolina Press, 1949.

Hare, Robert D., Ph.D. *Without Conscience: The Disturbing World of the Psychopaths Among Us*. New York: The Guilford Press, 1993.

Hinkle, William G. and Gregory S. Taylor. *North Carolina State Prison*. Charleston, S.C.: Arcadia Publishing, 2016.

Lee, Lawrence. *The History of Brunswick County, North Carolina*. Charlotte, N.C.: Heritage Press, 1980.

Lehr, Dick and Mitchell Zuckoff. *Judgment Ridge: The True Story Behind the Dartmouth Murders*. New York: Harper Collins, 2003.

Maisel, Larry. *Before We Were Quaint: The Southport Few Remember . . . and Others Can't Imagine*. Southport, N.C.: Southport Historical Society, in association with Years of Yore Books, LLC, 2009.

Millard, Candice. *Destiny of the Republic: A Tale of Madness, Medicine, and the Murder of a President*. New York: First Anchor Books, 2011.

Putnam, Carleton. *Race and Reason: A Yankee View*. Washington, D.C.: Public Affairs Press, 1961.

Reaves, William M. *Strength Through Struggle: The Chronological and Historical Record of the African-American Community in Wilmington, North Carolina, 1865-1950*. Wilmington, N.C.: New Hanover County Public Library, 1998.

Scharnhorst, Gary. *Julian Hawthorne: Life of a Prodigal Son*. Urbana, Ill.: University of Illinois Press, 2014.

Schenck, Carl Alwin. *Cradle of Forestry in America: The Biltmore Forest School, 1898-1913*, ed. by Ovid Butler. Durham, N.C.: Forest History Society, 1955, 1983.

Simpson, Bland. *Ghost Ship of Diamond Shoals: The Mystery of the Carroll A. Deering*. Chapel Hill, N.C.: University of North Carolina Press, 2002.

Smith, Sharon Claudette and Sherry Monahan. *Southport*. Charleston, S.C.: Images of America, Arcadia Publishing, 2012.

Sprunt, James. *Chronicles of the Cape Fear River, 1660 – 1916*. Raleigh, N.C.: Edwards & Broughton Printing Co., 1916.

Sullivan, Buddy. *Early Days on the Georgia Tidewater: The Story of McIntosh County and Sapelo*. Darien, GA: McIntosh County Board, 1990.

Umfleet, LeRae Sikes. *A Day of Blood: The 1898 Wilmington Race Riot*. Raleigh, N.C.: North Carolina Office of Archives and History, 2009.

Young, Virginia Heyer. *Becoming West Indian: Culture, Self, and Nation in St. Vincent*. Washington, D.C.: Smithsonian Institution Press, 1993.

Zucchino, David. *Wilmington's Lie: The Murderous Coup of 1898 and the Rise of White Supremacy*. New York: Atlantic Monthly Press, 2020.

Zweigert, Konrad, and Ulrich Drobnig. *International Encyclopedia of International Law*, vol. 12. Dobbs Ferry, N.Y.: Oceana Publications, 1973.

ARTICLES

Bryce, James and William Howard Taft. "Washington, The Nation's Capital." *National Geographic Society*, March 1915.

Carten, Don. "Schooner Trash," www.patch.com, August 6, 2011.

Deane, Gary. "Andrew and Virginia Stone: Noir to the Bone." *Bright Lights Film Journal*, August 10, 2018.

Gilmore, Glenda. "Murder, Memory, and the Flight of the Incubus," from *Democracy Betrayed: The Wilmington Race Riot of 1898 and Its Legacy*, Cecelski and Tyson, eds. Chapel Hill, N.C.: University of North Carolina Press, 1998, pp. 73-93.

Haley, John. "Race, Rhetoric, and Revolution," from *Democracy Betrayed: The Wilmington Race Riot of 1898 and Its Legacy*, Cecelski and Tyson, eds. Chapel Hill, N.C.: University of North Carolina Press, 1998, pp. 207-224.

Hindley, Meredith. "Chattanooga Versus the Supreme Court." *Humanities*, vol. 35, no. 6, November/December 2014.

Howard, Philip. "Vera Cruz VII." *Ocracoke Island Journal* blog, January 25, 2018.

Janken, Kenneth R. "Remembering the Wilmington Ten: African-American Politics and Judicial Misconduct in the 1970s." *The North Carolina Historical Review*, vol. 92, no. 1, January 2015, pp. 1-48.

Justesen, Benjamin R. "Black Tip, White Iceberg." *The North Carolina Historical Review*, vol. 82, no. 2, April 2005, pp. 193-227.

Korobkin, Russell. "The Politics of Disfranchisement." *The Georgia Historical Quarterly*, vol. LXXIV, no. 1, Spring 1990, pp. 20-58.

Laszkiewicz, Weronika. "Jack London: A Writing Sailor, a Sailing Writer." *Crossroads. A Journal of English Studies*, vol. 6, March 2014, pp. 16-27.

"Let's Talk It Over." *The National Magazine*, vol. XXXVIII, no. 38, April-September 1913, pp. 1113-1118.

"Munroe Rogers," *The Colored American Magazine*, vol. 6, no. 1, November 1902, pp. 20-25.

Murrell, David. "Murder on the High Seas: The Tragedy of the *S.S. Berwind*." *True Detective Mysteries*, April 1935.

Newkirk, Vann R. Sr. "Washed Down in Blood: Murder on the Schooner *Harry A. Berwind*," *The North Carolina Historical Review*, vol. 91, no. 1, January 2014, pp. 1-29.

Norrell, Robert J. "When Teddy Roosevelt Invited Booker T. Washington to Dine at the White House." *The Journal of Blacks in Higher Education*, Spring 2009, p. 63.

Parkinson, David. "Black Noir: 10 Essential Black Performances in Film Noir and Neo-Noir," www.bfi.org.uk, August 2, 2017.

Prather, H. Leon Sr. "We Have Taken a City: A Centennial Essay," from *Democracy Betrayed: The Wilmington Race Riot of 1898 and Its Legacy*, Cecelski and Tyson, eds. Chapel Hill, N.C.: University of North Carolina Press, 1998, pp. 15-41.

"Prison Reform: Helping the World's Unfortunates, An Interview with H.B. Warner." *The National Magazine*, vol. XXXIX, no. 39, October 1913-March 1914, pp. 19-21.

Rountree, George. "Memorandum of My Personal Recollection of the Election of 1898". Henry G. Connor Papers, Southern Historical Collection, Wilson Library. Chapel Hill, N.C.: University of North Carolina.

Ruckman, P.S. Jr. "Executive Clemency in the United States: Origins, Development, and Analysis (1900-1993)." *Presidential Studies Quarterly*, vol. 27, no. 2, Spring 1997, pp. 251-71.

Schubert, Frank N. "The 25th Infantry at Brownsville, Texas: Buffalo Soldiers, the 'Brownsville Six,' and the Medal of Honor." *The Journal of Military History*, vol. 75, no. 4, October 2011, pp. 1217-1224.

Tyson, Timothy B. "Wars for Democracy: African-American Militancy and Interracial Violence in North Carolina During World War II," from *Democracy Betrayed: The Wilmington Race Riot of 1898 and Its Legacy*, Cecelski and Tyson, eds. Chapel Hill, N.C.: University of North Carolina Press, 1998, pp. 253-75.

NEWSPAPERS

The Bangor Daily Whig and Courier (Bangor, Maine)

The Bar Harbor Times (Bar Harbor, Maine)

The Boston Globe (Boston)

The Boston Guardian (Boston)

The Broad Ax (Chicago)

The Brooklyn Daily Eagle (Brooklyn, N.Y.)

The Charlotte News (Charlotte, N.C.)

The Charlotte Observer (Charlotte, N.C.)

The Daily Free Press (Kinston, N.C.)

The Decatur Herald (Decatur, Ill.)

The Evening Telegram (Lakeland, Fla.)

The Farmer and Mechanic (Raleigh, N.C.)

The Fort Worth Star-Telegram (Fort Worth, Tex.)

The Gazette (Montreal)

The Greensboro Patriot (Greensboro, N.C.)

The Greensboro Telegram (Greensboro, N.C.)

The Houston Post (Houston, Tex.)

The Inter Ocean (Chicago)

The Lancaster News (Lancaster, S.C.)

The Morning Post (Raleigh, N.C.)

The New Berne Daily Journal (New Bern, N.C.)

The New York Daily News (New York)

The New York Times (New York)

The News and Observer (Raleigh, N.C.)

The North Carolinian (Raleigh, N.C.)

The Philadelphia Inquirer (Philadelphia)

The Semi-Weekly Spokesman Review (Spokane, Wash.)

The Southport Herald (Southport, N.C.)

The State Port Pilot (Southport, N.C.)

The Vancouver Daily World (Vancouver, British Columbia)

The Washington Herald (Washington, D.C.)

The Washington Post (Washington, D.C.)

The Washington Times (Washington, D.C.)

The Wilmington Dispatch (Wilmington, N.C.)

The Wilmington Messenger (Wilmington, N.C.)

The Wilmington Morning Star (Wilmington, N.C.)

ARCHIVES AND LIBRARIES

All cited government documents pertaining to the trials of Henry Scott, Arthur Adams, and Robert Sawyer, including but not limited to the trial transcripts, court documents, exhibits, photos of the defendants, correspondence among the defendants and judicial officials are preserved and catalogued as follows: *United States v. Robert Sawyer and Arthur Adams*, Case no. 126, Criminal Cases, 1904-1910, Box 1, Record Group 21, Eastern District of North Carolina, U.S. District Court, Wilmington Division; *United States v. Henry Scott*, Case no. 127, Criminal Cases, 1904-1910, Box 1, Record Group 21, Eastern District of North Carolina, U.S. District Court, Wilmington Division.

All cited government documents pertaining to the imprisonment of Robert Sawyer and Arthur Adams at the Atlanta Federal Penitentiary, including correspondence involving the prisoners, attorneys and others, are preserved and catalogued as follows: Robert Sawyer Papers and Arthur Adams Papers, Case nos. 1580 and 1581, Boxes 66-67, Record Group 129, U.S. Bureau of Prisons, Atlanta Federal Penitentiary, Inmate Case Files, 1888-1921, ACC No. 129-62-0269.

All cited government documents pertaining to the clemency proceedings for Robert Sawyer and Arthur Adams, including legal filings and correspondence, are preserved and catalogued as follows: Record Group 204, Office of the Pardon Attorney, Pardon Case Files 1853-1946, Record X, pp. 752-766, and Record Y, pp. 1-14, both in Box 504.

JUDICIAL CASELAW

Jamison v. Wimbish, 130 Fed. 351 (1904), reversed as *Wimbish v. Jamison*, 199 U.S. 599 (1905).

Martin v. Texas, 200 U.S. 316 (1906).

Patapsco Guano Co. v. Board of Agriculture of NC, 171 U.S. 345 (1898).

Sawyer v. U.S., 202 U.S. 150 (1906).

U.S. v. Hodges, 203 U.S. 1 (1906).

U.S. v. Klintock, 18 U.S. 144, 5 L.Ed. 55, 5 Wheat. 144 (1820).

ONLINE AND MISCELLANEOUS

"A Brief History of Bequia." Bequia Tourism Association, www.bequiatourism.com.

"Coastline: George Rountree III on Confederate Family History, Healing Old Wounds," WHQR Public Radio, Wilmington, NC; November 17, 2017.

Declaration of Intention, US Department of Labor, US Naturalization Service, filed by Robert Sawyer, February 15, 1918.

Garrity, Tim. Interview with Gail Reiber, by Mount Desert Historical Society, June 10, 2019.

"A Guide to Wilmington's African-American Heritage," published by City of Wilmington, NC, 2013.

North Carolina Journal of Law, vol. 1, 1904, University of North Carolina Department of Law.

Paddor, Scott. *The Big House*, History Channel documentary series, 1998. One episode describes history of the Atlanta Federal Penitentiary.

US Register of Historic Places, Inventory-Nomination form for South-port Historic District, 1979.

http://bermuda100.ucsd.edu/blanche-king/

www.cinemaretro.com

www.measuringworth.com

www.millbridgehistoricalsociety.org

www.penobscotmarinemuseum.org

http://shipbuildinghistory.com

www.waywelivednc.com/before-1770/plantations

ILLUSTRATION CREDITS

Illustrations are photographs unless otherwise identified.

5-6 Newspaper front pages, Thursday, Oct. 12, 1905 / clockwise from upper left: *NEW-YORK TRIBUNE. THE MORNING STAR*, Wilmington, N.C. *THE NEW YORK TIMES. READING* (Pa.) *TIMES. THE WILKES-BARRE* (Pa.) NEWS. *THE IDAHO DAILY STATEMENT*, Boise, Idaho. *THE HARTFORD* (Conn.) *COURANT.*

7-8 Newspaper front pages, Thursday, Oct. 12, 1905 / clockwise from upper left: *THE WASHINGTON POST. THE NORTH CARO-LINIAN*, Raleigh, N.C. *THE BANGOR* (Maine) *DAILY NEWS. THE MORNING NEWS*, Lancaster, Pa. *YORK* (Pa.) *DAILY. THE CONCORDIA* (Kan.) *DAILY KANSAN.* 10 *Harry A. Berwind* / *DAILY ARKANSAS GAZETTE*, March 10, 1912

16 Illustration of struggle on *Berwind* / *LOS ANGELES HERALD*, November 4, 1906

18 Capt. Edwin B. Rumill illustration / *BANGOR* (ME.) *DAILY NEWS*, October 20, 1905

21 *C.A. Thayer* / LIBRARY OF CONGRESS

23 *Berwind* Logbook / NATIONAL ARCHIVES, ATLANTA, AU-THOR PHOTO

30 Whittler's Bench / AUTHOR PHOTO

33 Old Brunswick County Jail and railroad station / COURTESY SOUTHPORT HISTORICAL SOCIETY. Jail, now museum, today / AUTHOR PHOTO

185 Article, "Sailors Convicted of Murder at Sea Freed by Actor" / *NEW YORK TIMES*, March 3, 1912

197 Naturalization document / U.S. DEPARTMENT OF LABOR

199 Rumill tombstone / COURTESY JOHN ZINN

203 1898 Memorial Park / AUTHOR PHOTO

208 Movie poster / METRO-GOLDWYN-MAYER STUDIOS INC.

212 Lobby card / METRO-GOLDWYN-MAYER STUDIOS INC.

INDEX

Hall, John T., 27, 48-49, 51-52, 92, 96-97, 102-6, 112-15

Hare, Dr. Robert D., 192

Harlan, John Marshall, 17, 122-23, 124; Alfred Davis appeal, 87-89; dissents in *Hurtado* and *Plessy*, 87

Harris, Charles, 86-87

Harris, John C.L., 86-87

Harry A. Berwind (vessel), *10, 16*, 29, 42, 41, 343-44, 71, 91; blood evidence found aboard, 53, 94; cargo of, 19; construction of, 15; depiction in *The Decks Ran Red*, 212; logbook, 22-24, 93; overrun by curiosity-seekers in Southport, 43; physical dimensions of, 15, 21-22; scene of murders, 17, 19-24; schedule of voyage, 22, 24; sinking of, 199-200; storm damage, 20-21, 24

Hawthorne, Julian, 1560-61

Henderson, William E., 57, 66

Hewitt, Isaac F., 91-93

Hilton, James, 7

Hose, Sam, 80

Howell, Clark, 130

Hunt, Jim, 206

Hurtado v. California, 83, 87

Hutchins, Styles L., 122

Hysom, Edna Rumill, 26, 198

It's a Wonderful Life (film), 200

Jamison, Henry, 83

Jeffries, William L., 40

John N. Smith cemetery, 31-32

Johnson, Ed, 122-23

Jones County, NC, 84

Jones, Thomas G., 83-84

Joyner, Irving, 206

Keith, Benjamin F., 59, 149

Kenan, William Rand, Sr., 60-61

Kerr, J.T., 61

Kirk, J. Allen, 63, 69

Knight, Thomas H., 162, 169, 205

Knight, Mary, 162

La Soufriere volcano, 282

Larsen, Wolf, 12

Lewis, William H., 177

Lindale, GA, 128-219

Loeb, William, 134

London, Jack, 13, 209, background as sailor, 11-12; writings, 11-12

lumber industry in southern United States, 14, 24, 27

lynchings, statistics throughout South, 40

Maine; shipbuilding industry, 12-13

Manly, Alex, 57, 59, *65,* 66, 72, 79; attacked in speeches prior to Insurrection, 61-62; background and parentage, 39; controversy over authorship of editorial, 40; escape from Wilmington, 66

Manly, Charles, 39

Martin, Rufus, 121-22

Mason, James, 211, 213

McKinley, William, 57, 74, 75

McRae, Hugh, 60

Meares, James Iredell, 149, 169

Melton, Joseph, 66

Millbridge, ME, 15

Miller, Thomas C., 57

Mitchum, Robert, 7

Mobile, Ala., 24, 51, 96

Moody, William H., 134, 153

Moore, "King" Roger, 34

ABOUT THE AUTHOR

From an early age, Charles Oldham had a feeling that he could write a good story, especially one about true crime.

He was born and raised in Sanford, North Carolina, the son of a community college professor and a math teacher. His parents instilled in him a natural curiosity, and a love for reading. Early on, Charles had a special interest in history and politics, most especially that of North Carolina, where his family roots go back more than two centuries. He also has a keen eye for mysteries, for searching out the details of a story that needs to be explored. It is a talent that led him to become an attorney.

Charles graduated from Davidson College, and from law school at the University of Georgia in 2000. Afterward, he practiced law in Sanford for a time, including a term as President of the Lee County Bar Association. He now lives in Charlotte, where for ten years he had a solo legal practice focused on criminal defense and civil litigation.

Ship of Blood is Charles's second book, which he wrote after having a wonderful time with his first, *The Senator's Son*.

In his spare time, Charles can be found doing just about anything outdoors, especially hiking and camping. He also loves spending time with his family in the summer at their favorite vacation spots, including Ocean Isle Beach and Lake Junaluska in the mountains.

www.CharlesOldhamAuthor.com